# INSIGHT GUIDES

*The world's largest collection of visual travel guides*

# Vancouver

Edited by John Wilcock
Updated by Pat Kramer
Principal photography: Stuart Dee
Managing Editor: Martha Ellen Zenfell

Editorial Director: Brian Bell

**APA PUBLICATIONS**

Part of the Langenscheidt Publishing Group

**INSIGHT GUIDES**
# Vancouver

© 1999 APA Publications GmbH & Co. Verlag KG
(Singapore Branch), Singapore. *All Rights Reserved*

**CONTACTING THE EDITORS:** Although every effort is made to provide accurate information in this publication, we live in a fast-changing world and would appreciate it if readers would call our attention to any errors or outdated information that may occur by writing to us at Apa Publications,
P.O. Box 7910, London SE1 8ZB, England.
Fax: (44) 171-620-1074.
e-mail: insight@apaguide.demon.co.uk.

*First Edition 1990*
*Third Edition (updated) 1999*

*Distributed in the United States by*
**Langenscheidt Publishers Inc.**
46–35 54th Road
Maspeth
NY 11378
Fax: (718) 784 0640

*Distributed in the UK & Ireland by*
**GeoCenter International Ltd**
The Viables Centre, Harrow Way
Basingstoke, Hampshire RG22 4BJ
Fax: (44) 1256-817988

*Worldwide distribution enquiries:*
**APA Publications GmbH & Co. Verlag KG**
(Singapore branch)
38 Joo Koon Road
Singapore 628990
Tel: 65-8651600
Fax: 65-8616438

*Printed in Singapore by*
**Insight Print Services (Pte) Ltd**
38 Joo Koon Road
Singapore 628990
Fax: 65-8616438

This guidebook combines the interests and enthusiasms of two of the world's best known information providers: **Insight Guides**, whose range of titles has set the standard for visual travel guides since 1970, and **Discovery Channel**, the world's premier source of nonfiction television programming.

The editors of Insight Guides provide both practical advice and general understanding about a destination's history, culture, institutions and people. Discovery Channel and its Web site, www.discovery.com, help millions of viewers explore their world from the comfort of their own home and also encourage them to explore it firsthand.

*Wilcock*

Vancouver's unique blend of pioneer spirit and Pacific Rim sophistication make it a near-perfect destination for Insight Guides, whose 190-strong series of travel books span the globe. And with a formula that combines frank writing with bold photojournalism, the series has the scope to do justice to Vancouver's energetic urbanity as well as the surrounding scenic splendour, not forgetting the historic town of Victoria.

The books are carefully structured, both to convey a better understanding of the region and its culture, and also to guide readers – whether on a short visit or a long-term stay – through its best sights and most interesting activities.

*Zenfell*

• To truly understand the West Coast of Canada, it's important to know something of the area's past. The first section, therefore, covers Vancouver's wide-ranging history and lively culture in authoritative essays written by local experts.

• The main Places section provides a full run-down of all the attractions and destinations worth seeing, with handy maps included whenever necessary. Specific sites can be found in bold lettering for easy reference.

• The Travel Tips listing section provides a convenient point of reference for recommendations on travel, hotels, restaurants, shops, sports, culture and local festivals.

*Dee*

*Young*

*Boulanger*

Heading the project was **John Wilcock,** who long ago mastered transatlantic spelling by exchanging a Fleet Street reporter's job in Britain for one on Toronto's *Saturday Night* magazine and then moving south to work on the travel desk of the *New York Times.* His many books cover something like 30 countries, several of which he has project-edited for Insight Guides from his Los Angeles base.

"Apart from the magnificent harbour," Wilcock says, "the thing I notice most about Vancouver is the inevitable rain. But when I started work on this book I came to appreciate how important rain is to an understanding of the place."

Inclement weather is something journalist **Martha Ellen Zenfell,** at the time Insight Guides' editor-in-chief of all of their North American books, knows about. A native of the American south now relocated to often rain-shrouded London, England, Zenfell steered Wilcock through the pitfalls and pleasures of putting together an Insight Guide. One of her first tasks was to hire photographer **Stuart Dee**, and, later, to sift through countless slides to put together the visual look of the book. Dee, who specialises in travel, people and location photography, spends four months a year working abroad, so a chance "to shoot my home town was a welcome assignment."

**Stanley Young** also has an English connection, having been born in London before moving to Los Angeles. Young continued his exploration of the origins of the West Coast by writing the history chapters of this book as well as researching the pictures that accompany it.

The rest of this edition was written by committed Vancouverites, even if many of them originally started out somewhere else.

Scottish-born Melanie Chandler has an explantion for her attachment to Vancouver's moody mists. "Water is like the blues," she suggests. "In the form of the ocean or rain, its moods externalise your own, so you are left feeling peaceful."

For choice, Montreal-born **Michel Beaudry** would prefer snow, having been a champion skier and a member of the country's National Telemark Team. Another fan of the outdoors is **Dan Hilborn**, who was born at Nelson, British Columbia, in the Kootenay region of the Rocky Mountains.

Author and poet **Sue Nevill** started out in England but has lived on and off for 30 years in Vancouver, which she describes as a city that meets at least "three quarters of her emotional, intellectual and physical needs." **Dianne McGuire** was raised in Jamaica and lived in three countries before returning "home," while Saskatchewan-born **Alex Gabriel** headed west after completing her journalism training in Calgary, Alberta.

**W. Ruth Kozak** says her love affair with Vancouver began at 13 after a long, cross-country journey across Canada, a trip that inspired her to write about the early pioneers.

"I love Vancouver," says Toronto-born but West Coast-based **Annie Boulanger**, "because it accepts everybody, no matter how different or wierd." **Angela Murrills** would no doubt agree.

Admiration for the city is something our last two contributors know a great deal about. **Chuck Davis**, a high-profile local writer and broadcaster, has written several books on the subject. He took time out from a hectic schedule to give us his personal view and favourite places in an essay.

**Pat Kramer** is also devoted to Vancouver. A busy writer and photographer with several books to her credit on all aspects of West Coast life, she is almost solely responsible for bringing this edition up to date. Attacking her task with a vengeance, she not only deleted now irrelevent facts, but also restructured part of the manuscript and submitted many new photographs to give the book a fresh new look. Only someone with files at their fingertips and enthusiam for the subject could have done such a comprehensive job, and we take our hat off to her. Of course, all that rain belting down may have contributed to a zeal for indoor work.

# CONTENTS

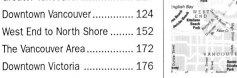

# SPECTACULAR BY NATURE

Vancouver, in the province of British Columbia (BC) just north of the US border, squeezed by the waters of Burrard Inlet, False Creek and Fraser River, bordered on the north by the sharp-shouldered Coastal Mountains, and positioned about as far west as you can go on the Pacific side of Canada, has always seemed to be poised on the sharp edge of something wondrous. It's a linguistic irony that the city's original centre, the historic district now called Gastown, was known by the native Indian population as *Luck-a-luck*. For luck has had much to do with Vancouver's boom-and-bust past, if not its present fluctuating fortunes.

Despite explorer Captain George Vancouver's exclamation, on his initial visit in 1792, that the area required only the trappings of civilisation"to render it the most lovely country," early settlers had trouble coming to terms with its immense forests, mountains and ocean inlets. British naval authorities created the first anchorage, not on the ocean but on the Fraser River at New Westminster, a tiny settlement declared capital of the new British colony in 1859. With the promise of a trans-continental railway from the fledgling government of Canada in 1871, the colony subtly decided its fortunes lay with Canada, not the United States, and its capital shifted across Georgia Strait to Fort Victoria on Vancouver Island. In the 1880s, it was the fiscally shrewd Canadian Pacific Railway (CPR) that selected the deep water port of Burrard Inlet as its western terminus, thus ensuring Vancouver's fortune.

The trans-continental railroads, linking Asia's goods with Great Britain's and Europe's burgeoning markets, brought prosperity. They also enticed some famous tourists. British author Rudyard Kipling proclaimed in *Letters of Travel* that "such a land is good for an energetic man," and added,"It is also not so bad for the loafer." The Queen Mother, during a royal visit in 1939, described Vancouver as "the place to live".

Nobody has ever questioned its natural beauty. "A clean, prosperous, lively city in the most magnificent natural setting," raves London's *Sunday Times*. "Once a setting in search of a city [that] has blossomed into one of the most attractive places in North America," opines *Saturday Night* magazine. Vancouver is indeed the city next to the wilderness, a metropolis strangely perched on the edge of vast forests.

Of course, it's only fair to mention the rain. The locals are used to it and some even claim they can distinguish different kinds. One local tour guide defined the words "expected showers" as "the original Vancouver euphemism used by forecasters to mean anything from light sprinklings to torrential downpours." What distinguishes the climate from the rest of Canada are year-round mild temperatures, lack of snow and the predictability of rain. However, no matter the season, say locals, "you don't have to shovel it."

Once you get used to frequent showers, they don't seem so bad and if you're prepared a rainstorm can even be fun, if only to see the incessant greyness punctuated by brightly coloured umbrellas. But if there is one colour really predominating in the environs of this lovely city, it's green, year round green. All because of the rain.

What makes Vancouver impressive? Members of a visiting delegation of US city planners were impressed by the night-time vitality of Robson Street. Vanvouver's penchant for high-density housing, much of it discreetly sited within the downtown itself, keeps the city core alive. Rather than emptying to the suburbs as other North American centres, Vancouver centre hums with activity day and night.

Vancouver's growth, both in multicultural population and new building construction, has astonished everyone, not least its own citizens. Though it has its critics, who consider it a rather loopy place, its reputation for racial tolerance and environmental awareness have earned it grudging admiration.

*Loopy?* That's the way outsiders talk, anyway. A certain freedom of spirit permeates the city separated from the rest of Canada by a reassuring barrier of nine mountain ranges. They act as a sort of protective filter against the niggling details of problems elsewhere. City administrators wrestle with growth and fail to relieve the occluded traffic flows in overbuilt corridors. So called "freeways" are referred to as "parking lots". In spite of the elevated rapid-rail public transport, *Skytrain*, getting around is time consuming. But with an eye on the snow-covered mountains and rugged ocean shores surrounding them, Vancouverites stubbornly resist growth, preferring congestion and a slower pace to altering one inch of scenery or giving up one iota of the hard-earned leisure life style that goes with it.

Even with a population approaching 2 million, the third largest Canadian city after Montreal and Toronto continues to relish its reputation as an outpost on some bright frontier. Likened to a popular actor, Vancouver continues to collect its admirers, a bit dismayed by its popularity, but continually refreshed by its natural beauty. "The best thing about downtown Vancouver is that you can catch a glimpse of freedom at the end of the street," wrote Allan Fotheringham, former *Vancouver Sun* columnist."Stand at Georgia and Burrard, or Georgia and Granville [streets], and there, at the end of the canyon, is a slice of blue water and green mountain. It's the tiny visual escape-hatch that Toronto or New York would trade a pack of skyscrapers for."

**Right**, gliding into the future.

Like Columbus three centuries before them, the first Europeans to sail western Canada's watery Gulf of Georgia flew the flag of Spain and were looking for a Northwest Passage. In 1791, Captain José Maria Narvaez and the *Santa Saturnina* charted the region naming its principal headlands. The following year, two more Spanish exploration vessels far from home crossed paths with *Discovery* and *Chatham*, ships of the British Navy. Under the command of 35-year-old Captain George Vancouver, who trained aboard Captain Cook's South Pacific expedition, the crew put traditional rivalries aside, enjoyed a hearty breakfast, set up a three week British-Spanish venture, explored the area by longboat, and then shared their maps and notes.

Near First Narrows, Captain Vancouver encountered the Coastal Salish-speaking inhabitants of the village of Whoi-Whoi. These indigenous people were well versed in trading sea otter pelts with outside traders – Russian, British and Spanish.

"These good people," Vancouver wrote of the Squamish nation, "finding we were inclined to make some return for their hospitality, showed much understanding in preferring iron to copper" and had an "ardent desire for commercial transactions." Vancouver named the long inlet "Burrard"and proceeded up the coast.

**First Nations:** Descendants of ancient Mongolian tribes who crossed the Bering Strait perhaps 10,000 years ago, West Coast tribes once based their livelihood on the copious migration of salmon and the adaptability of the cedar tree. An estimated 20,000 native peoples lived in great cedar plankhouses along the shores of Burrard Inlet. With a complex social structure and abundant surroundings, they enjoyed frequent salmon feasts and clambakes. Many of their villages, including Whoi-Whoi, were built on a moraine of mollusc shells up to 20 metres (60 ft)

deep. In fact, the first road around Stanley Park was surfaced entirely with these shells.

Much of our knowledge about the Kwakiutl (now called Kwakwakawak'wa), Coast Salish, Nootka (now called Nuu-chal-nulth), and Haida First Nations is thanks to the writings of Franz Boas. One of the founders of the academic discipline of anthropology, he wrote a series of ethnographic studies on the area.

Descendants of those West Coast natives continue to be noted for their distinctive artistic designs. While most visitors equate this skill with their prominent totem poles, this unique graphic sensibility seen nowhere else on the continent is also exhibited in elaborate masks, bent boxes, longboats and other wooden artifacts.

In earlier times, much of the tribes' elaborate artwork was devoted to creating ceremonial crests proclaiming their family clan rights. Their intricate organisation of social ranking included bottom ranking slaves: women kidnapped in slave-raids on southern villages or men whose tribes were uninterested in ransoming them back. The social zenith was occupied by the wealthiest individuals whose position was affirmed through the potlatch, a ceremony as unique as their artwork.

An important elder might mount two or perhaps three potlatches in a lifetime. The two-week-long ceremony included the conducting of trials and important marriages, granting property rights, settling feuds, granting titles and new names, and proclaiming noble births. In a society without a written language it was imperative to assure records were kept; thus during the potlatch, specific people were asked to remember or witness each proceeding and promise to testify if questioned in the future.

For their services, they were given gifts, the most important witnesses receiving longboats, carved chests and slaves, and were feted royally on shellfish, smelt, sturgeon and smoked salmon, with much dancing, drumming and singing. If a man died,

**Preceding pages:** drawing of the *Beaver*, the first West Coast vessel to trade for furs. Left, Haida totem of Bear.

credit or debit for his witnessing fell on his heirs. Over time, the wealthy tried to outdo each other, ceremonially providing greater gifts to their witnesses, so that eventually, regarding these gifts as wasteful and counterproductive to "assimilation", the (later regretful) Canadian government banned potlatchs from 1924 until 1952. Many elders were jailed or fined and their ceremonial regalia confiscated.

**Attraction of furs:** It was the sea otter trade and later, beaver pelts that drew the first Europeans to the area. Simon Fraser, a North West Company explorer, arrived by canoe in 1808 in search of the Columbia River and

John Jacob Astor's Pacific Fur Company at Astoria. His unsuccessful foray along a more northern river led to the naming of the major river in present-day Vancouver. For 50 years previous, Russians traders wandered up and down the coast in search of sea otter pelts, competing with enterprising Yankee skippers trading pelts for rum and ironware. It was, however, the redoubtable Hudson's Bay Company (HBC) that came to dominate the West Coast fur trade.

By 1827 the HBC had established Fort Langley, 49 km (30 miles) inland from the coast on the Fraser River. Eight years later

the company's pioneering steamship, the *S.S. Beaver*, a smoke-belching paddle-wheeler, as one HBC official put it, managed to "overawe the natives" as well as beat the competition. American captains at sea in their four-masters watched helpless and becalmed as the *S.S.Beaver* easily steamed up narrow inlets to make the first bid for a native village's supply of pelts. Symbol of the Hudson's Bay Company for over half a century, the good ship went aground off Prospect Point in what is now Stanley Park in 1888. For years, Vancouverites' favourite Sunday after-church sport was salvaging pieces of the wreck.

The clerks and factors who oversaw HBC operations in remote wilderness trading forts might easily have been mistaken for clerks straight out of a Dickens novel. Not so the fur traders who moved among the Indians. Sir George Simpson, sent out to reorganise north-west division in the 1820s, saw this mixed bunch of mountain men, adventurers and scallywags as "the very scum of the earth". "They are," he declared, "the most unruly and troublesome gang to deal with in this, or perhaps any other part of the world."

These colourful fur traders developed a trading jargon known as "Chinook"and introduced the pleasures of rum to local populations. The area, as one historian pointed out, was at that time little more than a "savage fur farm".

**Glitter of gold:** In 1858, the discovery of placer gold on the banks of the Fraser River brought a new band of rag-tag adventurers. Within months thousands of miners arrived, mostly from San Francisco. James Douglas, the HBC's Chief Factor and governor of Vancouver Island, lost no time in extracting as much as possible from the gold seekers. He established gold panning licences and fees, set up a monopoly on mining supplies and pressed men to construct roads to the gold fields in return for supplies. Unwilling to lose potential tax revenues to the royal chartered Hudson's Bay Company, the British Parliament quickly created the crown colony of British Columbia and extended to Douglas control of a vast area from the coast across the mainland to the highest peaks of the Rocky Mountains.

**Douglas makes it work:** Born out of wedlock to a Glasgow merchant and a black freewoman from Barbados, and raised in Scotland, Douglas was an able apprentice in the fur-trading business from the age of 17. After moving steadily through HBC ranks (and before any gold rush), in 1842 he was asked to fortify Fort Victoria on Vancouver Island against a potentially expanding Oregon Territory.

Douglas dealt well with relocating the local indigenous people, though with virtually no military, constabulary or judiciary, "he turned parsimony into an art form," said one historian. The whites, used to having from England. These Royal Engineers set about surveying Vancouver, New Westminster and environs. Besides naming Lulu Island after a comely lass in a dancing troupe sent to entertain British soldiers, Moody pursuaded men who would rather be prospecting to build a military road from the freshwater Fraser River to the salt-water anchorage in Port Moody. British naval ships now had a choice of ports linked by road. When the Fraser River froze in the winter of 1861–62, Moody's foresight was doubly rewarded.

**Call of the Cariboo:** In September 1861, the Fraser River rush expanded when rumours

their own unregulated way throughout this untamed wilderness, were less than enamoured of his governing abilities, especially after he forbade firearms, collected fines for public drunkeness, and brought in from London the flamboyant and handsome, mustachioed Matthew Baillie Begbie, soon to be known as the "Hanging Judge".

**Moving people and goods inland:** As prospectors continued to flood in, Colonel Richard Moody and a team of 25 sappers arrived

**Left**, Europeans and natives trade for furs. **Above**, miners of the Cariboo gold rush, 1858.

of especially rich deposits of gold came from Cariboo country, far in the British Columbia interior. Dutch Bill Deitz, then two lucky prospectors, Abbott and Jourdan, reported 120 ounces a day.

After Ned Campbell took out 900 ounces in one day, glowing newspaper accounts around the world picked up the news. By May 1862, a rush of reckless gold seekers had arrived from all corners of the globe – including many of California's "49ers" who by then were coming up empty-handed.

Even though the area was accessible only by river steamer followed by 200 miles along a treacherous canyon road, by 1863 4,000 men were dredging creeks and digging shafts. Barkerville, a boom town, overnight became the largest city north of San Francisco. Though few miners were successful, many eventually chose to stay.

**The Three Greenhorns:** In 1862, one apparently unlucky miner, John Morton, spotted a chunk of coal in a window in New Westminster. Having worked as a potter in his Yorkshire home, Morton knew coal often lay mixed with clay, so filled with ideas of potting rights, he hired a local native to explore present-day Stanley Park and Coal Harbour. Though his coal was unfortunately logically) started a kiln and brickworks in the midst of a heavily timbered forest. Hacking their way through more than a mile of rainforest, they cut a trail linking up with the military trail to New Westminster. Though full of money-making ideas, it was their grindstone that proved to be their salvation: "The Indians had never seen [one]," said a historian "and when they learned to use it they were overjoyed. In return for the privilege of using it, the grateful natives kept the shack well supplied with fish and *mowich* – deer, elk or any wild animal suitable for eating."

In 1884, the Canadian Pacific Railway began negotiating a site for their terminus,

embedded in sandstone, not clay, and his hopes seemed dashed, Morton subsequently convinced two of his prospecting countrymen, Sam Brighouse and William Hailstone, to join him and pre-empt or claim lot 185. This comprised some 225 hectares (550 acres) that would soon become the West End of Vancouver.

The "Three Greenhorns" as they came to be known, taken at first for fools by their gold-panning colleagues, cleared a small patch, constructed a shack overlooking the inlet just west of the present day Marine Building, planted a kitchen garden and (illogically) started a kiln and brickworks in the and the Three Greenhorns donated part of their parcel toward the venture. But holding on to the greater part, expecting a boom, they named the West End "Liverpool City". Two of the three were handsomely rewarded but until he was an old man, John Morton held onto his house representing the tiniest piece of the original parcel. Far from being embittered by the vagaries of fortune, Morton was full of life and humour. "Ay, lad, ay, I had [a lot of land]," said the old pioneer in 1911, "Then I fell among forty thieves…"

**Birth of Gastown:** Another refugee of the Cariboo gold rush was Yorkshire Englishman John Deighton who arrived by rowboat at Burrard Inlet on 29 September 1867 with his native Indian wife and mother-in-law, a yellow dog, two chairs, two chickens, a barrel of whisky and $6 in cash. Fresh from a squabble with his American saloon-keeping partner in New Westminster, Deighton embodied the get-rich-quick spirit rampant at the time.

At that time the entire shore was covered with forests of fir and cedar – the Indians called it *Luck-a luck* meaning grove of beautiful trees. Apart from a trading-post run by Portuguese Joe who sold a little rum, two thriving lumbermills were both dry: Captain

agents soon arrived from Victoria and forced him to add sleeping rooms. The subsequent Deighton House Hotel, its owner nicknamed "Gassy Jack" partly because of his lengthy monologues and partly because he was often "gassed" (inebriated) himself, was a thriving success. To soothe tattered guests after a night on his cheap pillowless beds, Jack provided a free morning "libation".

In 1870, as the Royal Engineers surveyed the nine buildings comprising the new town site of Granville, Gassy bought the first lot for $65. However, the little strip where Water and Carrall streets meet soon became informally known as "Gastown". Thus was

Edward Stamp's Hastings Mill, started earlier that same year, and across the inlet Sewell P. Moody's older Pioneer Mill. A good hand-logger could earn as much as $1,000 a month, and with the nearest tavern 20 miles away, Deighton was in the right place at the right time – accessible to both mills.

With the promise of free whiskey for all who helped, Deighton built his own saloon within 24 hours of his arrival. Government

**Left**, city officials met in a tent after Vancouver was destroyed by fire, 1886. **Above**, first trans-continental train, 24 May 1887.

born Vancouver, the only major city in Canada that was not originally a fur trading post.

Eleven years later Granville's first official census revealed a thriving population of 44 loggers, 31 millworkers, four butchers, two shoemakers, two ministers, one school teacher, one wine seller and a policeman – with no word on why the 28 saloon keepers were not included.

**Trans-continental railway:** British Columbia's entry into Canadian Confederation in 1871 was conditional upon completion of a trans-continental railroad. Only in 1885 did

Prime Minister John A. MacDonald finally comandeer financing for construction of the last section in the west. Unknown as yet was the exact location for the railroad's terminus, an anticipated complex of warehouses, railway yards, and repair shops – the money pot at the end of the steel rainbow.

Speculators first counted on the Canadian Pacific Railway (CPR) choosing an ocean inlet (a fijord) at Port Moody as the terminus, but William Van Horne, general manager for the CPR, preferred the quickest route to the open Pacific, the deepwater port next to the Granville townsite. Van Horne thus proclaimed, "This is destined to be a great

city in Canada. We must see that it has a name that will designate its place on the map. Vancouver it shall be, if I have the ultimate decision."

**Royal approval:** Van Horne had his way, and even as the city of Vancouver was given royal assent, on 6 April 1886, the land rush was on. Within three months, 500 buildings had been constructed and though Indians, Orientals, lunatics and women were not allowed to vote, the first city elections were held. The city councillors' first resolution was to set aside land for Stanley Park. Much acclaimed in later years, their underlying

motivation at the time was to safeguard a military reserve to the west of their new city, and to protect the value of their personal Gastown real estate investments against a huge parcel of pristine waterfront land coming onstream. Thus in the spirit of speculation, Stanley Park was born.

Two-man saws swiftly cut down the hemlocks and firs – some as much as 2.5 metres (8 ft) in diameter. Teams of oxen pulled stumps to clear new streets, and brush was quickly burned. One such fire got out of hand on 13 June 1886 and, although the conflagration lasted less than an hour, 20 people died and almost every building burned to the ground. But there was no holding back the energy of Vancouver's inhabitants. Within a day the City Council was meeting in a tent, and hotels were selling liquor before their roofs had been put on.

By the end of the year, the young city was handsomely rebuilt, with 23 hotels, nine saloons, one church, and more than 8,000 pioneering souls who called Vancouver home. When the first CPR train trundled into its new terminus on the eve of Queen Victoria's birthday, 23 May 1887, in the jubilee year of her coronation, Vancouver's future as the Canadian commercial centre on the West Coast was assured.

**Vancouver toothpicks:** Ever since the founding of New Westminster, it was obvious that the evergreen forests of the peninsula would supply wood for the world. The first sawmill, established in 1862 on the north shore of the inlet was soon exporting lumber to Australia.

By the 1880s Hastings Mill, was exporting millions of "Vancouver Toothpicks" – knotless timbers 1 metre (3 ft) square and 18 metres (60 ft) long. Churches and buildings around the world sported impeccable beams from Vancouver and environs. Many a clipper ship and naval vessel sported fine tall masts and spars hewn from Canada's primeval West Coast forests. Lumberjacks and millworkers received a handsome $1.25 for a 10-hour working day. Vancouver was on her way up.

<u>Left</u>, a new dance craze hits the city.
<u>Right</u>, law and order in a frontier town.

A year to the day after Vancouver's disastrous fire, in 1887, the *Abyssinia,* a CPR-chartered passenger ship from Yokohama, was the first to dock in Vancouver's new deep-water port. She carried 22 first-class passengers, a cargo of mail, tea and silk, and 80 Chinese in steerage. Little could any of those passengers realise the boom and bust ride they and their descendants would soon experience.

**Gold Mountain:** In Vancouver, products from far-off Cathay were clearly more valued than people from those distant shores. Tens of thousands of Chinese, most poor bachelors from Hong Kong and Canton, were already in British Columbia, having arrived to build the railroad for a dollar a day. Once the Canadian Pacific (CP) line was complete the "Celestials" attempted to compete with the European immigrants for jobs at every millsite, cannery and mine in the province – and they were willing to work for less money.

In China, news spread about "Gold Mountain," as Vancouver was known; how if you came without your family, worked hard clearing the stumps from the land, slaved night and day, did a little prospecting, helped to build the railway – how, if you endured all this, a better life was possible than could ever be found back home.

"My father worked all his life here and when I was four years old he moved back to China and bought land in Canton," recalled Sing Fung who once owned a store on Pender Street. "But when the Communists took over he lost everything. I came back to Canada, I worked hard every day – 10 days a week at least. I don't work eight hours a day, I work 16, seven days a week, maybe that's more than 10 days. If you don't work that hard you'll never make anything. But in Canada, if you make it you keep it."

Early settlement patterns were tense. In 1887 generalised prejudice was replaced by

anti-Chinese riots. Marauding settlers razed Chinese camps on False Creek and Coal Harbour; their shacks and tents were burned; men were tied together by their pigtails and publicly beaten. In September that same year the Asiatic Exclusion League demonstrated against the docking of the *SS Monteagle*: "900 Hindus, 1,100 Chinamen and a bunch of Japs" read the pierside sign. Within a month, a general economic boycott organised by local businessmen went into effect against firms trading with the Chinese. Stores which insisted on dealing with the "Asiatic hordes" had black crosses painted in front of their doors.

Anti-Chinese sentiment became a fixture of the young province of British Columbia and its largest city: from 1878 to 1913, more than two dozen anti-Chinese statutes were passed. As late as 1907, 30,000 people showed up on Cambie Street to cheer the Asiatic Exclusion League speakers at a parade.

**Chinatown puts down roots:** Still, Vancouver's Chinatown managed to take root. Dr Sun Yat-Sen found sanctuary in the Chinese Freemasons building at One West Pender for a time before returning home in 1911 to establish the modern state of China. Many buildings in Chinatown housed secret gaming rooms where "chuck-a-luck" was played, the participants dodging frequent police raids and shakedowns. Opium dens were commonplace, and the use of the drug was so widespread that its whafting smell offended the delicate sensibilities of those attending the city's first rudimentary Opera House on Dupont Street.

"If the disgusting perfume of opium which always hangs in the atmosphere were removed," exhorted a newspaper reporter in 1886, "there would hardly be anything to offend the nostrils in the balmy air." Two years later the City Council passed a law requiring all persons selling or manufacturing opium to pay $500 a year. The object of the law was not so much to diminish the lucrative trade, but to shift its profits from

**Preceding pages:** Kwakiutl people and Dzunkwa figures, *circa* 1910. **Left**, the Canadian Pacific Railway linked Vancouver to the rest of Canada.

the Chinese proprietors to white pharmacists – who were, as it happened, exempt from the annual fee.

**Millworkers and gold diggers:** Vancouver, far from the sedate and liveable metropolis of the present, was in those early days a rough milltown whose hardworking inhabitants lived a rowdy existence. An 1895 federal study showed Vancouver as leading the Dominion in per capita consumption of alcohol. Locals, of course, blamed the Indians. In 1898, the Yukon gold rush hit, with a new wave of gold seekers arriving and the general air of uproariousness increasing. Outfitters made a killing selling to mining aspirants the

kind of houses they were expected to work in. Brothier was not alone in making a fortune from prostitution, which in Vancouver, with its preponderance of single men, was rampant. "They say it doesn't exist," said a visiting police chief from Toronto in 1903, "but the social evil is spread all over the city."

**Railway robber barons arrive:** By 1902, Vancouver had a population of 30,000. The CP railroad had certainly made a city out of Gassy Jack's Granville, but the relationship between the Vancouverites and the CPR was fraught with tension. Railroad executives established their mansions in the city's West

necessary 450 kg (1000 lb) of provisions Canadian authorities demanded before each miner was allowed to enter the frozen goldfields.

Other would-be goldminers made their fortunes with less sweat and more certainty. Desire Brothier, on his way to the Yukon from France, landed in Vancouver, took one look at the situation and returned within the year with a shipful of shop girls. He convinced them they could make better wages as domestics in Canada, but knowing no English, and arriving illegally, the ladies dared not protest when they discovered just what

End and attempted to set a civilised tone in a rough town whose citizens bridled at the imperious attitude of a company that owned more than half the area's real estate. "With time," wrote author Eric Nicol, "the fairy godmother [CPR] came to look less and less like the matronly goodbody and more and more like the Wicked Witch of the East."

When the notorious American bandit Bill Miner (later immortalised in the film *The Grey Fox*) was captured in 1904 at Kamloops after the first series of train robberies in Canada's history, a hung jury acquitted him. "Bill Miner's not so bad," went the joke of the day. "He only robs the CPR once every two years, but the CPR robs us all every day." Miner was eventually sentenced to 25 years in a trial at New Westminster, but escaped from his Canadian jail in 1907 at the age of 67.

**Coming of the automobile:** The world was changed by the automobile and British Columbia was no exception. Beginning in June 1908, Vancouver's first gasoline station at the corner of Smith and Cambie supplied cars with fuel transported from the east in barrels. Much of it evaporated en route. And it was not much later that a Mr Annard turned his bicycle repair shop at Hastings and Co-

around 3,000 km (2,000 miles) – in just over 52 hours, a breathtaking average speed of almost 60 kph (37 mph). Motorists were soon demanding a cross-country highway but it was not until 1964 that the last section of the Trans-Canada Highway, and the long-awaited Port Mann Bridge across the Fraser River, were completed.

**Off to war:** On 4 August 1914, the city fathers claimed that Vancouver sent more soldiers to France than any comparably sized city in Canada or the United States. One of the local regiments, the 72nd Canadian Infantry Battalion, Seaforth Highlanders, was particularly decorated. Far from the scene of

lumbia streets into the city's first garage. Horse-drawn tankers delivered gasoline retailing for 20¢ a gallon. And there was no tax to pay. Twelve years later there were 28,000 registered vehicles on Vancouver's highways.

Before the decade was over, automobile endurance runs were popular. William Ball set a record in 1928, driving from Vancouver to Yreka, California, and back – a distance of

**Left**, the second of four Capilano Suspension Bridges, *circa* 1910. **Above**, forests removed, a city emerges, *circa* 1930.

battle, the city profited. The Vancouver branch of the Red Cross rolled bandages, the Council of Women raised money to equip a hospital ship. Local lumber merchants reacted favourably to an increased demand for their products, particularly Sitka spruce used for making lightweight airplane spars. Women were welcomed into the workplace during the war years and soon advanced the dual causes of suffrage and women's rights.

**Panama increases sea trade:** The opening of the Panama Canal in August 1914 also did much to enhance the young port's future.

The promise of the CPR to provide a fast land transportation route across Canada from Asia to Great Britain was now usurped. But in return Vancouver could cheaply ship wheat and wood to Britain and the Continent as well as the Far East. Vancouver now lay the same distance from England as the harbours of Asia, and so began its life as a bona fide world port catering to world markets, particularly Pacific Rim countries.

Vancouver soon developed many of the cultural accoutrements that make for international stature. The year 1918 that marked the end of World War I also seemed to be the city's first coming-of-age: movies, radios,

War industries, in particular shipbuilding, dwindled as the worldwide postwar depression affected Vancouver too. However, the city's deep-water, ice-free harbour soon became known as a convenient port for the export of wheat, and, as a short-lived Canadian experiment with Prohibition came to an end, contraband rum-rumming to the United States became the preferred get-rich-quick industry. Many a surreptitious BC vessel made the 80-km (50-mile) voyage across the international border to the American San Juan Islands where the liquor was dropped off on lonely US beaches for later retrieval.

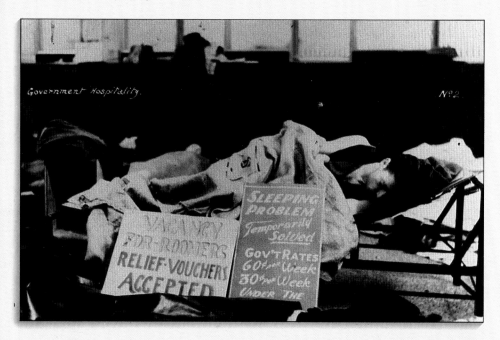

motor cars – and an upsurge in propriety – grew by leaps and bounds. "The practice of courting in automobiles in Vancouver has got to cease," reported one lady writer in a local magazine of 1920. "Inspector Hood, who is the moving spirit in the crusade, describes the habit as 'dangerous'." When the city won the Stanley Cup in the 1915 national hockey championship, it came as no surprise that the team's name was the Vancouver Millionaires.

**Rum running for profit:** As men came home from the front, they were greeted as heroes but most soon found themselves unemployed.

**Boom time again:** US President Warren G. Harding came to visit in July 1923. It was the first time an American president had paid a social call to Canada, and it also proved to be Harding's last public appearance: he died of food poisoning one week after his speech in the city. By the end of the Roaring Twenties, Vancouver was booming. Amalgamation with South Vancouver and Point Grey gave the city 79,000 additional inhabitants and more land.

Vancouver had blosomed into a city of middle-class homes, without architectural grandeur but also without slums like those in

Montreal or Toronto. It had accomplished the incredible: turning a pre-war boom town into a 20th-century metropolis within in a decade. But at a price. A historian described it at the time: "In downtown Vancouver… the air was heavy with grime and soot as boats and trains, sawmills and flour-mills, breweries and food-processing plants, shoe factories and clothing factories belched clouds of heavy smoke. The city was now held fast in the toils of industry."

**Stock market crash:** And Vancouver would also soon be held in the grip of the Depression. Following the October 1929 stock market crash, building came to a standstill, lum-

In April 1935, 2,000 unemployed men advanced on Vancouver City Hall demanding "work and wages". They invaded the Hudson's Bay Store, tangled with police and marched to Victory Square. A sympathy strike by local workers and a solidarity meeting of 15,000 people urged abolition of "slave compound" labour camps. With no unemployment insurance in place, conditions deteriorated. In 1938, 1,500 demonstrators occupied the Art Gallery, Hotel Georgia and the main Post Office at Hastings and Granville demanding a public works programme. The standoff lasted a month before the end: "Bloody Sunday". "Fleeing before a

ber sales shrank, sawmills closed, wheat shipments declined. By December, breadlines stretched outside the City Relief Office. The unemployed streamed in from shutdown mines, logging camps and fish canneries. By the winter of 1932–33, nearly 40,000 people, about 15 percent of the city's population, were on relief. To prevent schools from closing, local teachers agreed to work the month of December 1933 without pay.

**Left**, the Depression hits Vancouver, 1934–39. **Above**, Japanese children are rounded up during World War II.

barrage of tear gas bombs and the swinging batons of city police officers," wrote a reporter for the *Vancouver News-Herald*, "a swarm of shouting, blood-spattered men… looted stores and for more than an hour created a reign of terror in the city. It is hard to imagine how traumatic public violence on such a scale is for Canadians, especially outside the confines of a professional hockey rink."

**War again:** As elsewhere in North America, the September 1939 outbreak of World War II in Europe brought changes to the city. Guns were mounted along the coast and the old Hotel Vancouver first became a recruiting centre, then a barracks housing the headquarters of the army's Pacific Command. However, when the Japanese attacked Pearl Harbor in December 1941, the war came closer.

A nightly blackout was established and thousands of Japanese citizens were soon under suspicion. By the mid-1930s about 30,000 Japanese lived in British Columbia. About one quarter lived in Vancouver – most of them in Japantown, the blocks of Powell Street between Gore and Heatley. Most were *nissei* (Canadian-born). Though hundreds of Japanese-Canadians fought valiantly in Canadian regiments, an article in the *Vancouver Province* on 7 April 1937 summed up the feelings of the white majority: "The old Oriental immigrant was objected to because he brought to Canada the low standard of living... of Asia and because he worked for low wages and so tended to undermine the standards of white labourers [*sic*]..."

By January 1942, all Japanese males between 18 and 45 were ordered away from the coast to internment camps. All Japanese-owned property, including fishing vessels, homes and grocery stores, was seized and liquidated by the Custodian of Enemy Property. Newspapers were full of exceptional bargains on former Japanese property. Within three months, Vancouver's Japantown was wiped out. Little of what was seized was ever returned.

**Post-war boom:** The boom that followed the war quickly erased the memory of its hardships. Vancouver's population in 1941 was 275,000. Ten years later, the city proper counted 345,000 and Greater Vancouver numbered over half a million. Many new residents were immigrants from war-ravaged Europe or were eastern Canadian servicemen who had been stationed in the area. In 1954 Vancouver made the world's headlines

as the venue of the British Empire Games. Roger Bannister broke the 4-minute mile record and the world rejoiced.

The 1950s marked a period of similar advancement in the city's economic growth, centred primarily around Vancouver's position as a major port. During the 1960s the First Narrows was dredged to a depth of 15 metres (50 ft) to allow for new bulk carriers, and in 1970 Robert's Banks causeway opened to export western Canadian coal to Japan. John Morton's 1862 lump of coal finally bore anthracite fruit.

A newly aware population began to celebrate its raucous past. In 1970, a statue of Gassy Jack Deighton was erected in Maple Tree Square, at the intersection of Carrall and Water streets, and in 1972 Mayor Muni Evers unveiled a headstone to commemorate the unmarked grave in which Gassy's remains had lain for 97 years.

**Greenpeace begins:** Given its glorious natural setting, it is unsurprising that Vancouver then spawned one of the most celebrated environmental organisations in the world. When 12 activist members of the Vancouver group "Don't Make a Wave Committee" sailed their small boat out of the Strait of Georgia and into the US atomic test

largest and most beautiful city seemed finally to have come of age.

In an ironic twist, the city proceeded to welcome a host of immigrants from Hong Kong. Many chose Vancouver as a secondary safe haven in the event that the 1997 return of their territory by Britain to the People's Republic of China did not go as planned. These new immigrants, many of them wealthy, brought the imprimatur of international respectability. But the surge of Asian investment came to an abrupt end. The ensuing Asian monetary crises demanded cash injections, so recent immigrants have chosen to limit their Canadian investments.

zone off Amchitka Alaska in 1971, Greenpeace was born. Today, Greenpeace has branches throughout North America and Europe, and the gutsy environmentalists continue to draw public attention to issues of environmental abuse around the world.

**The world notices:** The coming of a World Fair, Expo 86, thrust Vancouver and its jewel-like setting onto the world stage. In the glare of fireworks and celebration, Canada's third

That and a downturn in the lumber industry thrust Vancouver into the doldrums yet again.

**Pacific rim player:** Modern Vancouver has come a long way from its rough and tumble frontier origins. In a world gradually turning environment-conscious, the city has evolved as something of a trend-setter. Hollywood producers, attracted by its unspoiled beauty, frequently choose the city as a location. Tourists come by the millions. It seems Vancouver's next logical step will be to find its way somehow to the centre of the world stage, to become a major North American influence on the vast Pacific Rim.

**Left**, City Hall in the 1950s. **Above**, Greenpeace sails into world headlines via Alaska in 1971.

Vancouver is a young city and, in many ways, an orphan. Cut off from the rest of the country by the Western Cordillera's mountainous barricade, and blessed with a climate that is decidedly un-Canadian, this coastal port has been left to its own devices for much of its history. The natural bounty of its surroundings, its isolation from the rest of the country, and its position as a seaport have combined to create an intriguing metropolitan area.

An object of desire for many urban Canadians, Vancouver has a character reflecting the irascible flavour of the Pacific Northwest. Its coat-of-arms, a logger and a fisherman, hold the provincial seal above the legend, "By sea, land and air we prosper." And while its burgeoning arts scene reflects its urban soul, the population's strong ties to its natural habitat are immediately apparent. Expanses of forested parkland paint swatches of green through real estate developments; world-class ski-runs rise directly above terraced suburban gardens. Today's Vancouverites are among the biggest outdoor sports *aficionados* in the world.

Little more than a century ago Vancouver was a frontier village, a logging backwater barely afforded a glance by the hordes of gold-maddened prospectors stampeding into the interior in search of fame and fortune. In 1883 there were just 145 registered white residents: loggers, mill hands, stevedores, fishermen and merchants, plus uncounted saloon owners. It was nothing like today's garden-loving, afternoon tea-drinking Victoria across the Strait of Georgia or booming New Westminster upriver on the Fraser.

But discerning entrepreneurs were already sizing up its awesome potential as a Pacific Rim trading centre. "It is only once in a lifetime that the public have such a chance as the present," wrote a writer for the Portland-based *West Shore Magazine* in 1884, "and we would recommend to those who have

**Preceding pages:** Vancouver character; fiddling around. **Left,** sporting style. **Right,** paddler.

money to investigate the merits of Vancouver… before making other investments."

It has often been said that the finest trees on the entire Canadian west coast once stood in the heart of what is now downtown Vancouver. Indeed some giants remain, mutely standing today in Stanley Park. Blessed with a seemingly inexhaustible source of wealth, few questioned loggers', miners' and fishermens' early exploitative methods. The land was so vast, the geography so over-

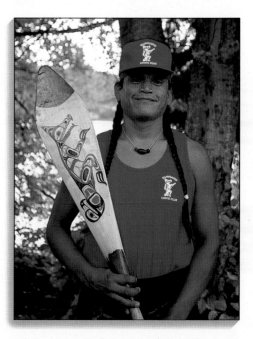

whelming, nobody imagined the well would ever run dry. For many years this led to an unimaginable harvesting of natural resources from the ocean, rivers, mountains, canyons and forests.

**Natural harbour:** Vancouver is blessed with a fine natural harbour – a critical factor in its rapid expansion. With the arrival of the Canadian Pacific Railway (CPR), linking this harbour to the markets of Asia and the world, Vancouver soon became an important cog in Pacific trade routes while also serving as the gateway to the wild and profitable gold-laden interior. Slowly the rough-hewn logging town donned a more gentrified skin, while never completely losing its rowdy boom-town roots. Immigrants who arrived with a European-orientation soon learned to look to the Pacific for their future and to form a new set of links to the land and its First Peoples.

**Casual chic:** And therein lie its charms today. For if Vancouverites have something of the entrepreneurial Californian in them, they also have the unabashed play ethic of the coastal Australian. The operative word is casual. Cotton slacks and open-necked shirts are far more popular than suits. And being fit is simply understood. Tight muscles and a

well-sunned skin are not only highly appreciated, they are *de rigueur*. You don't only do lunch here, you meet for a run or a swim or a ride. Tennis, golf, skiing, scuba diving, windsurfing, kayaking, climbing, cycling – they're all available within the city limits. In Vancouver, your quality of life is measured less by what you do at the office and more by what you do with your leisure time.

Eastern Canadians refer to Vancouver as Lotus Land – Canada's capital of hedonism. To them, Vancouver seems a sub-tropical paradise peopled by dreamers, schemers and eccentric New-Agers. Wrapped in the chill of winter, they wince when they see news clips of Vancouverites playing tennis or golf in January. They shake their heads despairingly as Vancouverites enthuse about snowboarding or bungee jumping. They can't understand why Vancouver has such inefficient highways. They sigh in exasperation when their western colleagues arrive at board meetings dressed in jeans and tennis shoes.

**First People's spirit:** It is at night, when the sound of drumming wafts along the shore lines and spirit dancers weave their magic within their longhouses, that Vancouver's secret wild-soul seems most apparent. Hidden behind a sumptuous golf course in Vancouver's posh Point Grey district, the modest wooden homes of the Musqueam village reserve sprawl across the coarse marsh grass that lent its name to this native tribe. The Musqueam are one of a handful of thriving native bands still inhabiting their ancestral lands within the city's boundaries.

Make no mistake, despite the encroachment of modern Canadian society, indigenous native cultures are very much alive. Hunters and gatherers as well as business people and bureaucrats; today's West Coast Nations continue to be consummate water-experts who look to the sea for their cultural affirmation. Salmon, prawns, clams, oysters and crab are bounteous in the oxygen-rich waters of the Fraser River estuary.

Almost annihilated by smallpox during the 19th century, the Musqueam, Burrards, Kwantlen and Squamish Nations have experienced a resurgence in recent years. Their voices can be heard in the day-to-day affairs of modern Vancouver. The Musqueam, for example, run a golf course, while the North Shore Squamish Nation leases out a major shopping centre, driving range, condominiums and desirable real estate beside Lions Gate Bridge.

Of even greater promise to the bands' future, however, is the curiosity shown among the young for the old ways. Once-forbidden rituals like the potlatch are now practised openly. "It is a way of reinforcing our own identity," says Wendy Grant, tribal chief of the Musqueam, real state developer and spirit dancer, "a way of finding within ourselves the power to resist the wholesale destruction of our culture."

A private ceremony, the spirit dance is but one of the sacred rituals of the Coast Salish-speaking people. Today, along with sweat lodge ceremonies, dances are sometimes used to reset the life course of a troubled youth or addicted adult. Inititiates do not choose to become dancers. Rather, they are chosen and may be taken against their will. "It can be a very traumatic experience," says Grant of the week-long initiation which employs fasting, meditation, exercise and sweat baths to reveal an individual's personal spirit guide (usually an animal: Bear, Wolf or perhaps

haunting geometric renderings carved in wood or precious metal. Coveted by collectors from around the world, they are a potent vision of a spirit world imprinted indelibly on the city.

**Denizen of Vancouver:** "How can a resident of this region ignore an art form so obviously in tune with its environment?" asks Vincent Massey, a third-generation Vancouverite and grandson of actor Raymond Massey. A successful potter and passionate outdoorsman, Massey lives in the popular alpine resort of Whistler, only 115 km (70 miles) north of Vancouver. "It is obvious from their art that the Coast Salish had a very deep kinship with

Eagle). "But," she adds, "it most always turns out to be a positive experience."

**Salish spirits:** British Columbia has the largest population of First Nations in Canada. The cultural fabric of the region's indigenous people infuses the spirit of Vancouver as in no other city in North America. The artistic incarnation of native power is perhaps most accessible to outsiders. Obstreperous Raven, leaping Killer Whale, soaring Eagle and playful Sea Otter are some of the

Left, gotta lotta latté. Above, a great way to get around – except when it rains.

their natural surroundings before the coming of the whites. For them, it wasn't a question of man against nature but of man existing within nature. Everything was in balance – everything had to be treated with respect." In many ways, Massey embodies that balance. He grew up on the far edges of West Vancouver, in a cliffside house designed by his architect father, Geoff Massey, overlooking the Straits of Georgia. Behind the house, rising in one solid wave of granite and fir, were the imposing North Shore mountains.

"The ocean was our playground," says Vincent. "Each summer my dad would pack us all in his boat and we'd take off for some destination up the coast. We'd fish and crab and dig for clams; camp on the beach and cook over big ol' driftwood fires. It was coastal adventuring at its best." In the winters, Massey Sr would lead his family into the mountains on skiing trips. "Dad wasn't into skiing the runs at the local ski hills," adds Vincent. "More often than not, he'd take us deep into the mountains for some backcountry exploring."

By the time he was a teenager, Massey was as comfortable taking an outboard engine apart as he was leading a party of skiers through a mountain blizzard. But that was

noons are often spent snowboarding at Blackcomb, mountain biking in the hills behind his house or windsurfing down on the waters of Howe Sound. "I like to have fun," he says. "Both at work and at play. For me, that's what life on the coast is all about."

**Quality leisure time:** Massey is not alone in voicing these sentiments. Vancouverites are almost rabid in their pursuit of the leisure life next to the land, which is not surprising: Vancouver's charms have always revolved around its physical attributes. The Coast Salish migrated here because of the abundance of food and the mild climate. The first white settlers stayed for the seemingly inex-

only half his education. His mother, a painter, encouraged her four children to develop their artistic talents early. "Pottery just felt natural to me," he says of his chosen profession. "It is a very physical activity. Yet there are subtle sensibilities involved, too."

**Coastal life:** Like the English potters with whom he studied, Massey works at home in a studio he built adjoining his house. Despite the growth in popularity of his pots and the consequent drain on his free time, Massey manages to maintain a balance between work and play. Mornings will often find him at his wheel or mixing a new batch of clay; after-

haustible supply of timber, game, minerals and fish. Today, tourists travel here to bask in BC's breathtaking scenery and take in leisure activities.

From the impossibly steep slopes of the North Shore mountains to the great sandy beaches of English Bay and Kitsilano, from Point Grey's spectacular Pacific Spirit Park to clothing-optional Wreck Beach, the city offers up a variety of outdoor settings. The denizens of Vancouver are quick to take advantage.

**Green space foremost:** Interestingly enough, the importance of protecting Vancouver's natural beauty was accidentally appreciated by its founding fathers. The primordial forest of Stanley Park – its 400 hectares (1,000 acres) within a short walk of downtown – is one of Vancouver's oldest features. The decision to acquire the peninsula of land and turn it into a park dates back to 1886; indeed, it was the first resolution of the city's very first council.

Despite being surrounded by wild rainforests to the south, east and north – and despite having to deal with the ravages of a massive fire that had completely destroyed the town only two weeks earlier – Vancouver's fledgling council considered preserving this tidal

**The outdoor scene:** Today's Vancouver is interspersed with walking trails, beaches and playing fields that have always set the tone for the city's sporting style. Walking is respected and pedestrians are generally given the right of way over all vehicles.

Nowhere is Vancouver's outdoor flair more apparent than at Kitsilano Beach (Kits) in summer. Minutes away from downtown, Kits Beach offers a microcosmic view of the city's hedonistic culture – along with a slough of bronzed bodies that belies Vancouver's reputation for grey skies and rainy days. From muscular body builders and sleek ocean swimmers to rangy basketball players; from

island of mostly-unlogged forest as its most important order of business. Though city fathers were partially motivated by a desire to keep pristine new waterfront lots from competing with their seedier holdings in Gastown, their action turned out to be an act of radical foresight. Initially treated as a joke in Ottawa – why do they want to save trees when they have so many? – Stanley Park provided the young city with a strong and impressive signature.

**Left** and **above**, quality leisure time is the measuring stick of success.

lean beach volleyballers to sculpted triathletes; from hackey-sackers to jugglers and acrobats: the extensive grass-and-sand area of Kits seems to display almost every kind of outdoor leisure activity. "It's a scene," says Joelle Smith, a longtime frequenter of Kits Beach. "There's no doubt about it."

**Fitness and vitality:** Places like Kits Beach have a sporting ethos with few urban peers in North America. Where other towns have developed a single-minded café culture, Vancouver has developed an obsession with physical fitness and remains devoted to its coffee houses as well. Packs of well-toned joggers in $200 running shoes churn up the paths of city parks; smooth-legged cyclists in racing jerseys and $2,000 bikes hammer through the streets. When the ski season begins, the action shifts to the mountains. One of the favourite ski resorts in North America, Vancouver's much-vaunted Whistler–Blackcomb, 115 km (70 miles) distant, is as hip as they come. Former Prime Minister Pierre Trudeau often takes a vacation here, as do a bevy of Hollywood stars like John Travolta, Darryl Hannah and Mel Gibson.

But Whistler doesn't diminish the attraction of the three North Shore ski and

snowboarding mountains – Cypress, Grouse and Seymour – each providing excellent conditions. Only minutes from downtown, all three offer day and night skiing from November until April. On a good powder-snow day many Vancouverites will *not* be found slogging away in stuffy, overheated offices. They hide from the boss in a cloud of powder-snow.

Vancouver's love affair with outdoor sports goes back a long way. One cherished figure was Jamaican-born "Black Joe" Fortes, who arrived as an able-bodied seaman in 1885. Fortes soon took on the responsibility for

policing the popular beach at English Bay. "He taught nearly all the boys and girls to swim," wrote novelist Ethel Wilson. "I can still hear Joe Fortes saying in his rotund rich voice, 'Jump! I tell you, jump! If you don't jump off that raft, I'll throw you in.' So we jumped. Mothers send their children to the beach with a nickel for Joe. 'Tell Joe to watch you.' Joe was a 'heroic' figure."

The city's obsession with fitness and sports has nurtured fine athletes over the years. Sprinter Percy Williams captured two gold medals in 1928 at the Olympic Games in Amsterdam. Although no Vancouver athlete since has managed to match Percy's feat, athletes from the Lower Mainland have always provided a large contingent to Canada's national teams.

Vancouver has also inspired visiting sports figures to amazing feats of excellence. It was here, at Empire Stadium during the 1954 British Empire Games, that Britain's Roger Bannister nipped Australian John Landry at the wire to win what was to become known as the Miracle Mile. For the first time in history, two men had managed to complete the gruelling run in under four minutes.

From Vancouver's international triathlon to its annual marathon and Dragon Boat races; from the World Cup ski races hosted at Whistler–Blackcomb to the prestigious Indy NASCAR race held in the city's downtown streets and the world-championship sailing regattas at Jericho Sailing Centre – the range of high-calibre sports events are wide-ranging. "It's one of my favourite places to compete in the world," says superstar triathlete Mark Allen. "Vancouver fairly oozes with vitality."

If watching team sports is your favourite pastime, fear not: Vancouver boasts a National Hockey League team, the Vancouver Canucks; a Canadian Football League team, the B.C. Lions; a National Basketball Association team, the Vancouver Grizzlies; a soccer team, the Eighty Sixers; and a triple A baseball team, the Canadians. All are strongly suppported by local fans.

**Endurance and style:** Vancouver's most fitting – and offbeat – event, however, is one that few people have heard about. It is the Knee Knackering North Shore trail run, a gruelling 48 km (30 miles) endurance test with nearly 6,000 metres (18,000 ft) of vertical change along a narrow path in West Vancouver's mountainous rainforest. The fastest runners complete the course (a journey that takes most backpackers two or three days) in just under five hours; the maximum time allotted is 10 hours.

Far from knackered, though, most participants seem surprisingly rejuvenated by their backcountry adventure. "It's the kind of race," explains perennial champion Peter Findlay, "where you need a wide range of skills: balance, agility, flexibility – not to mention endurance and strength. Besides, there is

Vancouver right of passage. Starbucks, the Bread Garden, and numerous independent coffee establishments glory in the flavours of deep French roast blends complimented in summer by iced latté "frappuccinos". To experience Vancouver is not only to show off the fit body, it is equally to lounge outdoors, learn a little java jabber, order a "long tall skinny," do a little people-watching, and savour the aroma of a fresh brewed cappuccino.

**Self confident at last:** Vancouver, Canada's orphan metropolis, youthful, hedonistic and showing the self-confidence of a major new world capital, is a blend of diverse influ-

something really special to running alone in the mountains. At times you reach this incredibly peaceful state of mind. It is," he pauses for a moment, then smiles broadly, "pure bliss."

**Coffee house culture:** Sporty Vancouverites also relish the chance to reflect upon their city's bounties, summer or winter, rain or shine, sitting in an outdoor café. Establishments seem to spring up almost every other day. The art of drinking java has become a

**<u>Left</u>, gazing out at the world. <u>Above</u>, three peas in a longboat pod.**

ences, shaped on the one hand by the mystic visions of the Coast Salish who first inhabited its shores, and on the other by the entrepreneurial spirit of the wild-eyed fortune-seekers drawn here during the 19th century. Today health-conscious, sports-crazy, liberal-minded Vancouverites live in one of the most beautiful natural settings on the planet. And the land shapes their world view. "I've travelled all over the world," says Vincent Massey, "and I wouldn't live anywhere else but here. Why should I? I've got everything I want in my own backyard."

# FRONT DOOR ON THE PACIFIC

With the mountains at its eastern side and tundra to the north, Vancouver has always looked for its identity to distant horizons towards both Asia and California. Here, on the coast, the Pacific is both the familiar ocean lapping at the beaches, and the doorway to fabulous and exotic lands.

Vancouver vibrates to the fact that the Pacific, with over a quarter of the world's population on its rim, is where the city's fortunes lie. The BC government maintains a trade presence in Taipei, Hong Kong, Singapore, Tokyo and Seoul, and the BC Trade Development Corporation continuously seeks Pacific-based export opportunities. And at the turn of the 21st century the population of the city of Vancouver approaches 60 percent Asian.

**Pan-Pacific focus:** The Pacific brings to Vancouver the Japanese current, the climatic modifier delivering continous rain and temperate seasons. The Pacific brought the first Europeans (around South America) and that ocean continues to be the most reliable and cheapest carrier for Vancouver's trade goods. More than 200 years ago, sea otter pelts satisfied the sartorial demands of mandarins in far-off China. To this day, fur is a valuable trade item as posh Vancouver hotel boutiques advertise Canadian furs to tempt the hundreds of thousands of Japanese tourists who visit each year.

Gift shops around fashionable hotels post Japanese and Taiwanese signs inviting tourists to buy "Canadiana" (Canadian-made goods), furs and local salmon; over 20 stores cater to the Japanese gift trade in an area sometimes called "Little Ginza". Vancouver has 33 foreign-based banks and, though the US remains BC's largest single trading partner, Pacific Rim nations combine to vie for equal footing.

Planeloads of Japanese and Taiwanese tourists arrive each summer to enjoy Canadian scenery, especially its national parks. Vancouver hotels give their employees courses in Asian customs and etiquette to better serve incoming visitors. For example, Japanese diners like fast, quiet, efficient service and small portions, while Chinese customers like more leisurely, convivial dining, though they rise immediately after a meal and leave.

The traffic, of course, is in both directions. Young Canadians with touring fever can economically explore Thailand, India and other Asian destinations, while Asian language courses are always popular at colleges and night schools.

**Asian immigrants arrive:** Asian influences are nothing new to BC. The first influx of Chinese workers arrived in the 1870s, following on the heels of those who came to search for gold in 1858 and others who may have arrived even earlier. From that time to this, the Pacific nations of China, Japan, Taiwan, Korea and the Philippines have provided hundreds of thousands of immigrants to "Saltwater City", as the Chinese once called Vancouver. In addition, hundreds of thousands more from the US west coast, Hawaii, Mexico, Australia, New Zealand and India have come to BC to seek their fortunes and sink their roots.

As early as 1860, Hawaiians, known locally as *Kanakas,* jumped ship at Vancouver to settle and work in Gastown; others went to work for the Hudson's Bay Company. The gold rush and the railway boom lured many Chinese, mostly from the poor province of Canton. There is no doubt that Canada greatly prospered through the muscle-power provided by these early immigrants.

At the turn of the 20th century, Japanese and East Indians, mostly single men, ventured across the Pacific to work at fishing and logging. Despite being highly visible targets and useful scapegoats for the dissatisfied, their diligence and good business acumen brought many of them prosperity. Sikhs from India made fortunes exporting BC lumber to Asia; the Japanese were expert fisher-

**Preceding pages: our future lies with Canada. Left, immigrants have long been an important part of Canada's culture.**

men and gardeners; the Chinese started small businesses, bountiful market gardens and the first florist industry.

**Exclusionary period:** With the wholesale importation of Chinese labour to build the railway, it was not long before anti-Chinese sentiment surfaced. The Chinese who settled this new land consistently sent their savings back across the Pacific to help their families, and many intended to return, though for most this would not be possible. As early as 1887, ruffians marched on Chinese camps, employers imposed hiring boycotts (except for the railway), inflamatory speeches were common and Chinese labourers suffered vicious

**Quiet evidence of Asia:** Today, in stark contrast to those turbulent beginnings, all around Vancouver quiet evidence of Asian contributions can be seen. In Stanley Park, a stone memorial stands under cherry trees commemorating Japanese Canadians who died for Canada in World War I. During World War II, a highly decorated contingent of second-generation Japanese-Canadians fought with the Canadian Forces in Italy. Near the park's shoreline, the replicated figurehead of the *S.S. Empress of Japan* still extends a silent greeting to vessels entering Vancouver's beautiful harbour. One of a whole fleet of elegant Empress steamships,

assualts. After a mob scene in which Chinatown was set on fire, on March 2, 1887, Vancouver's city charter was suspended pending the restoration of order. Though the activities of so-called exclusionary leagues were to continue for almost 50 years, the Chinese community came together to set up benevolent societies to care for their sick and elderly, and helped each other endure the periodic race riots as well as punative fines, immigration head taxes and unfair business practices. The same litany of hardships was also endured and overcome by Japanese "Asiatics".

it plied Pacific waters for 31 years carrying Vancouver's commerce to the Orient.

Bilingual street signs and recessed second-floor balconies on many of prosperous Chinatown's red-painted buildings are an echo of home to visitors from Hong Kong. On Pender Street, the charming Dr Sun Yat-Sen Classical Chinese Garden is a testimonial to the Chinese leader who in 1911 visited Vancouver while raising funds for the Chinese revolution. In 1985, the People's Republic of China sent 52 artisans, armed with a secret recipe for lacquer and knowledge of *feng shui,* to build an authentic copy of a Suzhou scholar's peaceful garden retreat. Now part of the Chinese Cultural Centre, the garden stages numerous events celebrating the city's Chinese heritage.

At the University of British Columbia, the beautiful Nitobe Memorial Garden, dedicated to the Japanese humanist Inazo Nitobe, provides a tranquil refuge for students and citizens alike. When Japan's Crown Prince visited the garden in 1980, he tellingly stated, "Now I am in Japan." Alongside the Nitobe Garden are the University of British Columbia's (UBC) Asian Centre for Oriental Studies and its Arts Centre, partly funded by Tom and Caleb Chan, wealthy expatriates from

working in real estate, Lam has given much of his wealth to various universities and foundations. He accepted the governorship in the interest of increasing inter-racial harmony. Son of a Baptist minister, he combined the philosophies of Christianity and Confucianism. During his tenure, he received up to 1,000 people each month at Government House. When a child asked him about his job, he quipped "I am here to deny the government absolute power."

**Exposed to Expo:** From the 1950s to the 1970s both immigrants and refugees arrived from the Korean and Vietnamese conflicts, as did East Indians expelled from the Fiji

Hong Kong who wanted to give something back. On the terrace of the Student Union Building, in honour of those who died at Tiananmen Square stands a replica of "The Goddess of Democracy," her light of freedom held high.

Other UBC buildings were funded through the philanthropy of Dr David Lam, a Hong Kong expatriate and British Columbia's recent Lieutenant-Governor. A millionaire

**Left**, Japanese Festival; Chinese New Year. **Above**, celebrations reflect Vancouver's Pacific Rim heritage.

Islands and Uganda. Then over 22 million visitors from around the world visited Vancouver's world trade exposition, Expo 86. Many liked what they saw and immigration soared in ensuing years. From the Philippines came nurses to work in Vancouver hospitals and families who despised the Marcos regime. As Asian immigration increased, so did their investment. Japanese trading companies, the *sogo shosha*, started the trend in the 1960s by investing in BC resource companies.

**The Hong Kong boomerang:** Hong Kong arrivals accelerated through the 1980s and early 1990s. These immigrants invested first in real estate, then in high-tech and the garment industry. Immigration from the crown colony grew by 44 percent annually from 1983 to 1987, until in the 1990s the immigrants' investment in Vancouver was estimated at around $150 million annually. The dominant language in Vancouver's Chinatown changed from Cantonese (descendants of railway workers) to Mandarin (Hong Kong residents). Long-time Cantonese expatriots felt great pressures from new self-assured Hong Kong arrivees.

In Vancouver, the years immediately preceding the Hong Kong handover brought a

As Hong Kong fortunes were quietly removed and new investment from Asia trickled to a standstill, Vancouver's real estate – commercial, industrial and residential – began a steady downward tick. Though the rest of North America's economy remained buoyant during that period, Vancouver and British Columbia entered yet another downturn in their infamous boom-and-bust economic cycles, evidence of the reliance on Asian investment and trade.

**English as a second language:** At the close of the 20th century, two-thirds of immigrants to Vancouver originate from Asia, many of them highly-skilled with both capital and

huge surge of investment and immigration. But in 1997, after the crown colony returned to Chinese rule, the Asian monetary crises struck and many new residents needed to sell their million-dollar Vancouver homes to recover what they lost in China. A great many recent immigrants pulled out their Canadian resources to save their Asian investments. Some returned to Hong Kong. All this had a devastating effect on Vancouver. However, since both housing and education continued to be cheaper in Vancouver, many of the well-to-do set about making their living in both regions of the world.

business acumen. However, the Vancouver school system is encountering a crisis in funding for English as a second language (ESL) instruction. In many schools at all grade levels, up to 80 percent of the children understand little or no English. This includes both the children of new immigrants and those of long time residents who are so integrated into a large Chinese community that there is little need to speak English to their children.

The school system is striving to adapt to the strain, with the proliferation of ESL-trained instructors in the Vancouver area spawning a pool of skilled English language teaching labour. Japanese nationals in Japan who want to equip themselves for world trade have wooed thousands of Vancouverites abroad to teach English in schools in Japan.

**Adapting to the Asian presence:** BC Hydro, a major electricity supplier, employs dozens of multicultural consultants, enabling the corporation to communicate with its customers in 24 languages. At the Vancouver General Hospital, a psychiatrist specialises in young people's cross-cultural problems. An active exchange programme between Vancouver's student population and Asian schools remains significant from a business perspective.

During the 1980s and 1990s, Asian investment changed the face of Vancouver's downtown, including the addition of the Hong Kong Bank, a modern office tower and Canada's seventh largest bank. Cathedral Place across from the Vancouver Hotel, together with adjacent Cathedral Park, is owned by Hong Kong film tycoons Ronnie Shon and Sir Runrun Shaw. The Ramada Renaissance Hotel (New World Developments, Cheng Yu-tung, Hong Kong) has been upgraded to the degree of luxury expected by affluent Asians. On the waterfront the Tokyu Corporation's aptly named Pan Pacific Hotel is topped with a glowing multi-coloured dome. At one stage in the 1990s, about 30 to 40 percent of Vancouver's hotel rooms were Asian-owned. Many of these hotels and other public buildings feature Asian ideograms on signs in elevators and washrooms.

The Vancouver suburb of Richmond is home to several all-Asian malls including the Aberdeen Centre, North America's largest Asian Mall, which is owned by the Sun Hun Kai group, one of Hong Kong's major business dynasties.

**Learning Asian ways:** The Chinese expression, *Gung Hay Fat Choy*, is heard as often in certain boardrooms in Vancouver as are the words "Happy New Year" the month before. The Canadian International Dragon Boat Festival on False Creek in June draws

thousands of Vancouverites each year, as does the smaller Powell Street Festival, the celebration of the Japanese community in August. Business people of all persuasions often proffer a business card held in both hands, a tiny tribute to Japanese ways. Asian customs permeate the city.

Vancouver realtors, for example, quickly learned what was necessary for a house to have good *feng shui* – that is, lucky and harmonious aspects, essential if you're trying to sell to Asians. This includes knowledge of the proper orientation of the front door, knowledge of districts where the sleeping dragon does not lie, avoidance of cul de

sacs and proximity to graveyards, beneficial colours like red or gold, and the use of mirrors or wind chimes to deflect unfavourable energies. The provincial government once ran seminars on how to cater to Asian customers, including hints on how to avoid the numbers 4, 14 and 24 – all of which have linguistic connections with death for the Chinese.

**Indelible exclamation marks:** The Asian influence has made an indelible mark on the West Coast way of life and will continue to do so. Throughout the city are exotic exclamation points reflecting Vancouver's Pa-

**Left**, Filipino native dance. **Right**, East and West make a marriage.

cific Rim heritage. The five golden domes of the Alkali Singh Sikh temple beside the freeway and the brightly coloured 10-metre (30-ft) dancing statue of Lord Chaitanya, a Hare Krishna saint, in the industrial area on Stewardson Way near Burnaby are two examples. On South Vancouver's Marine Drive is a dazzling white Sikh temple, its silver filigree onion dome designed by Vancouver architect Arthur Erickson. On the Steveston Highway in Richmond an ancient-style Chinese Buddhist temple, brightly decorated in red and gold with porcelain tiled roof, sits among western suburban houses near a traditional Shinto shrine. Off Canada Way in the

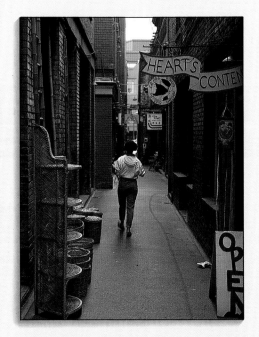

nearby area of Burnaby, behind the trees of its Taj Mahal-like forecourt, is the $10 million Ismaili Jamatkhana temple.

When a prominent Japanese artist, Noburi Toko from Kushiro, came to visit his home town's sister city Burnaby (a Vancouver suburb), he was so impressed by Canadian hospitality he created, in the style of the peoples of northern Japan, *The Garden of the Gods*, a unique collection of Ainu totem poles on Burnaby Mountain overlooking Vancouver. They include a cluster of bears, whales, owls and ravens, mutual symbols for both Ainu and BC native peoples. A pointer faces out over Burrard Inlet, indicating the direction to Kushiro.

**Multi-cultural media:** Vancouver has several ethnic television stations, so at any time you can switch your TV control and see an East Indian movie, an episode in a Chinese historical series, or a Japanese or Korean variety show. By law, cable companies must make at least one channel a local multicultural community channel. The city also has ethnic radio stations and non-English local publications.

Cathay TV's president, Lucy Roschap, born in Hong Kong to celebrated moviemaker parents, managed the family's chain of Chinese cinemas in Canada after graduating from the University of British Columbia. Then she was invited by the three Vancouver Chinese families who founded Cathay TV to take over its leadership. The station broadcasts in the Chinese, Vietnamese, East Indian and Thai languages, publicising local and community activities. "Not many people realise just what sacrifices many immigrants may have made in careers and salaries, to come to Canada for a chance to live under a stable government and get a good education for their children," she says. "These people are coming here to stay. They want to mix and be a part of this country, so a lot of our programming is geared to that need."

**Investing goes both ways:** China, for example, actively invites Western Canadian business people to invest there, and seeks their expertise. BC firms, such as suppliers of electrical high-voltage connections to mining and construction projects, have found China to be a good market for Canadian-made products. In return the People's Republic of China now has at least 40 companies doing business out of the Vancouver area. For example, a contingent from China is financing and redeveloping the town core of Maple Ridge, a Vancouver suburb.

When trading between Canada and Japan was reinstated after World War II, Japanese ships were loaded at night to avoid reprisals. Today, Japan is one of the largest Asian investors in BC to the tune of over $3.6 billion annually. Toyota's $58 million expansion to its Delta plant is turning out nearly a million automobile wheels every year. Included in the export business is one surprising venture: Mitsubishi/Chogoku owns the largest chopstick factory in the world. It is located in northern British Columbia and produces 10 million pairs a day.

**The Ka-shing dynasty arrives:** When the Expo 86 site went on the block, Hong Kong billionaire Li Ka-shing paid $125 million for it, perhaps the bargain of the century. He phased in the first stages of a $2 billion urban development on the site managed by Concord Pacific, originally under V. P. Stanley Quok, a Hong Kong architect, with expertise in developing large projects. Ka-shing's son,

BC's largest independent sawmill operators, he is a generous supporter of institutions such as the University of British Columbia and the Vancouver Children's Hospital.

Tiger Balm heiress Sian (Sally) Aw, from Hong Kong, bought IMPARK, Vancouver's largest parking management company, in the 1980s, and sold it 10 years later for $20 million.

**Pacific Rim Destiny:** "Vancouver seems destined to become an international city, almost a city-state unto itself," says Professor Jean Barman in her book, *A History of British Columbia*. A city on the Pacific Rim, but still a North American city, Vancouver

Victor Li, resides part-time in Vancouver to look after the family's Canadian investments in oil, gas and real estate.

Some Canadian-born Asians, such as former beauty queen Andrea Eng, president of the Hong Kong-Canada Business Association, have adapted to new markets and once handled real estate sales in the millions. Asa Jahal was only 18 months old when his family came to Canada from India and started work in a sawmill at age 14. Now one of

**Left**, alley in Chinatown. **Above**, Asian products for food and folk medicine.

offers citizens and business people the best of European, American and Asian cultures and worlds. Reflecting on Vancouver, Canadian opera conductor and impresario Irving Guttman says: "I get the impression that people of the West Coast, regardless of ethnic origins, are able freely to be themselves."

Vancouver's beginnings and its future are inextricably locked into the Pacific Ocean and its sister countries around its rim. After spending a century climbing the mountain ranges between itself and the rest of Canada, it continues to turn a welcoming face across the sea.

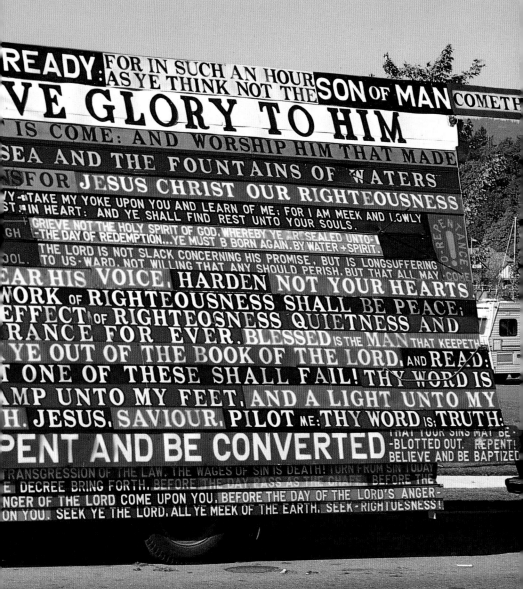

"Go west, young man," attributed to newspaperman Horace Greeley in 1851, has proven to be oft-repeated advice for persistent youths wanting to get ahead in North America. From Europe, America and Asia, the restless hordes have traditionally migrated westward across Canada where – stopped by the Pacific ocean shoreline and captivated by the mild climate – they stayed. Blocked from further wandering, it seems their arrested energy bubbles up in various types of West Coast looniness. At times hyperkinetic types east of the Rockies find it difficult to relate to Vancouverites' laid-back, somewhat off-centre lifestyle.

At the beginning Vancouver and its citizens didn't bother with many formalities. Morris Panych, the award-winning playwright and actor, when looking back on his adopted home, says, "Vancouver seems... an idea thrown together quickly, a hodgepodge, precariously teetering on the edge of civilisation, and sort of making itself up as it goes along."

**Odd from the start:** The first saloon keeper, Gassy Jack, dispensing opinions and liquor with equal generosity, was a unique host who chased drinkers out of his tavern at 10pm, saying he wanted them up bright and early to earn more money for him in the lumber mills. His saloon also doubled as the site for Vancouver's first church services, and stories are told of the first policeman, who having rounded up unruly Saturday night drunks, had them religiously wash their money on Sunday morning before they paid their fines. Otherwise, he said, when he counted it he felt sticky for a week. He accepted both British and American money, as well as anything of value and, for a time, this was Vancouver's only form of city income. Vancouver too is probably the only city that has named a street after an unknown leg. Downtown on False Creek is Leg in

Boot Square, commemorating all that was found of an unfortunate pioneer who set out to walk the 16 km (10 miles) to New Westminster through the bush.

**Confused politians:** The city was incorporated in April 1886, but the Great City Fire, almost a compulsory occurance in all boom towns, blazed out of control on June 13 that same year. Undaunted, the city fathers set up shop in a tent the next day and the first order of business was a group photograph in front

of the ruins (*see page 30*). Some say this was an early inkling of BC's political priorities.

BC politicians continue to be a special breed. Amor de Cosmos, the first premier, a displaced photographer from the California '49er gold rush, started a newspaper in Victoria. His specialty was criticising politicians – until, that is, he became one himself. His name, he claimed, meant "Lover of the Universe", but critics described him as a "waspish man with a venomous pen".

In 1897, on a boat returning from the Yukon, the bullet riddled corpse of criminal "Soapy Smith" was accidentally switched

**Preceding pages:** signs of his times. **Left**, squinty eyes, googly eyes. **Right**, scarlet is the colour of this true love's hair.

with the body of a vacationing passenger who happened to be former Vancouver mayor, Mr Fred Cope. In a lavish civic funeral, Vancouver citizens unknowingly buried the notorious outlaw.

A more recent premier who started his career in tulip bulb sales ended up owning a public show garden called Fantasy Gardens. Some say he kept confusing it with the entire province. His off-the-cuff pronouncements were considered bizarre enough to assemble into a little red book, *The Sayings of Chairman Zalm*. One of his predecessors as premier, nicknamed "Wacky" for his grandiose building projects, affirmed as Minister of

Highways a Pentecostal Revivalist nicknamed "Flying Phil". Phil, it seems, had an extensive collection of speeding tickets.

**Odd local laws and customs:** At one time or another Vancouver's lawmakers have decreed it illegal to sprinkle clothes by spraying water from your mouth, ride a camel down a major street, or run a three-legged race for money. Signs in certain Vancouver restaurants sometimes raise eyebrows too. Café Django once advertised "Jeffrey, the Headwaiter from Hell", and The Elbow Room once prided itself on its obnoxious service with the motto, "Abuse is our Game."

It must be something about the atmosphere – the air, the climate, maybe the barometric pressure – something seems to foster eccentricity both benign and bizarre. Some say Vancouver weather is enough to drive you mad. Although it's true you can golf in the morning and ski in the afternoon, you can also watch it mist, drip or pour rain all day for weeks. A local postcard once showed two identical dripping figures labelled respectively "Vancouver in summer" and "Vancouver in winter". There is, however, no truth to the rumour that 10 years' residence guarantees webbed feet.

**Watery masochism:** Water and Vancouver are synonymous, but its citizens demonstrate their affection for the ocean in unusual ways. The traditional Great Canadian Bathtub Race, a 61-km (38-mile) ocean race across Georgia Strait from Nanaimo in motorised, accessorised "bathtubs," seems as normal here as the Polar Bear Swim, a frigid English Bay experience on New Year's Day. The ultimate in hang-over cures, beginning the year with a dip in the sea has been a local custom since 1927, the idea being to see who can cavort the longest in the icy water, costumed either in formal dress or crazily attired. Vancouver author and humorist Eric Nicol describes it as "a form of mass dementia, demonstrating the city's penchant for masochism as an outdoor activity".

More uninhibited activities continue all summer at Wreck Beach where, on sunny weekends, more than ten thousand bathers bare all while similarly attired hawkers sell beer, hot-dogs, chocolate mousse, English trifle or chocolate-covered "magic" mushrooms. A beach wedding held here once saw the bride wearing only a veil and the groom a bow tie. Within the past decade, Vancouver has taken enthusiastically to the International Dragon Boat Festival. Local competitors have included a bank president and tellers against a rival crew composed of the VP of an airline and reservation clerks.

An even greater splash is generated by former football player and local businessman "Butts" Girard. He sponsors the Great North American Belly-flop at one of Vancouver's posh hotel swimming pools. The only athletic requirement is to have the build of a sumo wrestler. The winner is decided by the volume, sound and size of the splash.

**Eccentrics feel at home:** Flamboyant personalities seem to settle on the West Coast where they can feel comfortable among their own kind. The 1960s mayor Tom Campbell once said, "Where else could a loudmouth like me win an election except in a crazy city like this?" "Tom Terrific" won votes by threatening to "shave all the hippies".

Other cities had hippie colonies and flower children in the 1960s, but Vancouver was the only one that hired an official Town Fool. In 1967, Joachim Foikis, a philosophy graduate from Berlin and the University of British ver a unique reputation in a city where uniqueness is routine." In the same era, a citizen calling himself Mr Peanut campaigned for mayor in a giant nut costume. In his alter ego he called himself Dr Brute, appearing in a leopard-spotted costume playing a saxophone, often accompanied by his spotted wife, Lady Brute, and fellow artist Anna Banana, dressed as you might guess.

Colourful street people in Vancouver have a long tradition. In the 1930s Vancouver's eccentric-about-town was "Professor Francis", a talented pianist whose regular attire was bare feet, old shoes, a ragged overcoat with overflowing pockets and a

Columbia, received a $3,500 Canada Council grant to become Vancouver's Town Fool complete with a suit of motley and cap of bells. First outraged, then gratified, Vancouver city fathers revelled in the national attention he brought. However, when Foikis suggested citizens be taxed at 1¢ per citizen and 2¢ per politician for his continued street theatre services, his contract was not renewed. A professor of English, Warren Stevenson, said: "Foikis has given Vancou-

**Left**, nuke till you puke. **Above**, helping Lizzy relax on the set.

dead flower in his buttonhole. He frequently gatecrashed concerts and social events, where he cornered important people. One society matron and her prominent friends were approached at a lawn party with the sad story of the unhappy love that drove Professor Francis to be a derelict. As he talked, he rummaged through his pockets looking for his sweetheart's last letter, all the while handing the hostess various papers, unidentified objects wrapped in napkins and finally an old pancake. After many such incidents, the professor's appearance at a Vancouver social affair came to be considered a good omen.

Religious fanatics are legion, of course, but in Vancouver they come in amazing variations. During the 1950s, Vancouverites became inured to the sight of acres of bare flesh as large, heavy-set, elderly ladies stripped naked inside and in front of the courthouse at the height of the Doukhobour religious sect demonstrations. They were upholding their inalienable right to set fire to their own and dissenters' homes.

Also in the 1950s, a religious leader and convicted bigamist who called himself "Pope John" set up the community of the Temple of More Abundant Life on suburban acreage just outside the city. It flourished until he

His successor, Mayor Gerald McGeer, was a former milkman-turned-lawyer who favoured loud, checked suits and whose natural eloquence was criticised for "inflammation of the vowels". His reaction to the Depression was to build an expensive new monolithic City Hall and an illuminated fountain in Lost Lagoon, and to top things off with lavish Golden Jubilee celebrations. At least the city felt uplifted.

Mayor Dr Lyle Telford, a reformer with a tender heart, wanted to crack down on bawdy houses, but didn't want to throw the girls out on the streets, saying, "It's not fair to send them to Revelstoke, Calgary, Winnipeg and

gave a new meaning to the name of the church by running off with the funds and two of his young, nubile disciples. The building now houses Burnaby's popular Arts Gallery.

**Maverick mayors:** In the early years of the 20th century Mayor Louis D. Taylor bought a vacant lot and built a garage so its value would be assessed at over $1,000 to meet candidacy requirements. But he never lived there and didn't own a car. Somewhat accident-prone, he was nearly killed in 1928 when he backed into an airplane propeller, and had scarcely recovered a year later when he almost drowned on a canoe trip.

those other places." It's not clear to whom he thought this was unfair.

**Zany arts:** Though Vancouver has an active and talented arts scene, here too the bizarre sometimes reigns supreme. During a recent summer, tourists wandering Gastown streets were startled by a young actress dressed as a cat burglar scrambling down the side of a building – she was on her way to the outdoor set of an avant-garde production of *#5 Blood Alley*.

Visual art has managed to survive the assaults of a University of British Columbia professor, Dr Norm Watt, who for many years has roamed second-hand shops and garage sales collecting the World's Worst Oil Paintings. The annual auction of this artwork has netted the Canadian Paraplegic Association over a quarter of a million dollars. His "Salon de Refusés" once featured works rejected by the Louvre, the Smithsonian, and many a prestigious gallery.

The energetic arts community also includes BC artist Evelyn Roth who gained fame in the 1970s for crocheting Volkswagen covers out of film tape,then creating huge inflatable sculptures of salmon and Santa Claus. She once wrote: "There is certainly a spiritual something hovering on the Pacific Current

for the rest of his life. When he later went broke, he invited his creditors to a party to explain his plight. The menu consisted of one item: Boston baked brown beans on paper plates.

The monied do insist on indulging their foibles. The late "Chunky" Woodward, heir to a major department store fortune, once won a million dollars in a lottery. His comment was, "It'll come in handy." Jimmy Pattison, conglomerate owner and multimillionaire, sometimes plays the trumpet at his fundamentalist church on Sundays. Former Torontonian butcher Murray Pezim, a sharp shooting Vancouver promoter wins

that affects our lives." Yet when local artist Rick Gibson announced he was staging a public "happening" to kill a pet rat called Sniffy by dropping a heavy weight on him, there was a loud outcry. Vancouver can tolerate eccentricity, but not cruelty to animals.

**Money can be fun too:** Nelson Skalbania, former promoter and hotel owner, donated over a quarter of a million dollars to the YMCA for racquet ball courts on the condition that he get a permanent 5pm playing time daily

**Left**, hey, that's cheating. **Above**, light in a darkening moment.

and loses fortunes in penny mining stocks, while occasionally marrying and divorcing beautiful young women. Pezim once purchased the local football team, the hapless BC Lions, encouraging them to victory from the owners' box by waving his hands – encased in oversized orange gloves.

**Famous and wierd:** A good part of Malcolm Lowry's 1940s novel *Under the Volcano* was written in Vancouver in a ramshackle hut on the shores of Burrard Inlet. Lowry fitted comfortably into the local scene and local recollections include Lowry falling into the inlet from one of its windows while playing a guitar, or floating in a dinghy around the inlet in a drunken haze looking for Port Moody. Like all writers, Lowry hated deadlines and once took a hotel room downtown to hide from his New York agent due to collect a promised (and unfinished) manuscript.

Erroll Flynn, the swashbuckling actor, hardly had time to indulge in his famous eccentricities while he was in town. Stopping over to buy a boat in 1956, he passed away in a room in the Hotel Georgia. No word on who was with him. His body lay unclaimed in the Vancouver police morgue for several days.

**Alternative activists:** When a small dedicated band of environmentalists left Vancouver in a rickety boat to take on the French navy in the Pacific in 1971, the press thought they were crazy to protest about nuclear testing. Now they are known around the world as Greenpeace.

Dr Tomorrow, Frank Ogden, Vancouver's pre-eminent futurist, lives in an electronic floating cottage in the shadow of the high-rises overlooking Coal Harbour. Serviced by three robots, two satellite dishes and several computers accessing innumerable databases worldwide, he runs a future-predicting serv-ice. Constantly in demand for speaking engagements around the world he distinguishes himself from others who are only "using about 1 percent of their brainpower." Ogden says he gets paid "obscene" amounts of money by national corporations to tell them things like, "by the third millennium, you're going to see humans marrying robots." He is the epitome of the West Coast eccentric, his own man, sometimes outrageous, always entertaining, and sometimes even dead right.

**Transportation follies:** No one should be surprised that the first Canadian to jump from an airplane did it in Vancouver in 1912. The surprising thing is that he used a parachute. Vancouver had its first plane crash just six years later, when a local pilot (probably dissatisfied with the postal service) hit a West End roof while trying to drop a letter on his aunt's lawn. Not only daring but gallant, a Vancouver swain, George McKay, built one of Vancouver's longtime tourist attractions, the swinging Capilano Suspension Bridge, to amuse his girlfriend; it's been amusing generations of thrill-seekers ever since.

In 1900, young Bill Roedde, son of a bookbinder, achieved the lifelong distinction of being Vancouver's first pedestrian hit by a motorcar. The offender was no less than local sugar magnate, B.T. Rogers (the chauffeur did it!) but the highlight for the boy was being given sugar-treats and driven home in grand style. Not so lucky was the person who tangled with Vancouver's first ambulance. It accidentally ran over and killed a Texan tourist during its first emergency call.

Vancouver's generally well-mannered motorists still amaze tourists. Traffic can be backed up for blocks near the Lions Gate Bridge while a mother goose shepherds her flock of goslings across the road in front of a patient backup of stationary cars. Impatient visitors from other US and Canadian cities complain that the tempo here is too laid-back, easy-going, tolerant and eccentric. Sometimes Vancouverites agree, especially when they see how many of those same carping critics later decide to pack their bags and move in.

**Left**, street smart. **Right**, personal growth.

*Chuck Davis, noted broadcaster, writer and the man who has often been called "Mr Vancouver," describes in this chapter his affection for the city.*

I love Vancouver. When I arrived with my father in December 1944 there were flowers growing outside the Canadian Pacific Railway Station. We'd just come from my native Winnipeg, where temperatures of 20 below freezing were pretty normal for that

time of year. So the climate certainly got my affection for Vancouver off to an excellent start.

The waterfront was part of the attraction. Nothing quite equals a stroll along this crowded stretch of the inlet's southern shore, watching ships loading and unloading cargo, dodging big trucks as they rumble on to the docks, peeking into fish-processing plants, smelling the sea-wet air, and listening to the eerily beautiful screech of clouds of seagulls. The city's soundscape would be the poorer without them, and watching them fighting and diving for scraps is fun.

Speaking of sound, two unique examples are heard, unforgettably, every day in Vancouver. At noon, huge horns atop the BC Hydro Building startlingly blare out the first four notes of "O Canada", the national anthem; and at 9pm the famous Nine O'Clock Gun in Stanley Park booms out a one-bang time signal that, except for a hiatus during World War II, has been a city tradition for 100 years.

Europeans may be amused by our use of the words "tradition" and "heritage", given that we've been here at most 150 years. The aboriginal people here trace their presence back at least 10,000 years. One famous *midden* (refuse heap), at the time the largest one discovered in North America, is still down there under the parking lot of the Fraser Arms Hotel.

**Stunning sculpture:** On-site evidence of native life is hard to come by here in Vancouver. To get an idea of what life was like for the earliest residents, visit the UBC Museum of Anthropology on the campus of the University of British Columbia. The building is an airy, lofty marvel, designed by noted architect Arthur Erickson, and dominated at its entrance by gigantic totem poles and the stunning Bill Reid sculpture *The Raven and First Men*.

Reid's sculpture shows Raven prying open with his beak a gigantic clam, from which, blinking and fearful, the world's first people emerge. Reid, whose mother was a Haida Indian, is the Vancouver sculptor whose massive and powerful ebony-black sculpture, *The Spirit of Haida Gwai'i*, is set in the reflecting pool in front of the Canadian Embassy in Washington, DC. If I know friends are going to be visiting the city for just one or two days, this museum is the one location I tell them they must see.

I enjoy showing visiting friends other distinctive buildings in the city, too. The Marine Building at Hastings and Burrard, for example. This gorgeous Art-Deco creation, dwarfed now by taller, glossier neighbours, opened just in time for the Great Depression.

Even though it dominated the skyline of the time, for a couple of decades it sat mostly empty; no one could afford the rents. Then prosperity returned. For a great visual buzz, stand before the building's intricately carved main doorway, admiring the birds and planes, ships and seahorses, then afterwards step into the lobby.

Wow! The man who designed that lobby eventually went to Hollywood and became a set decorator. The elevators are a glossy

The Vancouver engineer who conceived this building, Bogue Babicki, also had a hand in the Bruno Freschi-designed Science World, an Expo 86 legacy, irreverently called the "golf ball", the gleaming spherical giant on Quebec Street to which I frequently point visitors. Lots of ever-changing science shows are held here, with an emphasis on hands-on activities for the kids.

**Holy structures:** Several of the buildings I like to show visiting friends are churches.

symphony of burnished hardwoods. The Marine Building is still the affectionate favourite of most Vancouverites.

**Another eyepopper:** The Westcoast Building on West Georgia is another eye-popper: it is suspended from giant steel cables and actually hangs from a central core. Its distinctive look earned it occasional appearances on the TV adventure shows and made-for-television movies.

**Preceding pages:** two of the city's notable facades. **Left,** Chuck Davis at the On On Tea Garden. **Above,** *The Raven and First Men.*

Built by its own priest, who died while finishing the little tower, there's the little Russian Orthodox church on Campbell Street with its bulbous blue steeple; St James's Anglican, a spectacularly Byzantine oddity designed by a man who had just finished working in the Middle East; and Holy Rosary Cathedral, a handsome Catholic structure whose placement is one of the great romantic traditions in the city. The bishop of the time, invited to choose the site for the placement of the new church, looked up into the lofty forest that covered most of what would become downtown Vancouver and the tallest of the trees. "There," he it there!"

...on to Glen Brae, built in 1910, the Shaughnessy Heights neighbourhood has dozens of huge and dramatic homes, many originally built for railroad executives. A drive along its curving, quiet, tree-lined streets is an experience to be savoured.

And there's Chinatown, not, as every city guide seems to have it, the second-largest in North America, but the third, because we're out-stripped by San Francisco *and* New York. When you visit you must see the World's Famous Building, so named by owner Jack Chow, a realtor. The 1912 Sam Kee Building

bought, and partly occupied, by the canny Mr Chow is just 2 metres (6 ft) wide, making it the narrowest commercial structure in the world. At one time, 14 separate companies were located in the building. A Chinese family of five once lived on the tiny top floor.

**Unusual facades:** The rest of Chinatown is also dotted with unusual facades. In fact, the north side of Pender Street has been called one of the finest groups of historic buildings in Canada. Constructed between 1886 and 1920 they demonstrate, said one admiring architect, a style "reminiscent of the commercial buildings in the proud cities of Shang-

hai and Beijing and the province of Canton. Recessed balconies, cornices and pediments crown the facades of brick, often with dates to testify to the year they were built."

Chinatown is always a visually and aurally exciting place to be: barbecued ducks hang in the windows, "hundred-year-old" eggs nestle next to the *bok coy*, other strangely-shaped vegetables share space with more familiar fare on a hundred sidewalk stalls, stores bulge with woks and lanterns, statues of Buddha, lamps, herbs, books and a million other colourful things. Bright neon Chinese characters tempt you inside scores of restaurants where gigantic menus open to page after page of different dishes. Saturday and Sunday are the busiest days, with Vancouver's thousands of Chinese doing their grocery shopping then.

If you've time for just one Chinatown restaurant, I'd recommend the On On Tea Garden, a small and informal gem that's been a favourite with my family for more than 25 years.

Although the building itself is unremarkable, you should set aside half an hour or so to visit the small, but densely packed Museum of Exotic World on Main Street. It's a huge, odd collection of photographs (many from *National Geographic Magazine*) and artefacts from far-flung corners of the world, in Africa, the Far East, South America and beyond, collected on their world travels by a retired gentleman named Harry Morgan and his wife. Harry is delighted to see visitors and tell them about the adventures that he's had and that *they* could have in these distant and exotic worlds. It's fun and free.

The modern trend of gussying up heritage buildings to convert them into glittering retail palaces has been in full flower in Vancouver. Two genuinely attractive examples among many others are the Sinclair Centre and City Square. Vancouver's Gastown area pioneered the concept locally: an entire block-long section of decaying warehouses and crumbling little office blocks was transformed several decades ago into a busy and hugely popular pocket of small shops, boutiques, bistros and cafés.

Gastown is still a fine place for strolling, with the harbour a few steps away, glimpsed between the old buildings. Art galleries, bookshops – with William Hoffer's big and unique collection of Canadiana worth a visit by the serious, and moneyed, book collector – souvenir stores, antique shops, ethnic emporia… lots to see and no shortage of places to eat an enormous variety of food.

**Random photo:** One of the town's more well-known sculptures is in Gastown. It purports to show Gassy Jack, the loquacious saloon keeper whose nickname was said to have inspired Gastown's name. I say "purports" because the sculpture, by Vern Simpson, is based on a photograph selected at random 20 years ago to represent old Gassy. A committee was leafing through some archival photos looking for someone who could have been Jack, and liked the look of one portly, bearded gent – name not known – leaning on a chair. Presto! He became Gassy Jack.

We seem to like statues of questionable lineage. A locally famous example is a full-sized Captain George Vancouver, standing on the north side of City Hall nobly pointing at something. That statue was based on a painting that once hung in an obscure corner elsewhere, because the curators decided they couldn't be sure it *was* Vancouver. There's a theory it may be George's brother, Charles Vancouver, a writer on botany. Incidentally, when I show a slide of that statue to Vancouver school kids during talks on the city's history and ask them who it is, they invariably reply: "George Washington".

The Vancouver statue and a great many others in the city were created during the 1930s and '40s by Charles Marega, a Swiss-born artist who fell in love with the city when he and his wife were here en route to somewhere else. They decided not to leave. Marega, over the years, provided us with many of our best statues as well as the dramatic Egyptian-style lions at the south end of the Lions Gate Bridge. His story has a sad ending, however: shortly after the Depression-era commission to do the bridge lions, he died with only $8 in the bank.

Speaking of sculptures, it's been said *The*

**Left**, horn of plenty. **Right**, the twin domes of Glen Brae, built in 1910, are a local landmark.

*Crab,* a gleaming and spiky George Nor creation in front of the Vancouver Museum/ MacMillan Planetarium complex (*see page 155*), is the single most photographed object in the city. A fountain jets its waters into the innards of this most unusual of Vancouver's outdoor artworks.

Vancouver has been made incomparably more interesting in the nearly 50 years I have known it through successive waves of immigrants. An astonishing variety of peoples has been drawn into the city: Greeks, Germans, Italians, Hungarians, Czechs, Poles, Thai, Chinese, Japanese, Vietnamese, Filipinos. Their restaurants and shops have enlivened

almost all of Vancouver's streets, and made it possible to dine and shop around the world at a moment's notice.

There are more than 2,000 restaurants in Greater Vancouver and I hope you'll have time to visit a flock of them. And I hope you'll have time to see a lot of Vancouver itself and environs.

If I were showing you around metropolitan Vancouver I might start or finish by driving you up on to the Upper Levels Highway, just across the inlet and halfway up the mountains. From here, you will be able to see all of the city all at once. The sight is stunning.

# HOLLYWOOD NORTH

When Vancouverites talk casually of a "shoot" on Georgia Street, they're not referring to downtown crime. Familiar with the caravan of trucks and limousines, the cables and sound booms that precede the making of a movie, they're comfortably at home with the jargon of what is one of their biggest industries – Hollywood North.

Established in 1978, BC's film making industry quickly grew from a mere $12 million a year, to an enterprise generating $650 million or so each year. That's not counting the billion dollars indirectly injected into British Columbia's economy. It's estimated 10,000 people are employed in film-making, so it's now one of the largest film production centres in North America.

Vancouver is often runner up to Los Angeles in its production of made-for-TV movies. In a recent year, for example, more than 80 assorted productions took advantage of BC's spectacular physical setting to produce 18 feature films, 16 television series, 5 animation productions, and 41 movies-of-the-week. The largest production ever shot here, a Walt Disney movie, required a crew of over 900 people. While California retains first place in major movie and television production, Vancouver and New York contend for second place in several catagories.

**Vancouver incognito:** Those wondering why the concept of Hollywood North comes as a surprise can forgive themselves. Vancouver almost never appears as itself in the entertainment world. It's gussied up, trashed up or fixed up to appear as any of a host of American or European locations. With its generic, architecturally anonymous, downtown towers side by side with older warehouse areas, Vancouver is a chameleon capable of masquerading as cities as varied as Seattle, Denver, New York, Hong Kong, Los Angeles, San Francisco, Detroit, London or turn-of-the-century Boston.

<u>Preceding pages</u>: long-stemmed roses. <u>Right</u>, a location shoot in the Kitsilano district.

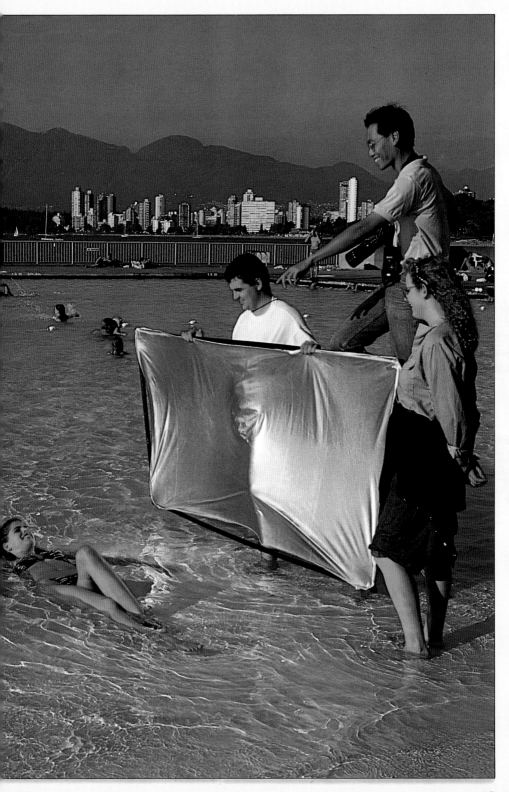

In the movie *Russia House*, starring Sean Connery, as he sat in an apparently secret and remote house being savagely interrogated by the KGB, only Vancouver audiences howled with laughter, recognising Horseshoe Bay and a regularly scheduled BC ferry gliding by in the distance. Yaletown, an enclave of recently gentrified old brick warehouses, and Gastown, with its flat-iron-shaped Europa Hotel and cobble-stoned streets, have doubled for such cities as Baltimore and Philadelphia. Gastown has appeared on-screen as Munich in *Neverending Story I* and *II*. The thriller *Shoot to Kill* was a rare exception where the city appeared as itself. Transform-

Formerly a bridge-building site (sections of the Golden Gate were fabricated here), Bridge Studios opened in 1987 with three sound stages and North America's largest effects stage. North Shore Studios, owned by Steven Canelli, has the second largest facilities. The facades of its seven sound stages and office buildings represent modern and period buildings from rowhouses to a small town streetscape, creating a virtual "back-lot on the front-lot". The animation sector is also a going concern with digital effects houses producing animation for films, television and music videos. Animated TV series created by Vancouver companies include *Reboot*

ing Vancouver into an American location is merely a matter of switching the maple leaf for the stars and stripes, adding a few mailboxes and stacking newspaper boxes with copies of the *Philadelphia Star*. Covering BC licence plates with magnetic US versions completes the illusion.

**Excellent facilities:** Proximity to Los Angeles – it's a scant three hours' flying time away – is only one reason movie producers are drawn to Canada's lower left-hand corner. Another is the availability of Vancouver's expert crews, excellent studios and state-of-the-art post-production facilities.

and *Transformers* for Mainframe Entertainment.

Unpredictable and unstable conditions in the rest of the world, as well as Canada's longtime favourable dollar in relation to the the US, have helped to establish the thriving entertainment business north of the border. But the *numero uno* reason why the city and its surroundings have become Hollywood North is the enormous variety of easily accessible locations. "If you can imagine it, the industry has used it, requested it or blown it up," says Mark Desrochers, former director of the BC Film Commission. "This land is your land," boasts a glossy brochure luring American producers to BC, "and we give it to you for a song."

**Quick change artists:** Vancouverites are famous for a shameless boast, "You can ski in the morning and sail in the afternoon." No longer mere braggadocio, this feat is *fait accompli* in the movie business. Uncut and unpolished, nature shows off its snow-capped mountain ranges, vast sandy beaches or sparkling blue waters. On the other hand, the writers and producers of *The X-Files* originally utilised Vancouver's sombre rain-soaked days to establish an ever-threatening shadowy gloom and in the process make

constructed a town on the shores of nearby Stave Lake for *We're No Angels* with Sean Penn. What followed was the coldest Vancouver winter ever. Attracted by the area's rainforests, the producers of the movie *Distant Thunder* brought cameras and crew to Vancouver, whereupon the city went a record 61 days without rain.

For the producer with a crew of 60 lighting experts to move, not to mention art directors, props people, camera persons, gaffers, best boys and actors – the fact that vastly varied locations are mostly within an hour's drive is a distinct financial advantage. In less time than it takes to sit through a soap opera, a

television history. Episodic TV or movies-of-the-week can be shot rain or shine: an average rainfall is rarely torrential enough to register on screen. If the script demands a heavy downpour, rain towers are used to boost the more common drizzle.

But sometimes Vancouver's legendary weather fails to cooperate. Having scouted Canada coast to coast and rejected most of it because of the severe winter, Paramount

professional movie crew can exchange downtown apartment blocks for a densely wooded canyon complete with a precipitous suspension bridge, or take a crew via cable car and chairlift to the ski slopes of Grouse Mountain.

**Chameleon city:** The mountaintop campus of Simon Fraser University and its futuristic glass domes are tailor-made for sci-fi adventures, while driving another 30 minutes brings movie-makers to Pitt Polder, a flat, tidy landscape that Van Dyck or Rembrandt might have painted. It's grass-covered dykes are a *tabula rasa* for set designers.

**Left**, crews move easily from mountain peaks to sea shore settings. **Above**, North Shore Studios is not open to the public.

Offering magnificent waterfalls, lush meadows, sweeping grasslands, country lanes, lakes and ponds, alpine meadows and even savannah grassland, Vancouver and its environs proffer a soup-to-nuts menu of nature. Apparently the only type of scenery missing in the Lower Mainland is "the big western look, deserts, tumbleweed, sagebrush". Surprisingly, that too is available a half day's drive away; in the rain shadow, Kamloops, BC's desert-like interior.

**Permanent sets abound:** Most appealing to dollar-conscious producers are locations that need little or no doctoring. The neo-classical Vancouver Art Gallery, formerly the provin-

cial courthouse, and Vancouver's City Hall chambers are frequently used for shoots needing a trial by jury. Many remakes of *Perry Mason* and *Ironside* with the late Raymond Burr took place here. Burnaby Heritage Museum is a restored late 19th century period town used for both interiors and exteriors; its buildings include a schoolhouse and a miniature train station. The *Royal Hudson*, Canada's last surviving steam train, and the *Love Boat* (actually a Princess Line cruiseship) at the downtown cruiseship terminal are also familiar sights to movie audiences, though they are never correctly identified.

Although little more than 100 years old, Vancouver has none the less managed to foster an astonishing variety of residential architecture. Apart from "Vancouver specials" – bland shoebox-shaped duplexes free from any form of ornamentation – there is no such thing as indigenous design. Nineteenth-century timber barons advertised their wealth with massive mansions, and every immigrant group has built structures embodying its own stylistic ideals: everything from English cottages thatched (uncharacteristically) with wooden shingles, to stuccoed and tiled Spanish style and exuberantly pillared Greek and Italian villas. Recent so-called "monster" homes are the unfortunate mismating of rococo, old English and Renaissance influences, an unsightly combination often garnished with wrought-iron gates flanked by stone lions.

What is generally termed "West Coast modern architecture", a harmonious melding of timber and glass, clings to the cliffsides of North and West Vancouver where it often stands in for Hollywood Hills or, as the BC Film Commission puts it: "Add a few palms and all you see is an exclusive home in an area of exclusive homes." But Art Deco, Victorian Gothic or ersatz San Francisco, for a film company, it all adds up to numerous location choices.

Like any seaport, Vancouver has its down and dirty side too. Warehouses, factories, docks and oil refineries line part of the waterfront and when action on screen demands an alley, Vancouver has some of the most photogenic ones around, including the evocatively-named Blood Alley in Gastown and what is reputedly the most photographed laneway in North America, the 100 block of East Hastings Street.

In the interests of hygiene for the crew and actors, high-pressure hoses wash away the real alleyway grunge, after which "clean" garbage, such as bags full of recycled styrofoam, are artistically spread around. Shooting completed, the alley is cleaned a second time. Yet compared with most North American and European cities, Vancouver is unusually pristine. The story goes that an American film crew, dismayed by the everyday cleanliness of a Vancouver alley, added more garbage, left for lunch and returned to discover that an all-too-efficient cleaning crew had made short work of their creativity.

**Movie legends:** Like its movie-making counterpart down the Pacific coast, Vancouver generates its own legends. There was the woman in the downtown ice-cream parlour who, finding herself next to Mel Gibson – "or it may have been Paul Newman" – distractedly dropped her double scoop of cherry ripple into her bag, snapped it shut and calmly asked for the star's autograph. Or the story is told of a group of British tourists who hardly believed their tour guide's tales of movie magic until ex-Beatle Ringo Starr casually

*The Man Upstairs*, with Ryan O'Neal and Katharine Hepburn; Ted Danson and Isabella Rossellini falling in love in *Cousins*; or Mel Gibson wooing Goldie Hawn in *Bird on a Wire*. Other movies present an odd look at the city, like *Deep Rising* and *Mr Magoo* for Disney Productions, or *Firestorm* for Fox. The largest budget for a Vancouver movie shot to date, costing $100 million, was the tentatively titled *Eaters of the Dead* for Disney Corporation.

Vancouver has played host to a number of long-running TV series, including *The X-Files, MacGyver*, starring Richard Dean, *21 Jump Street*, featuring the young Johnny

strolled by. The greats and the recently-greats of the movie star set regularly turn up for shoots. Recent made-for-TV or feature movies have starred Morgan Fairchild, Lindsay Wagner, Terri Garr, Elizabeth Perkins, Leslie Nielsen, Roy Sheider, Dom Deluise, Rob Lowe and Antonio Banderas.

In big-star movies, Vancouver continually pops up incognito in the background, as in *This Boy's Life* starring Robert De Niro and Ellen Barkin; the Burt Reynolds-produced

**Left**, Yvonne De Carlo in Stanley Park. **Above**, Mariel Hemingway as pin-up Dorothy Stratten.

Depp, and *Danger Bay* with its action centred on the Vancouver Aquarium and the picturesque village of Deep Cove. The producers of *MacGyver* once built a bunch of huts, spread some empty oil drums around and called it a Cambodian airport.

**Lights, Camera, Action:** Movie-making is a high-impact industry. It closes streets, re-routes traffic and takes up parking spaces. For some, the cables snaking across a suburban lawn, the spotlights and cameras are a nuisance; for others, a lucrative income. The BC Film Commission has over a thousand homes on file and talent scouts constantly knock on doors to find more. There is many a couple whose rundown home has been completely redecorated top to bottom in a mere 24 hours for a film shoot, "and not only that… they got paid for it!"

Production companies from around the world can access these files. On any given day, the BC Film Commission's flow chart lists anywhere up to two dozen projects being shot by production companies from the United States, Europe and increasingly, Asia. However, outside of a few main actors and producers, Human Resources Canada insists the entire production team, crew and extras all be Canadian.

south at the first opportunity in search of Hollywood fame and, in varying degrees, found it. Yvonne De Carlo, harem-girl star of *Salome Where She Danced*, *Songs of Scheherazade* and *Slave Girl* was born Vancouverite Peggy Middleton. Katherine DeMille, an orphan adopted by Cecil B. DeMille, played exotic leads in the 1930s and 1940s, and Barbara Parkins spent five tempestuous years as Betty Anderson on the TV series *Peyton Place*. All hailed from Vancouver.

On a tragic note Dorothy Stratten's walk down the yellow brick road to Hollywood led to life as a *Playboy* bunny, death at the

**Need nude cops:** Catalogued in the BC Film Commission's location files are everything from "airports" to "war memorials" but, even with more than 80,000 photos available, resources are occasionally taxed to the fullest. For the forgotten epic *Flesh Gordon Meets the Cosmic Cheerleaders* the producers sought a mountain range that resembled a pair of breasts, and the Commission was once approached by a US cable company eager to discuss the possibility of shooting a nude cop show.

Over the years Vancouver has produced its own home-grown stars. Many have headed

hands of her jealous husband and celluloid immortality as portrayed by the late Mariel Hemingway in *Star 80*. Dorothy was followed by another Vancouverite in *Playboy*'s life, bunny Kimberly Conrad, who until 1998 was Hugh Hefner's own truly wedded wife.

**Home-grown beauties:** Chosen by *People* magazine as one of the "50 Most Beautiful People in the World," Vancouver-born hunk Jason Priestly can just hold a candle to the bikini-clad star discovered at a BC Lions football game. Placing first in 1997 as the "Most Lusted After Women in America," few realise that CJ the Speedo girl, Pamela

Anderson Lee, comes from this area. Starting out as a player on TV's *Family Ties* and more recently *Spin City*, actor Michael J. Fox expected to be nothing more than a bit player when he left his Vancouver home.

In the more stolid, unsexy vein of most Vancouver-born male actors, Raymond Burr, *Perry Mason* for nine years and *Ironside* for eight, grew up in Vancouver's oldest suburb, New Westminster. Another local boy made good is James Doohan, best known for his role as Scotty in the *Star Trek* TV series.

**I wanna be a big star too:** Getting into the movies as an "extra" in Vancouver isn't much harder than picking up the phone. Any

huge crowd that cheerfully donned heavy winter clothing one sizzling summer day to observe the fight between Sylvester Stallone and Dolph Lundgren in *Rocky IV*. While rates can skyrocket to $200 or more an hour for a "specialty" role such as a cop or a lawyer, the going fee for being part of a nameless throng is minimum wage. "That's why we call them extras," says the casting agency. "Because it's only for extra money." Successful extras do know that the one unbreakable rule is never to approach or speak to the stars.

**Happy endings:** For all the talk about Hollywood North and hundreds of millions of

of Vancouver's 40 or more talent agencies will ask that "you come in and register with a résumé, giving height, weight and body size. We take a picture and then we send you out to work." The photograph should not require a fee of over $25.

Thousands of would-be stars, aged six to 90, are currently on file. Extras never get rich, but no matter, all are happy to work for little financial reward. A case in point is the

**Left**, actor Richard Dean has made two TV series. **Above**, stars of *The X-Files*, the series that made Vancouver's moody weather famous.

dollars for this and that, a recent novel *Beyond the Beyond,* by Lee Goldberg, now in production as a movie, is set in Vancouver and actually identifies it as such. Its hero intones, "With Hollywood invading... I figured it was only a matter of time before you all became aspiring actors or aspiring writers. And those who didn't aspire to be part of the industry would want to feed off of it, becoming as crass, greedy, and self-serving as the people they hoped to profit from... But instead [in Vancouver] I found [pure] people and clean air." Who said there are no happy endings anymore?

It laps at our feet and rather too often pours about our ears. Inevitably it seeps into our consciousness: the presence of water can't help but fill the imagination of Vancouver's inhabitants.

In summer, descending from the mistier North Shore, Squamish Nation people used to paddle up Burrard Inlet to dig clams. Then as now, locals had mixed feelings about the water. It was purifying, hypnotic to gaze at; it could also be oppressive. First Nations people told sea stories to each other while in their longboats, shouting across the bewhiskered, bobbing heads of harbour seals.

In one story, a youth plunges endlessly into the ocean to cleanse his body and spirit for impending fatherhood. Impressed, the Salish spirit *Sagalie* immortalises the man by turning him into Siwash Rock, ever to stand on the shores of Stanley Park – and be dutifully photographed by tourists. A less pleasant myth, reflecting the damper side of a watery clime, has *Sagalie* in an off-mood. He punishes a greedy native by changing the man into a sea serpent – a Siskiutl – who systematically thrashes longboats to bits and gulps down their paddlers.

Then as now, attitudes to the water shift. But the fascination never ebbs. At least the rain is comforting, or so thought Vancouverites who were seriously rattled when a government study branded their city the most depressing in Canada. According to the study, produced by the Treasury Board to calculate bonuses for civil servants, the rain and clouds that mist over Vancouver for weeks on end blight the psyche even more than the cold of Winnipeg or Whitehorse.

Reporters scrambled. They hunted out ex-residents of other climes, such as a former Whitehorse resident who willingly complained about her native city being "grey, dusty and dark". But Vancouver, she added, was "good for the hair and the complexion". Local climatologists felt personally affronted

by the study. The weather is "moderated", not depressed, insists Norm Penny, superintendent of climatological data services in the Lower Mainland. As for Ottawa, where he once spent a summer, "It was like walking around in a sauna the whole time."

In the main, Vancouverites seem perfectly able to cope with the 147 cm (58 inches) of water that falls on their downtown area annually. The North Shore receives even more, registering a soggy 173 cm (68 inches)

each year. Some wax quite romantic about the rain as they sit in cosy coffee houses dreamily studying the weeping patterns on the window.

Vancouver rain, though not the wicked acid variety of eastern climes, sadly bears tiny traces of sulphate, nitrate, ammonium, sodium, chlorine, magnesium, calcium, and carbonate. On the positive side, the black clouds that disgorge thunderbolts on the prairies further east and the funnel-shaped clouds that frightened Dorothy in the *Wizard of Oz*, rarely plague Vancouver, whose clouds are delicate, nimbo-stratus strands.

**Preceding pages:** a couple of swells. **Left**, rain has its compensations. **Right**, crab meet.

**On the boats:** *Pacific Yachting* editor John Shinnick, who with his blond hair and beard somewhat resembles popular depictions of Neptune, lives in a Canoe Cove 41 power boat. In the evening he and his wife sit on deck, contemplating the silhouettes of other False Creek Yacht Club boats. Sometimes Hank the blue heron perches nearby. On occasions they heave anchor and plough off to a more solitary patch. "There's something about looking outside to the clean horizon, the gorgeous water, the boundless pace, that pulls us out to sea," explains Shinnick.

The 35,000 vessels using the 222-km (138-mile) long, 40-km (25 mile) wide Strait of

kg (36-lb) salmon during the summer, but respecting the principles of Neptune, he throws most back. "People who think they have to fish to kill are prehistoric."

The once abundant pickings now vary in Vancouver waters. Bottomfish including flounder, sole, rock cod, and perch thrive, while the health of shellfish like crab, mussels, clams, oysters, and scallops is affected by toxins in the water. With new cleanup measures in place, prawns (shrimp) are thriving. But halibut have virtually vanished and overfishing has driven the lingcod to endangered status. Harvesting the tasty abalone is illegal though poachers continue to plunder

Georgia are divided about equally between sailboats and power boats, but a preference is developing for the latter. This Shinnick attributes to the aging of the current generation, who want more comfort. Shinnick's colleague George Will, an avid fisherman and editor of *BC Outdoors*, dislikes them all. A lover of the solitary, he deplores the tendency of "high-tech yuppies" to cram boats together in one spot. Huddling in crowds defeats the point of such a meditative sport as fishing, the ex-archaeology professor complains. "I don't like tangling my lines in other people's." Will catches at least a dozen 16-

them. Bottom dwelling rock fish are in rapid decline as are red snappers.

**With the fish:** All of the foregoing, however, is scarcely relevant to those attentive to life in the Emerald Sea, as the area's waters are known. The uniform temperature and salinity of the water off BC's deeply indented coast have nurtured some of the world's finest fish and fauna extolled by, among others, Jacques Cousteau.

Unaffected by the weather above, oceanographers in the University of Victoria's submersible *Pisces IV* toss gently about under the sea, studying the plant life and enjoying a rare, subterreanean panorama. They know that what you see is not always what you get. Brought to the surface, the most nondescript dark sponge may turn a stunning crimson. Water absorbs colour and grows inkier in depths away from the light.

The Lower Mainland's 50,000 skindivers are in a position to spot gangly kelp, whose thick elastic trunks rooted on rocks can withstand the fiercest currents. When parted, the kelp reveals red, white, green and blue cuplike anemones, ridged by dainty tentacles, and transparent moon-like jellyfish. A few lucky divers glimpse the world's largest seastar, the 24-rayed *Pycnopodia helianthodes*.

enlightened times, guidebooks cheerfully suggested visits to the Vancouver Aquarium in Stanley Park, promising that readers would enjoy observing the whales leaping about at the trainers' behest. As society's sympathy for wildlife increased, however, the sight of these wild creatures swimming endlessly in confined spaces became less entertaining. The aquarium was at the forefront of those concerned: it became the first in the world to decide against capturing more whales.

**Water into wine:** East and south of the city's Alex Fraser Bridge stretches Burns Bog, 10 times the size of the nearby park, yet barely

Sea-going kayakers may be less keen to come across one of the pods of killer whales which thrive off BC's coast. White-bellied and 9 metres (30 ft) long, the whales open their ominous black tops like automobile hoods to reveal rows of sharp, conical teeth – 40 or 50 in all. Swimming along at the pace of a slow-moving car, they whistle and warble to each other both above and below the water.

Despite their name, killer whales have been more harmed than harmful. In less-

known to anyone in BC. It is, according to University of Victoria biology professor Richard Hebda, "a 3,000-year-old super-organism, almost a conscious being, a strange symphony of collaborating life forms."

It may be the last major bog on the west coast of North America. Huge, wild orchids grow in its steamy depths. Blue dragonflies which could not survive in the climate of Vancouver itself flit across it. Black bears lumber by; strange mice jump in kangaroo-type arcs. So mystical has Burns Bog become, with its incongruous alpine and jungle ecology, that people lug away pailfuls of its

**Left,** ducks' delight. **Above,** bright sails in search of wind on the Strait of Georgia.

water to make wine. Local legends hold that the further you venture into the bog, the bigger its wild berries grow; and at night, be careful, dead trees turn into monsters.

If you visit Port Moody Inlet, you will see the tidal flats. In 1792, Captain George Vancouver sailed here along the 31-km (19-mile) Burrard Inlet. He met the Squamish Nations – and found himself looking down into the soulful brown eyes of harbour seals, which today still follow canoers. As the Captain chatted to the Indians, the seals little suspected he was discussing fur-buying, their own and sea otters' skins included. Port Moody's tidal flats are also the habitat for

sandpipers, geese, eagles, fan-tailed pigeons and tweedy, binocular-clutching bird-watchers. Until a law banning firearms was passed in 1958, hunting was a popular local sport.

**The beaches:** When Captain Vancouver's ships poked over the horizon, his men jumped into rowboats and headed to a beach off Point Grey. There the sun and surf lulled them into such comfort one sailor failed to awaken even when the rising tide began to carry him away. "I believe he might have been conveyed to some distance had he not been awakened by his companions," Vancouver remarked later.

The sailor's pleasure at sunbathing is shared today by the thousands who plonk themselves down on Vancouver's 16 km (10 miles) of sandy beaches. At Kitsilano, the worshippers are packed shoulder-to-toe – most insisting that Vancouver sun isn't strong enough to hurt the skin. Kits Beach is the finishing point of the Nanaimo Bathtub Race, a wild annual free-for-all that takes place every July.

West, Locarno and Spanish Banks beaches are quieter. Their shallow water is usually a bit warmer than the summer average of 18°C–20°C (64°F–68°F). Beyond these, and invariably snubbed by puritanical tourist board brochures, is the nudist Wreck Beach, discreetly shielded from the University of British Columbia by thick alders and maples. Vendors wearing nothing more than sun visors sashay up and down chanting, "Ice-cold brown, brown, brown cows, white Russians, black Russians."

Across the water, English Bay and several beaches ring Stanley Park. Landing at English Bay in 1862, Yorkshire potter John Morton rhapsodised about its "white sands" and "boulders overhung with branches lapped at high tide". The white glint in the sands probably came from bits of the clamshells the natives brought back from Port Moody.

Touring clockwise, North Shore beaches start with Cates Park on Indian Arm, where Malcolm Lowry wrote *Under The Volcano*. The serenity of West Vancouver's Ambleside is deafeningly pierced once daily by the steam locomotive *Royal Hudson*'s whistle, en route to the town of Squamish.

At Christmas, carol ships serenade most beaches. On New Year's Day thousands of the city's hardy, or perhaps foolhardy, jump into English Bay for the Polar Bear Swim. A few wiry old souls who still hobble into the freezing water were around for the very first plunge, back in 1927.

In their own eccentric way, special events laud the water. The Save The Strait Marathon, sponsored by the Save the Georgia Strait Alliance, reminds locals to care for their water now if they want to have marine abundance to celebrate in the future. Of the marathon's participating paddlers, swimmers, cyclists, snorkellers and rowers, one of the most ingenious is shipwright hobbyist Larry Westlake, who once set out in a "bubblegum kayak" constructed from 100 percent recycled materials.

**Saving the endangered:** Vancouverites are increasingly aware that our past behaviour has been very like that of the fabled fisherman's wife who asked and got great treasures from the sea until, in the face of her greed, the plunder ran out. Carcinogenic byproducts of pulp bleaching at Howe Sound mills, absorbed into the digestive glands of rock and Dungeness crabs, cause tumours, birth defects and reproductive failures. It took many years of bantering but a coordi-

There are rare oil spills, such as the one from the Japanese fish-processing ship in the Juan de Fuca Strait that killed 10,000 seabirds. Though the Canadian Coast Guard dispatched its submersible robot *Scorpio* down to siphon the oil with a hose, environmentalists shook their heads and lamented the damage.

As for the region's fabled salmon, they struggle to survive. University of Idaho scientists and others have suggested that the entire Fraser River Basin is endangered by a potentially deadly overdose of urban development, logging, grazing, railroad construction, dams and pulp effluent. One recent year the famed Georgia coho, the world's largest

nated effort to clean up the the Inlet is now underway with hopes that the US success with Puget Sound might be duplicated here – and surpassed. However, as ocean monitoring continues, more and more official signs dot beaches warning people not to catch and eat the local fish. Bob Lyons calculated, in his Greenpeace study *Dire Straits*, that enough waste was at one time being dumped into the Georgia Strait to fill BC Place Stadium 160 times over.

<u>Left</u>, sliding into the sunset. <u>Above</u>, Lost Lagoon during a rare freeze-up.

salmon run, failed to make its July date for spawning up the Fraser at Adams River. The fish did eventually turn up, but no one could explain the somewhat ominous delay. Now the numbers languish.

There are a few encouraging rays of light on the ecological front. Greenpeace once named North America's worst polluter as the pulp and paper industry. However, after much expensive research, the industry is able to produce chlorine-free pulp. It doesn't look quite so pristine but the world is ready to accept that in exchange for a cleaner environment and lovely fresh water.

# THE SEX LIFE OF SALMON

The sex life of the salmon is one of sadness and inspiration. Born already orphaned it never meets its children, yet the last stages of its life are a struggle in which it sacrifices everything to ensure their future. When it leaves the ocean, fully mature and ready to spawn, it can travel close to 50 km (30 miles) a day, dodging sea-lions, bears and other predators and battling fiercely against adverse currents to return to the place of its own birth.

There, with exactly the right temperature and climatic conditions, it fulfils its date with destiny, females depositing several thousand eggs in deep

gravel and males fertilising them before both drift away to die. The gravel beds, flushed by water that bears oxygen and removes wastes, protects the young until they can swim downstream and then in their turn grow to maturity in the ocean. The cycle is inexorable.

"Any real concern for self-preservation has largely left them," wrote conservationist Roderick Haig-Brown about the reckless drive of spawning salmon. "They are obsessed with sexual purpose and the imminence of death leaves no leeway for other concerns. Successful spawning is the preservation of the race."

Among the salmon's predators, of course, none are more deadly than humans. From the earliest

times indigenous people knew well the salmon cycle. It was easy to catch them as they cautiously bypassed currents and eddies, gathering for their magnificent waterfall leaps on the way upstream. Along the Fraser, Nass and Skeena rivers many native family clans held age-old rights to fish with seine net (a net used to encircle a school of fish), spear or a cedar-twined bag-shaped dip net. Sometimes wickerwork baskets were used and here and there wooden "fish wheels" would block specific channels, acting like miniature Ferris wheels to scoop the fish up.

The first salmon to be caught each season was embellished and painted red, and the event was celebrated with singing, dancing and praying and shared among all the people. It was a time to perpetuate ancient customs. Twins, believed to control salmon, were consulted; children were warned not to abuse the fish, even when dead. These ceremonies have survived to the present day. All along the Fraser River, drummers and singers head for the water as the run returns. If the first salmon is treated well – even if it is eaten – legend insists, many more salmon will follow from the city, where they live under the sea, and fishing will be good.

"O Swimmer, I thank you that you are willing to come to us. Don't let your coming be bad, for you come to be food for us," is part of the address made by Kwakiutl people at their First Salmon Ceremony. Like most tribes they assign the salmon as much importance as their counterparts on the plains did to the buffalo. In recent years some conservationists have speculated whether the salmon was not destined to suffer the same depleted fate as the buffalo. The assessments of officials from Canada's fisheries and conservationists differ only in the figures they give when calculating whether various species of salmon are "endangered" or merely "threatened".

Everybody agrees that the declining numbers have been caused by overfishing and poor water quality. What nobody can agree on is how to solve the problem. When Simon Fraser in 1808 first descended the river which now bears his name, he subsisted on the same type of dried salmon that was a staple for the natives. To this day, natives set up camps on canyon ledges and let the hot winds dehydrate the flesh, or else dry the hanging filets in smokehouses with alderwood fires.

In the 1830s the Hudson's Bay Company began buying salmon from native people and others and shipping them to Asia, eviscerated, scrubbed, salted and packed into barrels. At that time virtually every coastal river and creek up and down North America's West Coast teemed with the fish. Until the completion of the railroad in 1886, in fact, salmon was British Columbia's major export. By the end of the 19th century there were dozens of tiny canning companies up and down BC's coast. And devastation of the runs was under way. Extremely long traps wiped out entire runs and fish-lazy "sportsmen" casually tossed dynamite into pools.

Canneries sometimes dumped tons of fish to rot because the meat didn't appear red enough, and with the wasteful policy of catching virtually everything that swam by, there was too much to handle for early non-refrigerated canneries. Adding to the salmon's woes, the first mining

inland tributaries, the Adams, is responsible, once every four years, for the the red-fleshed fighting sockeye species.

Salmon numbers are greatly enhanced through the work of hundreds of BC Salmon Enhancement facilities. Technicians capture returning fish, fertilise their eggs, hatch them under optimum conditions and feed the fry (juvenile fish) until part grown. The scientific release of thousands of millions of healthy fry has vastly improved the fish supply, and today many First Nations, as well as others, are in the business of spawning and releasing healthy salmon into BC's rivers. The task is to keep ahead of the fishery industry and sports fishers. In recent years, BC has also embraced the fish farm movement and the salmon

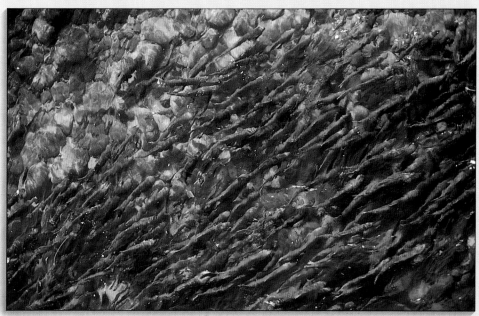

enterprises seriously polluted certain rivers and the early lumber industry let fallen trees clog pristine streams. Of commercial interest today are four principal salmon types: chinook (king); coho (silver); pinks; and sockeye. All head inland from May to October – the major runs arriving in August and September – bypassing the odd river obstruction like Hell's Gate by means of specially constructed "fish ladders".

Each year, the undammed Fraser River has an abundance of all species of salmon. One of its

**Left**, BC's rivers hold the key to a salmon's life. **Above**, sockeye salmon spawning in the Adams River, after which both male and female will die.

farming industry is competing with wild salmon producers. Millions of pounds of farmed fish are now sold alongside the wild-caught variety with the result that there has been a dramatic drop in per pound prices. Salmon farms work continuously to satisfy inspectors that waste droppings will not unduly pollute the water, and to convince them that flash diseases spreading through confined areas will not threaten other marine life.

Conservationists remain alert to declining salmon stocks and the governments of British Columbia, Alaska, Washington state, and federal governments too, are constantly arguing over conflicting data. Meanwhile, the salmon's upstream struggle continues. ■

Forests cover almost two-thirds of the Canadian province of British Columbia (BC), and what a vast area of trees and mountains that is. With an area of 952,000 square km (366,000 square miles) BC as a whole covers 9.5 percent of the land mass of Canada and 64 percent of the world's land surface. Approximately 1,450 km (900 miles) in length and 640 km (400 miles) in width, comparisons of the size of this single province to whole other nations boggle the mind. British Columbia is four times larger than Great Britain; 2.5 times larger than Japan; and equal to the combined sizes of France, Germany, Austria, Belgium and the Netherlands. Comparing it to American states, it is smaller than Alaska, but 1.35 times the size of Texas or about as large as Washington, Oregon and California combined.

That's a lot of land – 95 million hectares (235 million acres) – and with 67 percent covered in forests, it is a lot of trees. The challenge of managing these immense stands to the satisfaction of all the stakeholders and interested parties, as well as protecting the wildlife that inhabits them, all adds up to a huge responsibility. All the province's cities, towns and roads developed for human inhabitation take up a mere 2 percent of BC's total area. Barren mountain peaks and forests cover just about all the rest. So perhaps the most underrated precedent-setting commitment the provincal government has made in recent years is to set aside the best bits, the most beautiful wilderness areas, indeed 12 percent of the land of this massive province, as untouchable parkland for future generations. One single provincial park in the north of the province, for example, is larger than Switzerland. Several others are almost as big.

**A walk in the rainforest:** The best way to get into the gentle spirit of the temperate rainforest is to begin with a walk in the woods. Pack a picnic lunch, wear good shoes, block out a morning or an afternoon and choose one of several rainforest walks, all within Vancouver. All have well maintained trails.

Near the University of British Columbia (UBC) campus is Pacific Spirit Park; enter on Camosun Street. Though people are surprised at its lush fullness, this is a healthy second-growth forest of the usual BC conifers plus hardwood species such as maple, birch and alder. Evidence of old logging

practises are found in the great stumps. Since it takes cedarwood more than 150 years to decay, the notches cut for lumberjacks' springboards in pioneer days are still in view.

In Stanley Park it's a pleasure to enjoy the historic tall trees around Beaver Lake; enter at Pipeline Road and Beaver Lake Trail near the miniature railway. Despite its history as a native settlement, military reserve, logging site and urban park, Stanley Park remains largely forested. In fact, the landscape is still dominated by the very trees Captain George Vancouver described in his ship's log upon sailing into Burrard Inlet in 1792.

**Preceding pages:** each year over 300 million seedlings are prepared, then cold-hardened for new BC forests. **Left,** Cathedral Grove on Vancouver Island. **Right,** someday a forest giant.

The densest stands of temperate rainforest, with centuries old western red cedar, Douglas fir, Sitka spruce and western hemlock in an unbroken canopy, are found on the North Shore. Here, there are three recommended walks.

Seymour Demonstration Forest, a 5,200-hectare (13,000-acre) reserve, is over the Second Narrows bridge to the third exit (Lillooet Road). Follow the gravel road to the forest. Its trails combine a stroll through mixed age conifer forests with stops of interest illustrating how a multiple-use forest is managed. Like much of the area cleared to make room for the city now standing here,

arbutus and contorted shore pine. One of the many species of birds residing here is the bald eagle.

A deep, winding gorge, whose sheer granite cliffs were carved by natural water courses after the last ice age, Capilano Canyon is across the Lions Gate Bridge; take North Vancouver's Capilano Road to the Regional Park signs. The upstream Capilano Watershed provides 40 percent of Vancouver's drinking water. After a stop at the Capilano River Hatchery, the Coho Loop Trail is a 45-minute walk among rock outcroppings and mature forests of western red cedar, Douglas fir and hemlock. The massive trees crowding

the Lower Seymour Valley was intensively logged near the turn of the 20th century. Again, many people are surprised to learn that nearly two-thirds of this forest is second-growth. Frequent rain and good soil make for fast growing trees and Rice Lake, a pleasant stop on the way, is stocked with trout.

Lighthouse Park on Point Atkinson is next to the ocean, across the Lions Gate bridge; take West Vancouver's Marine Drive to Beacon Lane. Riddled with criss-crossing trails and towering centuries-old forests of Douglas fir and western red cedar, its rocky bluffs and tiny beaches also grow red-barked

the canyon are 90 to 120 years old, interspersed with massive stumps left behind by intensive 19th-century logging activity.

Slightly farther afield, about a 50-minute drive from the city centre, is the UBC Research Forest; travel 8 km (5 miles) north of Highway 7 (Lougheed Highway) on 232nd Street. Created to facilitate research in forest ecology, integrated resource and watershed techniques, as well as sustainable forest management procedures, there are a number of well maintained trails through these old- and new-growth forests, as well as a number of ongoing experiments to view.

**Commercial resource:** It was not until 70 years after Captain Vancouver had marvelled at "the trees of large growth" in his ship's log, that the pioneers of BC's lumber industry looked to the great forests for commercial purposes. The first influx of people in 1858 carried gold pans, not axes, and the second influx cried "coal". Though a corps of army engineers did hack out a trail between Vancouver's waterways in 1860, it was 1863 when the first sawmill was built at Lynn Creek in North Vancouver, and 1864 when the first cargo of lumber, 50,000 board feet of three-inch planking, clattered off the green chain bound for New Westminster.

developed around the dozen or so sawmills and logging camps that sprang up on either side of Burrard Inlet and False Creek. Teams of oxen dragged huge logs to the water's edge on greased "skid roads". Splendid timbers, some more than 100 feet in length, went to China to build the Imperial Palace in Peking. Other fine wooden beams were shipped to England for lavish country estates.

**Green from the start:** From between the stumps, the city of Vancouver – its homes and offices, streets and parking lots – slowly emerged. But even then, when trees were viewed as a nuisance, the citizens showed their perversity: the beauty of the great forest

By the year of Confederation, 1867, when Canada was declared a Dominion, several million board feet had been exported from the province. Under the Land Ordinance Act of 1865, the first piece of forestry legislation in the province, Captain Edward Stamp acquired the rights for virtually all the timberland in what is now metropolitan Vancouver for the princely sum of $250. Stamp then proceeded to build Hastings Mill.

For the next 25 years, small communities

Left, Vancouver's first real estate office, 1880s.
Above, Stanley Park's famous hollow tree, 1890s.

was appreciated and great swaths of green were left in place. When the city was incorporated in 1886, the first act of the first city council was to set aside a 400-hectare (1,000-acre) forested park in the city – Stanley Park. When the request was forwarded to Ottawa for approval, officials delayed answering for over a year, laughing all the while at those loony West Coasters, surrounded by pesky forests, yet wanting to preserve them.

British Columbia's forests first came into the international limelight in January 1889, when Ross McLaren Sawmills spent $350,000 on constructing the Fraser Mills plant, the world's largest sawmill at that time, about 30 km (20 miles) from Vancouver. But Fraser Mills faced tough times. As the timber business evolved, its boom-and-bust nature became evident. In 1907, the first big financial bust hit the marketplace; wages dropped from $35 to $25 a month. However, less than three years later, spurred by the opening of the Panama Canal, boom times suddenly arrived again. US industrialists invested about $65 million, representing at that time 90 percent of the growing industry.

**Knock on wood:** These developments startled the provincial government into calling the first British Columbia Royal Commis-

sion of Inquiry on Timber and Forests. A few people were surprised when in 1909, W. R. Ross, Minister of Lands, delivered this insight into the state of the industry: "An epoch, sir, is drawing to a close – the epoch of reckless devastation of the natural resources which we, the people of this fair young province, have been endowed by Providence." Based on the state of knowledge about forests at the time, new regulations were imposed, revised and reimposed. BC foresters were then quietly called upon to make an important contribution to the World War I effort. BC sitka spruce, the lightest of all woods for its

strength, was sought after to build early aircraft frames. In the 1920s and 1930s, lumber practises were modernised and a reforestation programme was put in place.

The trend has been towards forest renewal, not only in planting new trees, but in adapting and readapting policy to reflect changing forest practises. After a boom period in the 1950s and 1960s, the lack of enforcement of certain regulations led to tense and potentially violent stand-offs in BC's forests. Environmentalists argued convincingly against the destruction of habitat for rare and endangered species and logging damage to salmon-breeding streams and rivers. After a time, these protesters were successful, turning several valleys into dedicated parks. Macmillan Bloedel, a huge forest company, bowed to the pressures in 1998, agreeing to ignore current practise and discontinue clearcutting. Other companies followed in its wake.

**Save the trees:** It took a decade for large corporations and governments to realise that environmental activism was not simply a passing fad. Big-name musicians and celebrities joined the rallying cry and the state of the forest slowly came to the forefront of the public agenda. Throughout the 1980s and 1990s, as citizens became more environmentally aware, corporations and governments changed their attitudes too. Fearing for their children's future, people from all walks of life exerted various forms of pressure, and identified themselves with forest "stakeholder" groups: environmentalists, "tree huggers", union members, native bands, free trade agreement negotiators (in Canada and the US), government officials and people dependent on the industry. Even tourists came to be recognised as stakeholders in the process. All had a say in a BC Forest Policy.

Publicised incidents when loggers confronted protesters were but the tip of a much larger iceberg of complex priorities. The intricacies of land use disputes today reflect the size and scope of the province itself. While sensationalist headlines focus on protesters chaining themselves to trees, the public has shown an equal concern for the well-being of thousands of forestry jobs. Both companies and the government have multi-million dollar programmes in place to renew the forests even as they harvest them, and independent entities including medical research bodies do a great deal of research and development involving forests. For example, research proves that wildlife thrives in new clearcut forests better than in deep, dark old forests because the former have more food on the forest floor.

**You're sure of a big surprise:** As well as amazement at the enormity of BC's protected parks, if you go into the woods today you're sure of another big surprise... About 80 percent of BC's original temperate rainforests have never been cut. And because it is protected as parks or is unsuitable terrain

203rd street in Maple Ridge). This represents at least 10 percent more than the number of trees being cut.

Clearcutting has been greatly reduced and BC's Forest Practices Code imposes million-dollar fines for non-compliance with its strict reforestation and wildlife protection regulations. Many First Nations, far from being opposed to forestry, own their own silviculture and timber harvesting operations, milling and manufacturing plants and other forest sector operations. They also hold forest tenures and provide jobs for their people in forestry operations. Today, an extract from the yew tree, still growing abun-

for logging, 75 percent of what remains will never be harvested.

BC's reforestation programme is well over 75 years old, so many second-growth forests are ready for harvest or have been harvested a second and even third time. An entire reforestation industry is devoted to growing and replanting, then verifying the survival of more than 300 million cold-hardened seedlings each year. (Pelton Reforestation Ltd, the largest reforestation centre, is located on

**Left and above**, environmentalists think the forests are being destroyed.

dantly, is showing exceptional promise against certain types of female cancers.

**Sensible forestry:** Today, though the forest industry remains the economic engine of the economy, BC is still a looney place where the rainforest is not simply viewed as black (cut it) or white (don't cut it) but as shades of green (sustainable wilderness). Home to wildife, including more than 10,000 grizzlies and 150,000 black bears, place of peaceful contemplation and recreation, and source of medication, BC's forests today are treated as they have always been by some: as a huge and precious wilderness.

# PLACES

Vancouver ranks enviably high on the Good Life Meter. You can see that in the faces of bikinied windsurfers at Jericho Beach. You can spot it in the lazy lope of visitors to historic Gastown and in the comfortable stride of weekend fitness gurus who hike the circumference of what someone once termed "the 1,000-acre therapeutic couch that is Stanley Park". You can identify it in the media back-patting that's followed Vancouver's reputation as a fine restaurant and good eating town.

The Good Life is equally obvious during a walk through the arts-and-crafts area of Granville Island or along the up-scale blocks of fashionable Robson Street. Most of the people you see *want* to be here; they don't just *have* to be here. This includes many former Hong Kong residents who moved to Vancouver as a safety precaution when Hong Kong reverted to China. One such immigrant, Victor Li-Kashing, son of one of the richest men in Hong Kong, runs the old Expo 86 world exposition site on the north shore of False Creek. He's slowly developing it into a housing and business district that will expand the size of Vancouver's downtown area by one-sixth.

And this is a city that, agreeable as it is, people can't wait to get out of – not to escape Vancouver itself but to enjoy some of the awesome charms that surround it. They head north and east to the mountains for skiing, snowboarding, hiking, invigorating air or just the inspiring views; south to the lovely Gulf Islands, the US state of Washington or quaint Victoria. Across Georgia Strait, Vancouver Island stretches northwards for more than 400 km (250 miles) dotted with enough attractions to demand a week of anybody's time from big-city museums to small-town fishing piers. At its southern end, the charmingly quaint city of Victoria sits on a busy harbour.

Thousands of people travel on boats every day around the waters of Vancouver. If places were judged by the quality of their waterfront, this city would rate about as high as they come. Not only does it have hundreds of miles of waterfront, but its vast harbour, English Bay, is one of the world's most spectacular.

**Preceding pages**: the Pacific's Japanese current helps produce a mild climate; high-spirited Vancouverite; tanned skin is *de rigueur*, a club where anyone can be a member. **Left**, Lions Gate Bridge.

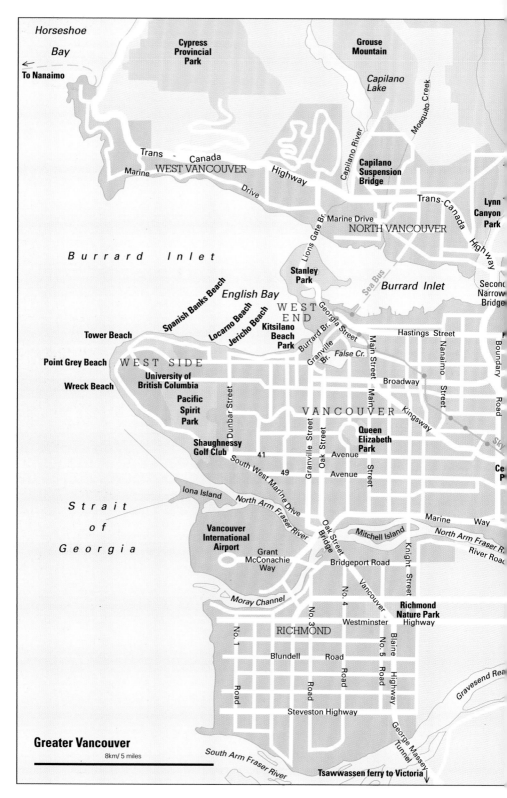

Greater Vancouver

8km/ 5 miles

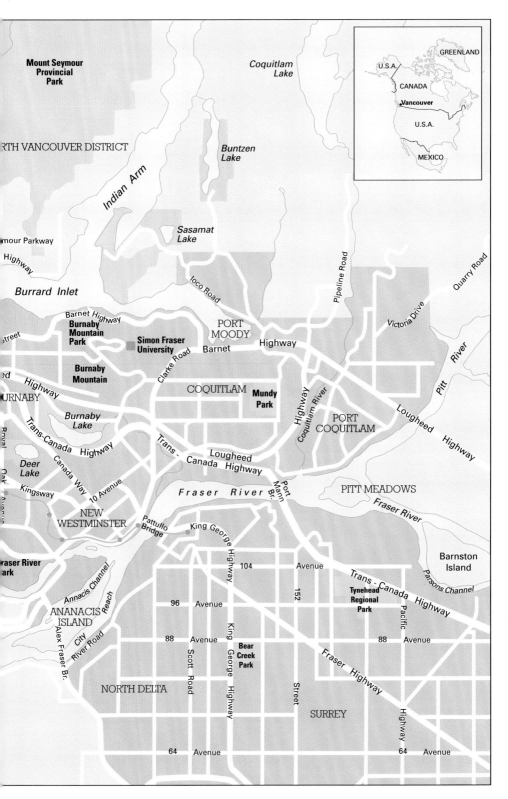

# GASTOWN

Vancouver is a city whose geography and climate one needs to understand as early as possible. First, remember the rain and be prepared. "Rain dominates Vancouver," wrote Donald Stainsby 30 years ago. "To understand the city you must study rain and its variants, wet snow and fog. Rain affects the life of the whole city. Even the absence of rain is notable." Once rain starts, Stainsby said in his book *Vancouver Sights and Insights,* "you don't make a dash for the bus hoping it will clear up; you put on a raincoat and prepare to use it for several days." That takes care of climate.

The easiest way to begin your geography familiarisation is to head for the landmark white sails at the north foot of Howe and Burrard streets; after a stop at Canada Place, head over to Water Street and nearby Gastown.

**Cruise ships and Canada Place:** For an overall impression, it would be hard to beat the view from **Canada Place**, nick-named "Under the Sails" for its huge **Trade and Convention Centre**. From the exterior levels, various Vancouver landmarks, such as **Stanley Park**, are clearly and interestingly identified by means of carefully-positioned plaques at the edge of the various decks over-looking the water.

Inside are two eating places which overlook the harbour: an inexpensive cafeteria and the classy **Prow Restaurant**. Visitors can watch ships traverse the harbour, identifying their flags or silhouettes from explanatory charts beside one of the stairways. A glass elevator connects the different decks and floors: below are promenade shops, fast-food counters and an immense arrival hall to serve the 120 or more sleek white cruise ships with 600,000 passengers bound for Alaska. From May to Sep-

**Left**, downtown and the white sails of Canada Place.

tember one or two of these magnificent cruise vessels are moored, one on each side of Canada Place, with another couple down the way at **Ballentyne Pier.** At the end of the promenade is IMAX, a giant five-storey high screen presenting one-hour features on natural wonders or amazing adventures shot on special wide-angle or 3D cameras.

Part of the Canada Place complex is the luxury-class Japanese-owned **Pan Pacific Hotel**, which has thick carpets, soft sofas, waterfalls, a piano bar and big windows overlooking the harbour. Across the street is the equally luxurious 23-storey **Waterfront Centre Hotel**, one of the Canadian Pacific (CP) chain. Nearby is the restored Post Office, now the **Sinclair Centre,** 757 West Hastings, where Haida native **Dorothy Grant's** boutique is a fun place to shop for West Coast *haut couture.*

**Best high overlook:** Just east of Canada Place, towering above the corner of Hastings and Seymour streets, is the 169-metre (553-ft) tall **Harbour Cen-**

tre. Both the revolving restaurant and the observation deck, **The Lookout,** offer what is perhaps the best view of the city. Ride up the glass elevator, skip the banal "multi-image extravaganza" mini-show and concentrate on the outstanding view.

Looking to the west, **English Bay** laps at the shores of the peninsula which separates Vancouver from the **Strait of Georgia**, the northern part of the peninsula looking much as it must have done when it was occupied by the Salish First Nation whose only means of transport were longboats carved from red cedar trees. The first roads in Stanley Park were built from the piles of shells salvaged from their refuse heaps.

Back in 1863, when Canada was still unsure of its mighty US neighbour, a tongue of land was set aside as a military reserve; eventually by a stroke of good fortune it was turned over to the city and became **Stanley Park**. Indented under Stanley Park's south shore, **Coal Harbour** – a seam was worked here briefly

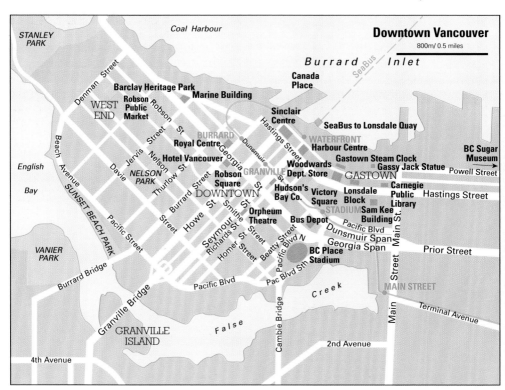

a century ago – is host to a number of marinas, floating gas (petrol) stations and docks for float planes providing flightseeing tours.

Visible to the southeast on a clear day is 3,000-metre (10,000-ft) **Mount Baker**. Named after Captain George Vancouver's third mate, it is 80 km (50 miles) away, just the other side of the Canada/US border. A dormant volcano (its last eruption was in 1843), it has been popular with mountain climbers since the first known ascent in 1868, and offers skiing and snowboarding on its rugged slopes.

Across the inlet is the **North Shore**. The Canadian Pacific Railway quickly developed the harbour with wharves and hotels; by World War I, North Shore shipyards were turning out a non-stop stream of cargo and supply ships, tugs, icebreakers, fishing boats and barges, many built with wooden hulls because steel was scarce.

**The city's charm lies in its setting next to the wilderness.**

Today, 70 million metric tons of bulk materials and 3000 foreign ships leave from the score of terminals every year, bound for the ports of 90 different countries. Shipments include coal, chemicals, various grains, wood chips and lumber, and the main components of the world's agricultural fertilizers – sulphur, phosphates and potash.

The first ferries chugged across the inlet in 1900, forerunners of today's **SeaBus** which takes approximately eight minutes to cross to **Lonsdale Quay**, the North Shore's fresh food market, restaurants and shopping centre.

To the east, the **Second Narrows bridge** crosses Burrard Inlet, latest in a long succession of bridges which were damaged by ships and eventually demolished. Rare sightings of killer whales have been made in the harbour. Boatloads of salmon, once plentiful here, used to be delivered to the big, red **Canfisco building** where from 1918 they were cooked and canned.

Below you are many old brick buildings, originally grocery or outfitters' warehouses. The first non-CPR finan-

cial entity in the new city after Hastings Mill store, established 1865, was the wholesale grocery firm founded by Bavarian-born David Oppenheimer (1834-97). His brick-built grocery warehouse still stands on the southeast corner of Columbia and Powell streets. Groceries enabled him to expand into steamship connections, development and contracting operations.

Oppenheimer and his brothers Isaac and Charles built their fortune at Victoria and Yale, supplying mule trains en route to the Cariboo goldfields. By the time David Oppenheimer settled in Vancouver in 1885, he was rich enough to buy all the land between the present-day streets of Carrall and Gore.

Oppenheimer was elected as mayor and soon afterwards gave a boost to his part of town, in 1889, when he and brother Isaac established the Vancouver Street Railway Company to run electrified trams. "There is no doubt," remarked the *Vancouver Daily World* on 14 January 1890, "that the electric light

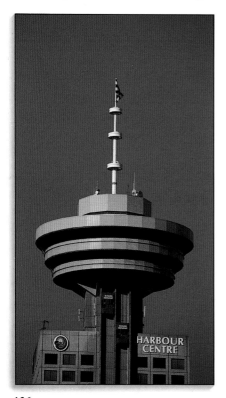

HARBOUR CENTRE

wire is dangerous, that it has killed a great many people… But notwithstanding frequent appalling accidents we now know that railway travelling is much less dangerous than travelling by coach." The city abandoned electrified streetcars in favour of buses in the 1950s.

**Entrance to Gastown:** One block east of Canada Place, the columned **Canadian Pacific Railway (CPR) terminal**, which in 1914 replaced an earlier building on the site, is now a terminal for the **SkyTrain**, the elevated rapid transit system, the city's **SeaBus** and **West Coast Express**, a commuter train to the Fraser Valley. When CPR's first train, festooned with flowers, steamed into the station here on 23 May 1887, the whole town turned out to celebrate. An endless stream of grain, lumber, even immigrants, could now travel with relative ease from coast to coast and at last Canada, and by extension Great Britain, had a Pacific-based deepwater port from which it could trade with the exotic Orient on a regular basis. The old CPR building is one of the city's most impressive, its soaring interior decorated with romantic pictures of the Rocky Mountains by the wife of a railway executive.

Just down the street stands the old Kelly-Douglas grocery warehouse, yet another supplier to the gold miners. This warehouse is now completely refitted as elegant shops such as **The Landing**. Douglas, one of the two partners, died in 1901 when aboard a ship that hit an iceberg, but Kelly, who got his training working for David Oppenheimer, continued to prosper. His brand-name Nabob goods were promoted by the Nabobettes singing group who had an early hit on commercial radio, and a 1940 advertisement for a soap in the Vancouver *Province* was at the time a sensational new gimmick.

Today, The Landing is a delightfully user-friendly shopping mall. It's two levels filled with eating places and such stylish stores as Ralph Lauren, the Edinburgh Tartan Shop and Snowflake. The

Up the glass elevators to the far-reaching view.

boast of **Pastel's Café** – that it offers a "beautiful view of the North Shore" – is a correct one.

**The Gastown experience:** Standing at the corner of Cambie and Water streets, Gastown begins with a unique sight: the world's first **steam-powered clock**. Every quarter-hour, crowds of spectators assemble to watch synchronised jets of steam announce the time from noisy whistles far above their heads. Built by horologist Ray Saunders, who maintains a basement workshop nearby, the clock was not erected until 1977 but the original design for its mechanism dates back to a century earlier. An outer bronze case hides an elaborate system of steel weights on a chain, plus a music box that plays the Westminster chimes every 15 minutes, all powered by an underground steam heating source. On rare non-rainy days crowds throng to the Parisian-style sidewalk tables of the **Water Street Café**, opposite the clock.

Gastown's main drag, **Water Street**, is composed of interesting souvenir shops, touristy restaurants and galleries including **Hills Indian Arts** and the **Inuit Gallery**, both selling exclusive West Coast native arts. **The Old Spaghetti Factory Restaurant** at 53 Water Street, with its charming, antique-filled interior, occupies the ground floor of what was once a warehouse built by Staffordshire-born William Harold Malkin. Malkin left England as a teenager and arrived in Vancouver in 1884. He and his brother became rich provisioning prospectors heading for the Kootenay goldfields and later the Klondike. In 1928 he, like Oppenheimer, became mayor of Vancouver, partly as a result of his pledge to build the Burrard Bridge and then to fund the Sea Island City Airport.

**Maple Tree Square** marks the spot where, back in 1868, a river boat pilot named Jack "Gassy" Deighton, a Briton who had been running a saloon in New Westminster, landed in a canoe with his native wife and a yellow dog, rolled a keg of whisky ashore and started a sa-

**Curled up in the sun.**

loon in an old wooden shack. Though the beds in his hotel lacked pillows, he was soon advertising that his establishment was replete with all the comforts of home. When Gassy died at the age of 45, his last words cursing a barking dog, his funeral included plenty of free drinks and cost a whopping $165. His infant son was immediately nicknamed the "Earl of Granville".

A rival saloon keeper, Joseph Manion, later described Gassy as "a man of broad, ready humour, spicy and crisp and everflowing of grotesque Falstaffian dimensions." Deighton died in 1875 but when the hotel burned down in the Great Fire of 13 June 1886, its new owner needed less than 24 hours to be back in business dispensing "encouragement" from an open-air bar consisting of nothing more than a plank resting on two kegs. Today, at the corner of Carrall and Water streets – the site where not only Gastown but the city itself began – there is a life-sized **statue** of **Gassy Jack** atop a barrel.

In 1885 an old maple tree grew here and it was under the shade of its branches that the West Coast pioneers met to choose the name Vancouver. The tree was one of the town's better-known landmarks, sloping at such a steep angle that one man had trained his dog to run up the trunk to retrieve things. It was on this tree that the notice of the first civic election was posted in 1886. A local paper, the *Herald*, urged citizens to "vote early and vote often".

The **Byrnes Block** building behind the statue went up that very year, one of the first to be constructed after the Great Fire. Behind it is another reminder of that era: **Gaoler's Mews**, now a brick-floored alleyway with ivy-covered walls, shady trees, lanterns and a **carousel clock** that musically greets the hour. The mews was the site of the log-cabin police station of Gastown's first police chief and postmaster, Jonathan Miller. Miller had his prisoners, lightly chained at the ankle, work on road-clearing projects. Behind the mews, **Blood Alley**

still has a cobbled yard with iron stairways and a sleepy air.

**Hotel boom:** Across Water Street beside the railroad tracks, several restaurants have decks from which diners can enjoy West Coast cuisine while watching trains shuttle back and forth. Gastown ends here, just beside the gridiron building that once was **Hotel Europe**, 43 Powell Street, the first fireproof hotel in the entire city. Water Street's turn-of-the-century boom encouraged Angelo Colari in 1908 to replace his first Hotel Europe with the present-day reinforced concrete, flat iron-shaped version. Still dominating the eastern end of the street, it is now an apartment house.

Among a score of the city's oldest buildings dating back to this era, at least half a dozen were Gastown hotels: the 1900 Dominion (its brick arches added in the 1960s) at **92 Water Street**; the Carlton (1899) and Commercial (1896) hotels at **300** and **340 Cambie Street**; the Italianate Grand Hotel, built in 1890 at **26 Water Street**; the bay-windowed Terminus whose customers were mainly sailors, miners and loggers, two doors away; the Kings Hotel at **208 Carrall Street**; and the deluxe Alhambra with fireplaces in every room for which guests paid as much as $1 a night when it first opened in 1887. The **Edward Hotel** at 300 Water Street was built in 1906 on the site of the Regina Hotel which had been the only building in Gastown to survive the fire of 1886.

**Just beside Gastown:** The now abandoned Woodwards department store, whose mail-order catalogues supplied isolated western communities for decades after it was founded in 1892, has stood at the corner of Hastings and Abbott since 1902.

This end of Hastings Street is now a seedy mélange of cheap hotels, cut-priced restaurants and low-budget shopping; be sure to note Sikori's Classical Records near Abbott. Check out **Funky Winker Beans Pub,** 37 West Hastings, with its brass rails, marble-topped bar, wooden balustrades and silent-movie nudes. One block north, at 15 West Cordova where sailors once caroused in the stand-up bar of the anything-goes Stanley Hotel, stands the **Pig & Whistle Pub.** The old Travelers Hotel (now a residence) in the white, four-storey **Fortin Building** (1893) and the **Lonsdale Block** (1889) across the street recall an earlier age.

**Sugar and sweeties:** Eastwards along **Alexander Street** is an industrial area of warehouses of little interest to visitors. An early sudsmaker, the Columbia Brewery, stood on the north side of Powell Street between Wall and Victoria in what was then Cedar Cove at the edge of the forest.

In the years preceding World War I, Alexander Street was rife with brothels, their doors wide open to the street into which flowed the melodious tones of piano rags. At 623 Alexander, the "House of all Nations" offered (according to a 1912 edition of *The Truth*) "everything from a chocolate-coloured damsel to a Swedish girl." The following year saw a police crackdown that netted 133 "keepers of bawdy houses" and 204 "inmates". By 1914 the red-light district was virtually no more.

The **BC Sugar Refining Co. Ltd.** warehouse dominates the eastern end of Powell Street. The **BC Sugar Museum**, at the foot of Rogers Street, recounts the saga of 24-year-old Benjamin Tingley Rogers who founded the company in 1890 and agreed to employ only white labour in return for 10 years' free water and 15 years without taxes. Mayor David Oppenheimer was an early investor in this firm, the city's first industry not based on fishing or forestry. Today the company's raw cane comes mostly from Australia and the province of Alberta. Generations of Canadians are familiar with Rogers' Golden Syrup whose pails served as lunch buckets during the 1930s Depression. The museum is free, friendly and is open every weekday, but it gets very few visitors, possibly because of its location.

**Gassy Jack marks the spot where the city first began.**

# NEAR THE STADIUMS

The triangular area between Hastings Street and the end of False Creek includes Chinatown, a new NHL hockey and NBA basketball arena nicknamed the "garage", Science World, B.C. Place Stadium and Yaletown, Vancouver's trendiest shopping area.

**The Chinatown experience:** Vancouver's **Chinatown**, the third largest in North America after San Francisco and New York, began with the influx of gold seekers in 1858, and was augmented by the need for labour to build the Canadian Pacific railroad.

For the instant ambiance of an old China market, stroll along **Pender Street**, admiring some of the city's oldest buildings with their characteristic recessed balconies: the **Chinese Benevolent Association** building (1909), formed in response to racial discrimination; **Ming Wo Cookware** with its dramatic green banners; and the **Wing Sang Building** (1889), 51 to 69 East Pender Street, probably the oldest on the street, behind which lurks rundown **Market Alley**. This once housed one of the area's many opium factories in the days when the manufacture of the drug, but not its consumption, was legal. The street is even livelier at night during the Friday Night Market. Of particular note are the fanciful neon signs of the **Sun Ah Hotel** and the **Niagara Hotel** (four blocks west).

Everybody comes to stare at the world's thinnest inhabited building (so it is claimed), no wider than the outstretched arms of Barbara Chow whose father Jack owns it and from which he operates his insurance business. Subject of countless magazine stories and featured in the *Guinness Book of Records*, the **Sam Kee Building** at the corner of Carrall and Pender streets is a mere 2 metres (6 ft) wide and 30 metres (100 ft) long, enlarged with bow windows on the upper floor and a basement

under the sidewalk. Jack Chow jokes about the highly publicised building: "We have no secrets; we can't hide anything in here." A local magazine once described the building as "as much showbiz as real estate".

In the 1930s, Chinatown was regarded with suspicion by the white establishment which, among many exclusionary acts, prohibited white women from working in Chinese restaurants. "In view of the conditions under which the girls are expected to work," said police chief W.W. Foster as he closed down two cafés for infraction of this by-law, "it is almost impossible for them to be so employed without falling victim to some immoral life."

Two **Chinese Cultural Centres** on Pender Street near **China Gate**, with changing art exhibitions and a free museum open to the public, are the main focus for the community today. The *Chinese Times*, located in a 1902 building at the corner of Carrall and Pender streets, once employed typesetters who

laboriously set type one character at a time from 5,000 separate pieces. Today, computers do the job.

**Authentic scholar's garden:** The intricate **Dr Sun Yat-Sen Classical Chinese Garden** was modelled after a Ming Dynasty scholar's garden in Suzhou, Jiangsu province, by artisans from that Chinese city. Contained within the walled garden are a jade green pool, a dripping waterfall, special Taihu rocks, several pavilions and an upturned T'ing. To fully appreciate the garden's *chi* or lifeforce, it's best to take the guided tour. No power tools, only traditional methods, were used on the wood and tile work. Office workers bring brown-bag lunches on sunny days and enjoy the duck pond and pavilion in the free admission portion of the garden. "In Vancouver," wrote Eric Nicol in a biography of the city, "a heat wave is defined as a warm sunny morning followed by a warm sunny afternoon."

For those in search of a little variety in their diet, Pender and Main streets feature non-stop Chinese street markets with exotic vegetables, dried edibles, live fish and hanging ducks *(see page 65)*. To overcome the objections of Vancouver's City Health Department in the 1970s, Chinese meat merchants marched to Canada's capital, Ottawa, and gleefully served up hundreds of pounds of their famous barbequed, open-air-preserved duck to Members of Parliament. Their traditional methods were allowed to continue. Traditional apothecaries too, will provide you with special items promising to restore your lost vigour. Nearby **Keefer Street** is famous for its Chinese bakeries.

Between Cambie and Hamilton on Hastings Street is one of the downtown's few parks, **Victory Square**. In 1924, the Southam family, then owners of the city newspaper, the *Province*, donated money for the square's rehabilitation which included the erection of the **Cenotaph**. At present, however, homeless people have taken the park over for themselves.

Chinatown began in 1858.

134

**Trash to very trendy:** A few decades ago it was little more than a cluster of dilapidated warehouses delighting film crews who needed gun-peppered flight scenes or drug-bust sets, but not too interesting for casual strolling. Today, **Yaletown**, the area along Mainland and Hamilton streets, sports the trendiest addresses in town. Historic warehouses have been converted Vancouver-style into restaurants, designer lofts, trendy pubs, chic boutiques and funky art galleries. Many of the old warehouse loading bays were ideal for restaurants which now spill over onto outdoor patios.

One hot spot, Vancouver's original brew pub, **Yaletown Brewing Company**, 1111 Mainland, combines the roles of brewery, pub, restaurant and people-watching venue. The young and trendy feel at home perusing the latest clunky shoes, chic accessories, innovative jewelry or unusual fashions in tiny sizes. Cigar lovers too will want to explore the area, as will book lovers who love to cook.

**The Sam Kee Building is in the *Guinness Book of Records*.**

**The Opera House rises again:** On the north side of Pender Street at Beatty was once an old drill shed which sheltered the 298-member Yukon Field Force en route to the Klondike in 1898. It had opened a decade earlier as the Imperial Opera House but was never as popular with the rough-and-tumble loggers, miners and sailors as the Grand Theatre on nearby Cordova Street, where audiences paid 25¢ to sing along to crudely tinted lantern slides spelling out "On the Banks of the Wabash" before the silent movie programme began.

Today, only a block or two away is the **Queen Elizabeth Theatre** which has concert and recital halls, a playhouse and an opera season. Beside it, between Georgia and Robson, is the architecturally acclaimed, rosy beige coloured **Vancouver Public Library**, curling open like a sea shell and often compared to the Coliseum in Rome. This library reverses standard library designs by clustering books in the middle and placing study-tables next to the scene-

studded windows. Even if reading-research is not part of your holiday plan, the main rotunda contains bookstores and coffee houses, and a walk across the suspended catwalks is an adventure.

Across from the library is the top-flight **Ford Centre for the Performing Arts.** If you missed *Starlight Express* or *Phantom of the Opera* in London, or *Showboat* on Broadway, check out the programme here. This is the venue for long-running, internationally popular, crowd-pulling performances.

**Jet engine-supported roof:** The 60,000-seat **BC Place Stadium**, 777 Pacific Blvd South, at the end of False Creek, sports a 4-hectare (10-acre) air-supported dome, strung like a tennis racket and one of the largest in the world. When it went up in 1982 it was the first covered stadium in Canada. The Teflon fibreglass roof, stronger than steel and light permeable, is held aloft by 16 revolving jet engine fans. If they all failed and the roof deflated it would still clear the uppermost seats. The stadium, the scene of numerous horse shows, trade shows, concerts and exhibitions, is also home to the Canadian Football League's BC Lions and has hosted several Grey Cup championship games.

Open every day at BC Place Stadium Gate 5 is the **BC Sports Hall of Fame and Museum**. Besides moving tributes to disabled heroes Rick Hansen and Terry Fox, there is a recreation of British contender Roger Banister and Australian John Landry setting the first track record for the four-minute mile in 1954 at Vancouver's Commonwealth Games.

**Cheers for a second stadium:** Canadian passions soar during National Hockey League (NHL) games at the new home of the Vancouver Canucks, **General Motors Place**, 800 Griffiths Way. Cheers erupt skyward from this second stadium, side-by-side with BC Place Stadium and nicknamed "the garage". Not only hockey melées, but the hype of the National Basketball Association's (NBA) Vancouver Grizzlies sets normally complacent Canadian passions Learning about *yin* and *yang* at Dr Sun Yat-Sen Classical Chinese Garden.

soaring. What could be more rewarding than a hard-checking Canadian hockey game or the bounce of a 100-point professional basketball match-up when Michael Jordan is in town?

Nearby, one of the city's best-known landmarks is the giant, silvery geodesic sphere containing **Science World**. Exhibits here demonstrate such principles as sound and light, as well as offering whole rooms full of ingenious games and puzzles. Ever changing displays may include devices to create gigantic bubbles, music studios enabling anybody to compare melodies, or sudden flashes of light that imprint visitors' images on the wall.

This futuristic museum also features **Omnimax**, a 12-storey high screen of stupendous proportions, complete with wraparound sound. Each frame is 10 times the size of conventional 35mm movie film, making a plunge into the Grand Canyon, a closeup inspection of the world's volcanoes or a walk in space a vivid experience.

**Industrial, no more:** The SkyTrain **Main Street Station** lies across from the Science World not far from the majestic, old **Canadian National Railways (CN) Station** now serving VIA rail and as the **Bus Depot**. Since 1919, it has occupied land reclaimed from False Creek. Today it stands "in majestic isolation… a wonderful survivor of its era," according to architectural columnist Robin Wood. **False Creek**, 3 km (2 miles) in length, once extended all the way east to Clark Drive, but was in-filled to provide more industrial land. City officials never liked the name – given by the Royal Navy – and in 1891 petitioned the Dominion Government to change it to the more attractive appellation "Pleasant Inlet". However, False Creek it remains.

Each June, False Creek reverberates with excitement as teams arrive for the **International Dragon Boat Races,** a thrilling exibition of races interlaced with Asian cultural performances and a great deal of food.

**Below left, Chinese therapeutics. Right, the Dominion Trust building.**

# MIDTOWN AND THE WEST END

At the corner of **Georgia** and **Granville** streets stands one of Vancouver's oldest and least noticeable landmarks, a mere 15 years younger than the city itself, the four-sided **Birk's clock**. Built in 1902 and moved in 1913, it has stood for most of its existence in front of a Montreal-based jewellery store, **Birk's**. From the clock south on Granville Street, a local author wrote in 1962, lies "Vancouver's gaudiest avenue". Not much has changed on Granville, though the word "seedy" now comes to mind. Georgia Street, on the other hand, presents a more sophisticated face. Having nothing to do with the state of Georgia in either the USA or Russia, Georgia Street's name comes from the Strait of Georgia which, in turn, was named after England's King George III.

Almost immediately after Vancouver's Great Fire of 1886, the Canadian Pacific Railway laid the foundations for the first wooden, four-storey **Hotel Vancouver**, thus moving the city centre a few thousand feet further "inland". One week before the CPR's first transcontinental train arrived on 23 May 1887, the hotel – where "on quiet nights, the creak of ships at anchor can be heard" – was open for business. The building survived until 1916 when it was replaced by a larger hotel with ballrooms and a glassed roof garden on the site of the present Eaton's store. In its turn, this incarnation was replaced in 1939.

**VIP guests:** The chateau-roofed *grand dame* Hotel Vancouver, 900 West Georgia, in its various forms has played host to royalty, politicians, writers and business tycoons, including Mark Twain, J. Pierpont Morgan, Rudyard Kipling, Winston Churchill, Clark Gable, Jane Fonda, Indira Gandhi, Romania's Queen Marie and a variety of British royals. "Its spacious suites," reported the *Vancouver Sun* in 1939, "seem...strangely and commodiously out of place in this day of cubbyhole bedrooms ar supper places." The present 508 rooms, many elegantly furnished with antique mahogany and Chippendale, and still among the largest in town. The five-bedroom Royal Suite (today partitioned into several rooms) was inaugurated within days of the May 1939 opening, when King George VI and Queen Elizabeth the Queen Mother arrived on their first royal visit to Canada. A decade later a dishevelled and unshaven Bing Crosby, returning from a backwoods fishing trip, was at first refused admission to the hotel until the manager was summoned and recognised the famous singer in his unfamiliar casual state. However, in 1986 royal visitors, HRH Prince Charles and Diana, Princess of Wales, shunned the usual royal arrangements and chose to stay at the new waterfront Pan Pacific Hotel.

**Good gifts:** Across from the Hotel Vancouver is **Cathedral Place** and in its courtyard the **Canadian Craft Museum** showcasing excellence in Canadian craft and design. The museum shop is whispered to be the best place to find well designed one-of-a-kind Canadian crafts.

Also across from the Hotel Vancouver are the stone walls of the Anglican **Christ Church Cathedral**, one of its stained-glass windows depicting Captain Cook, its beamed Douglas fir roof soaring to the skies. The cathedral, conceived in 1888, at first suffered funding problems, and the congregation were only able to afford the granite basement. Thus it was nicknamed "St Root House" until six years later new Gothic-style wall buttresses announced its completion. Across Burrard Street, adjoining a mini-park with a waterfall, is the **Skytrain Station**.

The **Hudson's Bay Company store** (The Bay), erected in 1913 at the corner of Georgia and Granville, was the firm's fifth outlet in the Vancouver area. One of the many legacies established by the royal chartered fur-trading company founded in 1670, its cream coloured Corinthian columns are yet another of

**Preceding pages: the courts of justice. Left, pulling some strings.**

ancouver's many and varied architectural attempts to inspire grandeur. The HBC's **Market Square**, an enticing collection of mini-shops and eating areas in the store's basement, should not be overlooked.

**Going underground:** The Bay is connected to the **Pacific Centre** whose 200 stores, most of them underneath the street, stretch for blocks. **Eaton's**, the most visible entrance to the underground complex, vies with **The Bay** for department store shoppers' attention. **Galloway's Specialty Foods**, 25 H Pacific Centre, seems wonderfully out of place among all the glittery stores but it's worth dropping in just for the exotic aroma of spices and curries as well as jams, chutneys, nuts, dates and a thousand and one imported foods.

Two blocks further west, along ragtag Granville Street, is the extravagantly opulent, 2,800-seat **Orpheum Theatre**, Smithe at Seymour, with its domed ceiling and dazzling crystal chandelier. Opened in 1927 as a combination vaude-

ville hall and movie palace to replace an earlier 1891 theatre, in 1973 the Orpheum was put up for sale and almost certain demolition by its movie chain owners. After thousands of voters petitioned the mayor, the city refurbished it at a cost of $7 million. Periodic guided tours are available. Charlie Chaplin, Bob Hope and Margot Fonteyn, among countless others, have graced its stage. The Vancouver Symphony Orchestra now performs here.

**Strolling Robsonstrausse:** Robson Street's nickname "Robsonstrausse" comes from its slight European flavour, reminiscent of when the street was predominantly populated with German restaurants all serving *Wiener schnitzl*. A compulsory stop along Robson is at one of the many coffee houses along its length. Classic java offerings are advertised alongside new inventions including frappuccino and flavoured iced coffees. For the diet conscious all are made with low fat milk alternatives. Made popular by Starbucks Co. in

Hotel Vancouver, Art Gallery and Robson Square on top; shopping malls underground.

nearby Seattle, Vancouverites enthusiastically embrace specialty coffee drinking as a way of life, adding yet another dimension to their already leisure-conscious lifestyle.

The standard-setting **Starbucks** is found in more than 70 locations throughout Vancouver. This major player continues to set the pace for its competitors, whose valiant strivings to gain custom please coffee drinkers even more. On Robson Street, ever-competitive Starbucks can be found occupying two diagonal corners of the same busy intersection.

But Starbucks is a brash newcomer in comparison to the venerable **Murchie's Tea and Coffee Ltd**, 970 Robson Street. Its aromatic interior hearkens back to the 19th century when billowing clipper ships called in at the port of Vancouver en route with their tea cargoes to the "mother" country, Great Britain. With well over 100 years' experience in the spice, tea and coffee trade on these Pacific shores, it is well worth a visit.

The section of **Robson Street** that thinks of itself as Vancouver's answer to LA's Rodeo Drive, with its designer boutiques, *haute couture* and names like Gigli, Ferragamo, and Chanel, is actually found off Robson on Hornby between Robson and Georgia, on Burrard between Robson and Georgia, and on Alberni parallel to Robson at Burrard.

Northwest along Robson Street at Bidwell is **Robson Public Market**, a glass-enclosed complex filled with enticing stalls and snack bars. It is worth heading up here just to eat some of the most reasonably priced food in this part of town.

Robson Street is the location where one of several crowd scenes characterises the livability of Vancouver. On almost any warm evening in summer, and on most Fridays and Saturdays throughout the year, crowds turn up on Robson Street between Hornby and Jervis, just to stroll, shop, visit, see and be seen. It's a recurring, spontaneous Vancouver "happening."

**Shopping on Robson Street.**

**Lonely lions:** Across from the Hotel Georgia stands the sandstone and granite **Vancouver Art Gallery (VAG)**. This domed and columned edifice features an eclectic collection of modern works mixed in with others dating to the 16th century. Its pivotal paintings are by local artist Emily Carr (*see page 147*). Even non-art lovers pop into the VAG to check out the outstanding gift shop. Once the city's courthouse, the VAG was one of several prominent BC buildings designed by Francis Mawson Rattenbury – who, on returning to his native England in 1934, met an ignominious end bludgeoned by his young wife's lover, the chauffeur.

The VAG's original entrance is flanked by lions overlooking Georgia Street, but much was lost when the place of entry was changed from the front to the back, writes architectural critic Robin Wood, leaving "lonely lions to guard a purposeless portico". The lions, copied exactly from the New York Public Library, also guard the outdoor **Centen-**

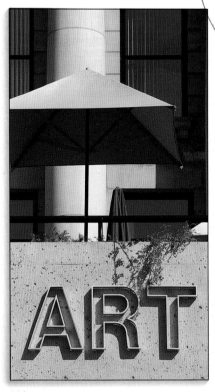

nial **Fountain** and watch over bands of rent-a-crowd protesters (the same faces, often paid for their participation, appear at many demonstrations) that Vancouver seems to spawn on a regular basis.

Pop into the **Hong Kong Bank** across Georgia Street to admire Alan Storey's enormous sculptural work *Pendulum*. It serves a functional as well as decorative purpose, to keep the atrium well ventilated.

The intersection of Robson and Burrard is dominated by the trendy **Robson Square.** It's a good idea to explore its lower regions for the latest mini-trade show or public lecture in progress. Robson Square plaza is also used for concerts in summer.

**Architectural studies:** Most of the architecture around this neighbourhood is worth a look, particularly Arthur Erickson's stylish **Courthouse** between Hornby and Howe (the present seat of provincial justice), with its sloping, glass roof. Architect Erickson's rationale for the profuse play of light is that "justice must be seen to be done". The area is a delight for pedestrians with its profusion of little plazas, waterfalls, seats and flowers.

Closer to the inlet, the **Sinclair Centre**, at Cordova and Granville near Canada Place, is a textbook example of how to renovate with taste and imagination. Based on the original 1910 post office together with its 1939 extension and two adjoining buildings, it is an artfully appealing blend of old and new designs, an attractively lit atrium surrounded by shops and offices connected with a granite staircase. The "Dickensian-looking" former **Customs and Excise Building** (1912) at the corner of Howe and Cordova streets and the **Winch Building** (1909), in wildly different styles, complete the quartet, each facade preserved to reflect the architectural taste of its era.

**Banks rule:** Still dominated by banks, this part of town just back from the water was always a business centre. **For Art's sake**

Across the street from the **Bank of Commerce** was the old (1889) Strand Hotel, where ship owners and brokers met for business lunches. Among the customers was Captain Alex Maclean, a belligerent fur trader, said to have been the model for one of Jack London's characters in his novel *The Sea Wolf*.

The corner of Granville and Hastings was the site of two "firsts" – the city's first modern skyscraper, the **Royal Bank Tower**, erected in 1929, and the first traffic light installation. It was known as McKinnon's Corner in the 1920s after Constable Duncan McKinnon, whose white gloves and white baton were a familiar sight to motorists. He was hired by the newly created Traffic Department in December 1921, two weeks before the rule of the road was changed to enforce driving on the right-hand side. Vancouver motorists expected a disaster. "It was prophesied that there would be a scene of wild confusion... that there would be innumerable accidents; that people would be killed every 10 minutes and the gods of old customs would rise up and demand a continuous stream of sacrifices," said a columnist in the *Province*. "But there were no sacrifices and no confusion."

**Art Deco masterpiece:** Past the premises of the sedate and private **Vancouver Club** (1913) are a gleaming rosy-gold skyscraper, its colour created by actual gold dust embedded between the layers of glass, and the magnificent 25-storey Art Deco **Marine Building**, 1055 West Hastings. With its terracotta friezes of Neptune and sea creatures, decorative tiled entrance and elegant lobby complete with stained-glass window, "its architectural conception," wrote its designers, McCarter and Nairne, "suggests some great marine rock rising from the sea clinging with sea flora and fauna, in sea green, flashed with gold." As well as inspecting the building's *Les Arts Decoratif* facade, it is acceptable to enter the building under its dramatic deco-sunburst and through its brass doors, to view the exceptionally ornate lobby.

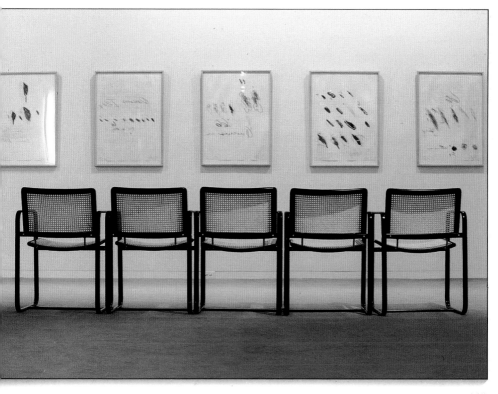

Constructed in 1929, the Marine Building was placed under the care of London-born Albert Cadman, superintendent. Unfortunately, he once fell down the elevator shaft. A clerk from one of the offices was sent down with a glass of brandy until a rescue crew could arrive. The clerk took one look at the battered Cadman and drank the brandy himself. Cadman survived and went on working for many years.

**The West End:** Vancouver's **West End** is not to be confused with the West Side which is across the Burrard Street Bridge to the southwest. In the 1960s and 1970s city planners went a bit berserk and permitted developers to replace hundreds of large, old single family homes with a jungle of concrete apartment blocks. At one time not so long ago, it claimed to be the most heavily populated district in Canada.

Some of the city's oldest wooden houses, Edwardian and Queen Anne buildings whose attractive gingerbread-type facades include balconies and stairways, remain in the area around **Nelson Park**, Comox and Bute. Nine old homes were transplanted to Nicola and Barclay where, renovated by the city as the **Barclay Square Heritage Park**, they are now being used as community activity centres.

**Denman Street** is not for shopping though there is good energy here and it's fun to walk south to very beautiful **English Bay** and the entrance to leafy **Stanley Park**.

**Commercial Drive** represents the multicultural character of the city. Sometimes impassable by car on summer evenings, being chock-a-block with locals patronising the many small shops, restaurants and outdoor cafés, there's some serious jazz and good food here.

On the southwestern side, **Sunset Beach**, running all the way up to the south entrance of Stanley Park on English Bay, is popular on any summer day it doesn't rain in Vancouver. It's especially busy during the annual Earth Day celebration in April.

Pacific Centre's miles of aisles.

146

# AN ARTIST'S LIFE

Emily Carr, one of Canada's most important artists and an award-winning writer, was considered an eccentric character in her own time. In her shapeless coat, sturdy laced shoes, her grey hair tucked into a hairnet with velvet band, and with only a dog or parrot for company, she often went sketching and camping in remote forests and Indian reservations. Her "modern" style earned her much derision, but British Columbians are now proud to claim this remarkable woman as one of their own.

Daughter of a successful Victorian merchant, she was 19 when, in 1890, she persuaded her family to send her to San Francisco's California School of Art. When she returned to her studio in Victoria, a reconditioned barn, she taught art so she could pay her way to a London art school. Later, in France, she became influenced by the painters of the Fauve school.

This "new art", which in the main is so much lighter and more brightly coloured than her "Canadian" paintings, was unacceptable to Vancouver and Victoria's less enlightened society, so Carr gave up teaching in 1912 in favour of other means of earning a living. Constructing a home on her father's land, she bred sheepdogs and made pottery, digging her own clay and wheeling it home in an old pram which doubled as a shopping cart. Her simple pots bore authentic West Coast native designs.

Carr's eight trips to sketch and paint the cultural scenes of northern British Columbia and Alaska in villages of the Nootka, Salish, Haida, Kwakiutl and Gitksen peoples, as well as her powerful renditions of totem poles, gave her credence with her peers, the reigning Group of Seven artists in eastern Canada, and increasingly with anthropologists seeking records of such artefacts.

In the 1920s Carr switched her affections from sheepdogs to Belgian griffons and expanded her menagerie: she had a cat, parrots, a cockatoo, a white rat named Susie and a Capuchin monkey called Woo for which she made pinafores so they could take winter walks together in the park.

She painted on manilla paper, using oils thinned with gasoline or even house paint. Adding boxes to an old caravan for her pets, she created a mobile shelter in which she could work on her visits to Goldstream Park and the Metchosin region of Vancouver Island. By the 1930s, her work was internationally recognised, but it had brought her scant financial reward.

While recovering from the first of four heart attacks, Carr began to write about her experiences. She was 70 when her first book, a collection of stories about her travels among the Indians of the Northwest, was published. It won the Governor General's medal for general literature. This first book, *Klee Wyck* (meaning "laughing one", the nickname given to her by the Indians of Ucluelet) is still in print, as are *The House of All Sorts* (about her days as a landlady), the *Book of Small* (based on her childhood) and *Growing Pains,* her autobiography.

Carr died in 1945 and her birthplace, 207 Government Street in Victoria, has been restored for public viewing. A museum of Carr artefacts is housed in the nearby Wharf Street building which her father owned and in which he operated a grocery store. The Vancouver School of Art on Granville Island is called The Emily Carr. ∎

**Emily Carr's *Street Scene*, 1911.**

# WEST SIDE STORY

An unwary visitor can easily be confused by the profusion of "wests" in and around Vancouver. West Vancouver is a separate North Shore municipality to the west of the Lions Gate Bridge. The West End's residential apartments and beaches join downtown Vancouver to Stanley Park.

**The real west:** The **West Side** of Vancouver, stretching from Cambie Street to the **University of British Columbia**, has been home to upwardly mobile Vancouverites since the early 1900s. There they are joined by scores of university students and countless others who worship the sun (when it shines) at one of **Point Grey**'s many beaches.

However, one of the great benefits of living in a rainbelt is the resulting greenery. Everyone delights in the major show gardens full of colour and scores of verdant parks in this part of the city. And the area also has a large number of high quality museums.

**False Creek**, the West Side's northeast boundary, was originally a 5-km (3-mile) inlet extending east from English Bay through marshlands and mud. Its south shore now harbours one of the most vibrant crowd scenes in the city, **Granville Island.**

Not really an island, but a narrow-necked peninsula, 15 hectares (38 acres) of mud flats built up by dredging and dykes. The original contractor hired to dredge the channel somehow managed to convince the city to expend funds simultaneously to expand the shoreline. By combining the two jobs, and being paid for both of them, he made a handsome profit.

**Shopping island:** The heart of the niftily infilled island today, nestled under the Granville Bridge, is a mosaic of colour and life made up of a **Public Market**, dozens of art studios, playhouses, restaurants, and charter crafts offering all sorts of boating adventures from a day on the water to dinner cruises. All are housed in what were once industrial warehouses.

The farmers' market, the anchor tenant, offers fresh seafood and good local produce, as well as imported gourmet items interspersed between kettles of fudge and mounds of strawberries. All of Vancouver heads here for Thai spices, fresh pasta and more than 150 different types of cheeses. Take-out stalls provide spontaneous casual meals, eaten on the pier among pigeons, jugglers, boat masts, street musicians and balloon clowns.

The best craftspeople display their ceramics, jewellery and art in jazzed up studios that were once part of the industrial heart of Vancouver. Sawmills, processing plants, cooperages and foundries smoked and clanked away until 1973, when an ambitious city redevelopment scheme introduced a new mixed-use policy.

The policy meant that cars, industry, breweries, commerce, shipping, restaurants, art studios, theatres, houseboats, marinas, a fresh food and fish market and of course people, now meld into a delightful hodge-podge of activity. Today, the island represents just about everything Vancouverites like best about their city.

Get a free map of the island at the **Granville Island Information Centre**, across Johnston Street from the public market, and watch a short video on the island's history. Then head for **Granville Island Brewing Company** on Anderson Street. In 1984, when this micro-brewery opened its doors, its aim was to make good old-fashioned beers. It takes as its gospel the Bavarian Purity Law of 1516: unpasteurised beers and ales without chemicals or preservatives. There are free tours and ongoing tasting sessions daily.

Granville Island's atmosphere is overwhelmingly marine-based. The **Maritime Market** deals in everything from boat sales, charters, repairs and sea-going hardware, to build-your-own model schooners and fish-themed jewellery. **Sea Village**, behind the **Emily Carr College of Art and Design** and its free art galleries, is a permanent enclave of floating homes.

Aside from the market, the most interesting eating places are **Mulvaney's**, hidden behind the Creekhouse, serving fresh northwest seafood in a New Orleans atmosphere; **Bridges**, the big yellow building, convivial and trendy, outdoors or in, with a great view of False Creek; or the **Granville Island Hotel** and its microbrewery, at the quieter far end of the island.

Students from the **Pacific Institute of Culinary Arts**, at the entrance to Granville Island, showcase their culinary talents for the public Monday through Friday for lunch and dinner.

The island also features a **mainstream theatre**, and a **revue stage**. Working studios demonstrate ceramics, weaving, dyeing, glass-blowing and papermaking, and visitors are more than welcome. Children have a two-storey department store all their own – the sparkly **Kids Only Market**, one of the more than 260 businesses and facilities now occupying the island.

**Getting to the island:** There are several ways to get to Granville Island. For sanity's sake, put your automobile at the bottom of the list. Although there are a thousand free three-hour parking spaces and several pay lots, you are likely to circle endlessly around the cobbled one-way streets.

A more relaxed approach is via the bathtub-shaped **electric ferries** which chug to the island from the **Vancouver Aquatic Centre** off Beach Avenue, or from the foot of **Hornby Street** on the north side of False Creek. Ferries depart every few minutes from early morning till 8pm. For a small bus fare, you'll get a seal's-eye view of water birds, expensive yachts and towering luxury condominiums. You can also get to Granville Island on foot, by bicycle or by BC Transit bus.

Most attractions on the West Side lie in a roughly circular route from the beaches at the western end of the Art Deco-style **Burrard Bridge**, around Point Grey and back to the Granville Street Bridge.

**Kitsilano Point** (Kits Point) was once home to the Kitsilano Indians. In 1870 their village called Snauq became a government-decreed reservation. In

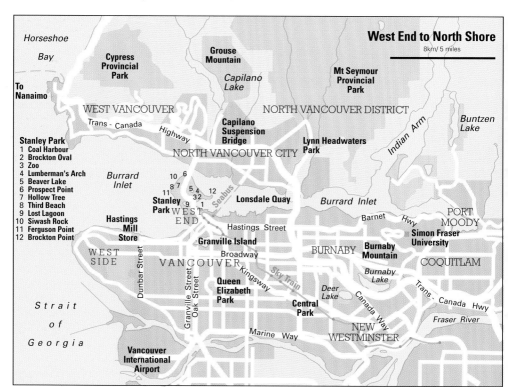

1901, the natives were forced off the land and most relocated to the North Shore. Provincial authorities tried to use the Point as an industrial site, but the influential CPR turned it into a residential area.

Today, Kits Point off Chestnut Street is the location of **Vanier Park** where kite flying is a major pastime as long as a major festival isn't in progress.

Besides the popular **Children's Festival** in May, and **Bard on the Beach** from June to September, Vanier Park is home to numerous special events. Within the park are the **H.R. MacMillan Planetarium**, 1100 Chestnut Street, featuring informative astronomy presentations and laser light shows.

**The Vancouver Museum** showcases local cultures charted back to 6,000 BC. Both the museum and the planetarium are housed in a building designed to resemble, not a spaceship, but a Coastal Salish person's rainhat. The small **Gordon Southam Observatory**, also on this site, offers use of a free stargazing telescope on clear nights.

**Marine heritage:** Nearby, where False Creek meets English Bay, the **Vancouver Maritime Museum's Heritage Harbour** accommodates classic and restored vessels. Tall Ships visiting the region tend to dock here, too.

The harbour-side museum's permanent gallery features plenty of sea lore and maritime disaster relics. Adjoining the museum is an A-frame building, the *St Roch* **National Historic Site**. Here stands an important Royal Canadian Mounted Police ship which gained international fame for her 1930s and 1940s voyages through Canada's Arctic waters.

In 1950, she was the first ship to circumnavigate the North American continent, a feat duplicated by the Royal Canadian Mounted Police again in 1999. Short guided tours are available.

**Kitsilano Beach** occupies the west side of the Point. In the summer, the grassy areas close to its tennis court are packed with unbearably fit single people, waiting for their turn at the nets and "catching some rays". Kits Beach in-

**Granville Island market.**

# HASTINGS MILL

Not many cities can point to a solitary log cabin as "the place where it all began", but no building in Vancouver could make a better claim than the Hastings Mill Store. As the hub of the tiny community on Burrard Inlet since its beginnings in 1865, the store was one of only a handful of buildings to survive the city's devastating Great Fire of 1886.

The Hastings Mill (which was originally the headquarters of the British Columbia and Vancouver Island Spar, Lumber & Sawmill Co.) was the town's first employer and its store the first meeting house, the first post office and the first church. After clearing some adjacent land, the mill then built Vancouver's first school. All this took place at the foot of what is now Dunlevy Street, a site marked today by a cairn which commemorates the mill's first export of lumber back in July 1867. The cargo was destined for Australia, "thus beginning Vancouver's prime function, the supply of her great timbers to the

world" as the inscription on the granite monument puts it.

"Magnificent Douglas firs and Western red cedars... some of the finest timber the world has ever seen" was grist for the mill around which the settlement of Gastown quickly developed. Today the old mill store is located 8 km (5 miles) from its original site, preserved as a museum in Pioneer Park at the foot of Alma Street.

Captain Edward Stamp's mill was not the first on Burrard Inlet; that honour goes to one on the North Shore which, after various financial problems, was eventually acquired by Sewell Prescott Moody and which spawned the town of Moodyville. But Stamp's mill was better situated and the decision of the Canadian Pacific Railway to run right into Vancouver clinched its leading role.

The demand for wood in the 19th century was almost insatiable: masts and spars for sailing ships, sturdy timbers for European mansions and beams and immense planks for the palaces of Asian emperors. Between 1867 and 1868, Vancouver's legendary timberman Jerry Rogers felled and shipped 2,000 spars, which even in those days fetched $200 apiece. Each massive, 800-year-old tree would take a day to bring down by axemen working from "springboards" notched into the tree several feet from the ground and 10-foot saws whirring away at the other side.

Captain Stamp's lease for the mill cost what was then the equivalent of about $250; until it was ready for operation he busied himself building the harbour's first tug. Within weeks of the mill starting production it was loading as many as four ships simultaneously. Soon Stamp converted to steam power and his mixed crew of native people, penniless gold prospectors and deserters from sailing ships were working around the clock to ship the timber out, spending their free time in Gassy Jack's tavern. On 11 April 1869 the mill transmitted the first message (to Moodyville across the inlet) on a newly-installed telegraph line.

By the time of Vancouver's disastrous fire, Captain Stamp was long gone – he returned to his native England after heavy financial losses – but, almost alone among the town's buildings, the mill survived.

Catch a No. 4, 7 or 32 bus running along Fourth Street to Alma Street, then walk three blocks to the museum. ■

**Hastings Mill: Vancouver's oldest building.**

cludes **Kitsilano Pool** – in 1931, when it was built, the largest salt-water pool in the British Empire.

West of the pool, Point Grey Road leads past assorted sailing clubs and beautiful but expensive waterfront homes to **Pioneer Park**. This is the site of the **Hastings Mill Store**, built in 1865 (*see page 154*) and the oldest building in Vancouver.

After the disastrous fire of 1866, which nearly destroyed the entire town, the stunned community gathered in the only surviving store to plan their future. It now serves as a fascinating if under-appreciated museum.

The museum houses a wonderful clutter of glass cases and rickety shelves piled high with old dolls, sewing machines, native baskets and wooden kitchen chairs used in early trams. Its single centre beam invites contemplation of the immense size and height of the trees that originally covered most of this area.

**Battle of Jericho:** The end of Point Grey Road leads to one of several entrances to **Jericho Park**. The park has 54 hectares (130 acres) of nature trails, picnic sites, 640 metres (2,100 ft) of beachfront as well as the **Vancouver Youth Hostel**. "Jericho" is either a distortion of "Jerry's Cove" or "Jerry & Co," in any case named after legendary 19th-century logger Jeremiah Rogers, who discarded the standard English broad-axe and invented his own.

The battle bit comes from an 1920s newspaper article that refers to the "Battle of Jericho" when the police chief and a posse cornered two murderers who had taken refuge near the site.

A Royal Canadian Air Force base dominated the property for decades. After a period of confused ownership, it was turned over to the city in 1973 to be massaged into its present incarnation as one of the best city parks for birding among duck ponds, bridges and paths.

The **Vancouver International Folk Festival**, held here annually in July, unfailingly attracts thousands of enthusiastic music fans.

MacMillan Planetarium, Vancouver Museum, and crab honouring Canada's 1 July birthday.

**More beautiful beaches:** West of Jericho, **Locarno** and **Spanish Banks** offer almost a mile of continuous sandy shoreline. These two beaches are the very best in the city for swimming, ship-watching and sunsets.

Every day a cavalcade of fishing boats, oil tankers, container vessels and grain ships makes its way through English Bay to port facilities on Burrard Inlet and beyond. **Locarno** is the board-sailing capital of BC's Lower Mainland. Tides at **Spanish Banks** retreat as much as half a mile off shore.

On a good day it is possible to enjoy abundant intertidal life including purple starfish, barnacles, mussels, whelks and crabs. All are strictly off-limits to collectors, however, and it's a good idea to leave them for others to enjoy.

**Northwest Marine Drive** leads from Spanish Banks into the campus of the **University of British Columbia (UBC)**, the third largest university in Canada. UBC was incorporated in the first decade of the 20th century, but World War I and financial crises stalled construction. Disgruntled students, fed up with temporary quarters, took part in the Great Trek of 1922 to focus public attention on the delay. The buildings are a hodge-podge but glorious trees and lawns help to visually unify the campus.

**First people's culture:** On the water side of Marine Drive, between Gates 3 and 4, the acclaimed **UBC Museum of Anthropology (MOA)** draws attention to the grandeur and intricacy of local cultures that new settlers once minimalised. This outstanding building, designed by Arthur Erickson, is sited on a grassy slope near a cliff overlooking the Strait of Georgia.

The soaring glass structure houses a collection of antique totem poles and, on its grounds, the traditional **Northwest Coast Indian village** evokes ghosts of the past. The superlative setting for the huge totem poles, as well as masterworks by contemporary native carvers and artists, that intrigue visitors. The MOA, a teaching museum and an academic storage centre for university

Quarry Garden Wedding, Queen Elizabeth Park.

anthropologists, also features an innovative sliding storage tray system to allow visitors to view thousands of small artefacts, both local native items and those of other indigenous cultures around the world.

The **Nitobe Memorial Garden**, just across from MOA, is a serene example of Japanese gardening art. Designed by renowned Japanese landscape artist, Kannosuke Mori, and said to be his finest work, it takes the art of the "borrowed landscape" to new heights. At its best in spring, summer and autumn, its stark forms are also acclaimed in winter. Containing a carp-stocked lake, a tea garden and 10 bridges, this Asian art form begs to be investigated.

**Clothing optional:** From June to September, you might encounter a mini-traffic jam not far from the museum. This attraction is the city's only nudist beach, 237 steps below the cliffs. The steep descent doesn't deter either the thousands of people who gather monthly on **Wreck Beach** *(see page 70)* to soak up Vancouver's sporadic sunshine, or

the entrepreneurs who serve them. Beer, fast food, jewellery and novelties are for sale here, as well as other more exotic substances. The very idea of Wreck Beach isn't overwhelmingly popular with more sedate local residents, but their fellow Vancouverites have been coming to this 6-km (4-mile) strip of foreshore since the late 1920s, and the beach's clothing-optional status is "unofficially official".

The entrance to the **University of British Columbia Botanical Garden** is just past the storage grounds turnoff. First assembled in 1916, the show garden now encompasses several sub-gardens. **The Asian Garden** occupies a patch of virgin forest, a former Royal Navy Reserve that supplied timber for masts for British sailing ships. Some of the trees here are over 60 metres (200 ft) high, and their trunks are frequently covered with a mass of climbing vines. This garden contains one of the largest collections of Asian plants in North America, including 300 different species of rhododendron.

"Clothes-optional" Wreck Beach.

Through a circular Chinese Moon Gate, and a tunnel under the highway, lies the **Lohbrunner Alpine Garden**, a collection of plants from the mountainous regions of the world; the **B.C. Native Garden**, a series of aromatic trails through woodlands, meadows and a peat bog; and the **Physick Garden**, a 16th-century medicinal herb garden that was originally started with transported plants from the Chelsea Physick Garden located in London, England.

The Chelsea garden became an important research and resource facility for gardens around the world. Herbal favourites such as datura, comfrey, valerian and witch hazel thrive in the Canadian garden; the symptoms they purport to treat are described on accompanying signs.

**Pacific spirit:** The second growth forest of Douglas fir, cedar and hemlock, to the right of 16th Avenue, is **Pacific Spirit Regional Park**: 763 hectares (1,885 acres) of native flora and bog life criss-crossed by a 50-km (31-mile) network of riding and jogging trails. The former UBC Endowment Lands are presently dedicated as regional parkland though they are subject to ongoing land claims from BC's First Nations.

Acclaimed by *Horticulture* magazine as one of the world's top 10 botanical gardens, **VanDusen Botanical Garden** at 37th and Oak, was originally a small golf course. When it was threatened with redevelopment in the 1970s, philanthropist W.J. VanDusen helped an enthusiastic group of citizens turn it into a first-rate show garden.

Its 22 hectares (55 acres) include thousands of ornamental plants including fuchsia and rhododendron, a hedge maze and intriguing sculptures. There is a special interest garden show here almost every weekend in summer. In June, the largest **outdoor garden show** in North America attracts hundreds of thousands of visitors.

**Railway barons' mansions:** Several miles east of UBC, 16th Avenue enters the world of Vancouver's early aristocracy. The Canadian Pacific Railway (CPR) was granted extensive land holdings in Vancouver (and throughout Canada) in return for constructing the railway that crossed the breadth of the country. In 1901, it turned one piece of land into an exclusive residential area called **Shaughnessy Heights**, named after its chairman, Sir Thomas Shaughnessy.

Within two decades, many influential families had a Shaughnessy address. Their vast mansions reflected a wide variety of architectural styles, from Georgian to American Gothic, with a slight preference for half-timbered Tudor Revival.

In the 1920s, the area was at the centre of a vibrant social scene revolving around costumed balls, croquet and tennis matches. In the 1930s, the Depression hit hard and by the end of the 1940s many of the largest mansions had been carved up into rooming houses or pressed into service as makeshift hospitals. In the 1950s a concerted effort was made to preserve the area.

Today, many of the houses are international consulates. The streets between 16th Avenue and King Edward still curve

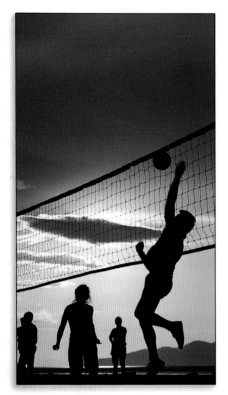

**Net gain.**

along the contours of the land in a leisurely, heavily-landscaped fashion echoing old money and Vancouver's early railway and timber prosperity.

The best examples in the district include **Villa Russe**, at 3390 The Crescent. Built by a Russian émigré in 1921, this building once hosted composer/pianist Serge Rachmaninov and the Grand-Duke Alexander. Thirty-room **Hycroft House**, at 1498 McCrae Avenue, was constructed between 1909 and 1912 and is now the University Women's Club. The beautiful pillars and porte-cochère of this Italianate mansion are visible from the gates.

Twin-domed **Glen Brae**, at 1690 Matthews Avenue, was built in 1910; the third-floor ballroom laid over a padding of seaweed to give it spring, quickly became the talk of the neighbourhood. Glen Brae's neighbours had even more to talk about in 1925, when the Kanadian Knights of the Ku Klux Klan paraded up Granville Street to take possession of their newly purchased headquarters. Their proprietorship didn't last long.

Shopping is varied and interesting on South Granville between 10th and 16th avenues. Along this corridor, there's an array of stores selling up-scale fashions, oriental rugs, antiques, art and country home-furnishings.

**The Queen Mum's park: Queen Elizabeth Park**, at 33rd Avenue and Cambie Street, built on **Little Mountain**, the highest point in the city at 150 metres (500 ft) above sea level, offers splendid panoramic views. This basalt hill was the source of crushed stone used to cover Vancouver streets until 1908. On top of the mountain are the free **Quarry Gardens**, created in the abandoned basalt quarry.

They are especially lively on Saturday afternoons in summer, when bridal parties arrive with the regularity of incoming airplanes at an airport. Nearby is the triodetic glass dome of the **Bloedel Floral Conservatory**, home to 500 varieties of tro-pical plants and noisy maccaws. The park also features **Henry Moore's** bronze sculpture *Knife-Edge Two Pieces*.

**Sunset, Kits Beach.**

# STANLEY PARK AND NORTH VANCOUVER

Both Stanley Park and North Vancouver lend a special "fresh-from-the-forest" quality to Vancouver which few other urban centres can claim. Stanley Park, a wilderness area set in the heart of a metropolis, is the image of Vancouver itself – a city set in the heart of the wilderness.

If visitors need a potent reminder of just how close to the wild Vancouver lies, North Vancouver, across Burrard Inlet, is a cogent example. City parks on the outskirts of North Vancouver, only minutes from residential neighbourhoods, have signs at the start of hiking trails explaining what to do if attacked by a bear. Bears admittedly are dangerous, but the untamed beauty of the city's wooded areas remains one of Vancouver's greatest attractions.

**Monumental Stanley Park**: A 400-hectare (1000-acre) peninsula with seascapes, a major aquarium facility, formal gardens, harbour views, thick rainforest and open picnic areas, **Stanley Park** is a fine area of sylvan calm, with enough activities and sights to fill the longest day. The park is encircled by a promenade, the low **sea wall**, which begins beside a bronze **statue of Queen Victoria** paid for by local schoolchildren on her death in 1901.

Near the main entrance, hidden in the trees at the western end of Georgia Street, is a **monument to Lord Stanley**, the former Governor General. Lord Stanley is equally remembered for this park and for donating the most coveted hockey prize in North America – the National Hockey League's Stanley Cup.

One-way traffic loops anti-clockwise on an 8-km (5-mile) road around the park. Pay parking is mandatory; save the ticket for your next park stop. There are also bicycles for rent near the park, cycle paths adjoin the promenade, and it is also possible to take a tour of the park in a **horse-drawn covered wagon**.

First stop is hidden **Malkin Bowl** and its **cafeteria**. This area is the site of an **open-air night-time theatre**, the **children's zoo**, and a **miniature railway**. The nearby **Rose Garden** contains 5,000 bushes which bloom in early June. Along the ring road is the virtually unmarked **Vancouver Aquarium** where dolphins, beluga and killer whales can be viewed through underwater windows.

The road travels first along the shore of **Coal Harbour** past the moored craft of the Vancouver Rowing Club and Royal Vancouver Yacht Club. A short causeway leads to **Deadman's Island**, a former First Nations burial place where bodies were once ceremoniously placed high in the trees.

World's most viewed totems: Most of the park's totem poles, visited by an estimated 8 million people a year, represent the Kwakiutl and Haida Nations. They are clustered around the **Brockton Oval Sports Field** where you may see white-clad sportsmen playing cricket in summer. Further east is **Hallelujah Point**.

The caged cannon fired nightly at 9pm, and sensibly called the **Nine O'Clock Gun**, was originally a re-

Preceding pages: Stanley Park's Royal Vancouver Yacht Club. Left, police park patrol. Right, the Capilano Suspension Bridge.

minder that fishing was finished for the day. **Brockton Point** and its little lighthouse take their name from the chief engineer of *HMS Plumper*, the first ship to first survey this area in 1859. Here there are views of **North Vancouver**'s busy shipping activity and its piles of non-odorifeous yellow sulphur.

Among the monuments in a hidden section of the park are a **statue of President Warren Harding** sculpted by Charles Marega, commemorating the United States' president's 1923 visit to Vancouver, and also the **Japanese War Memorial** amidst spring-blooming cherry trees.

**Roadside viewpoints:** Rejoining the circular road just beyond the *Empress of Japan* figurehead, a fibreglass replica from a CPR ship that serviced the Asia and the Pacific route from 1891 to 1922, sits the *Girl in Wetsuit* sculpture.

Often mistaken for a mermaid, she's a favourite place for high school students to lob their school hats. The next landmark is **Lumberman's Arch**, the original one built to welcome the Duke of Connaught who visited the city in 1912. Before Europeans arrived, this area was a village called Whoi-Whoi and a summer home to the seafaring Musquem people.

Just before the 2-mile mark along the circular road, **Ravine Trail** heads to hidden **Beaver Lake**; its bewhiskered inhabitants were removed because they threatened to flood the surrounding area by damming the lake's outflow. In addition to a mass of colourful water lilies, waterfowl and herons frequent the shallow lake today.

West of the road leading to the Lions Gate Bridge, the park's northernmost section, **Prospect Point**, was the site of an early semaphore station – which failed to prevent British Columbia's first fur trading steamship, the *SS Beaver*, from capsizing on rocks in 1888. A cairn commemorates this event. The Prospect Point concession is a pleasant spot to stop and contemplate traffic crossing the **Lions Gate** bridge, but in summer many people prefer to head slightly further into the park to one of many organised picnic areas.

**The Hollow Tree:** One of the park's most famous landmarks, an immense **red cedar tree**, was already hollowed out when the first Europeans arrived more than a century ago *(see page 106)*. It now stands as a symbol of the great forest that once extended through the region and still covers the park. In dusty attics all over Canada are faded photographs of people snapped by a photographer who plied his trade beside the tree in the early years of the 20th century. Trails from the tree lead to the offshore **Siwash Rock**, which native legend holds was once a young man who was turned to stone as a "reward" for his unselfishness.

**Ferguson Point** is named for an early member of the Parks Board, and the cement embankment in front of the **teahouse** is all that remains of what was once a World War II defence station. The park's only marked grave is near here: that of a local poet, Mohawk princess Pauline Johnson, who wrote lovingly about her adopted home of Vancouver for most of her life.

Cricket players in Stanley Park.

**Beaches and birds:** Next comes **Third Beach**, the precurser to Second Beach and the beach at **English Bay**. Below **Second Beach** with its saltwater **swimming pool**, is a large recreational area which adjoins Lost Lagoon. There are **playgrounds**, a **miniature golf course**, **tennis facilities** and an **outdoor dance floor** on which various ethnic groups perform folk dancing.

The lagoon once flowed into Coal Harbour. Now the tidal flow is blocked, **Lost Lagoon** is a freshwater haven for a delightful variety of birds including heron, Canada geese and black swans. Across the water, on the far side, is a choice of popular trails for rollerbladers and cyclists.

Stanley Park ends where the sea wall terminates in front of the offices of the Parks Board on Beach Avenue. Opposite is a **statue** of Vancouver's four-time mayor, **David Oppenheimer** (d. 1891). Here too is the hidden **Ted and Mary Greig Rhododendron Garden**, especially beautiful for its magnolias and rhodos in May.

**Onward to North Vancouver:** A trip acro Burrard Inlet to the North Shore offers visitors a chance to see the city to its best advantage. The two bridges across the narrows are exceptionally frustrating during rush hours.

Alternately, the **SeaBus** runs from just beside Canada Place in downtown Vancouver to its landing point, **Lonsdale Quay Market**. Seabus is probably the most economical as well as pleasurable way to get yourself onto the water, offering stunning views of Vancouver and its busy harbour.

North Vancouver city and district was established in 1907, extending from Horseshoe Bay eastwards to Deep Cove. The northside of Burrard Inlet was the site of the earliest saw mill, the now defunct Moodyville, and today it is mostly a dormitory suburb for Vancouver proper.

The waterfront area of North Vancouver is very much a working port with grain elevators, chemical production facilities, shipyards and the odd sawmill. First stop is the free **Capilano Salmon**

*Girl in Wetsuit.*

**ement Facility**, an architect-
... working salmon hatchery ex-
... the life cycle of the salmon and
the importance of conservation. Several
trails here lead into the West Coast
rainforest.

Next stop is **Capilano Suspension
Bridge**, 3735 Capilano Road. This most
recent version was built in 1956; the
original cedar plank bridge was built by
an early settler named George Grant
Mackay with the help of local natives,
August Jack and Willie Khahtsahlano,
back in the 1880s. A second bridge
replaced it in 1903 and a third in 1914.

The Capilano footbridge has always
been a tourist attraction, offering a mi-
nor thrill to adventurous visitors who
delight in crossing the 107-metre (350-
ft) wide canyon at a height of 70 metres
(230 ft) above the river. The bridge does
sway a bit, but the view down the gorge
of clear river amidst dense forest is
certainly well worth it. On the far side of
the bridge are short well-marked nature
trails into the forest.

The first **totem poles** adjoining the
bridge were created by two Danish immigrants, Aage Madsen and Karl
Hansen, in the 1930s; the others were
carved by local natives in honour of
Mary Capilano and Chief Mathias Joe
Capilano. More totems are added each
year (*see page 50*).

The **Cleveland Dam** here regulates
the source of much of Vancouver's fresh
water supply. It inadvertently blocked a
productive little salmon run, which is
why the enhancement facility was placed
just downstream.

A trio of Coastal mountain peaks –
Grouse, Seymour and Cypress – are all
accessible on the North Shore, and have
ski and snowboarding facilities, but only
**Grouse Mountain** offers the attraction
of an enclosed gondola ride to the top:
**Skyride**, 6400 Nancy Greene Way. The
top of the mountain is open all year
round; you can watch the hang gliders
launch, take in a periodic logger show,
or stop at the **native dinner longhouse**,
the Hiwus.

After a traditional meal, native dancers perform a West Coast button blanket
dance. Try the ascent on a crisp evening
when you may be able to catch the
twinkling lights of Victoria 80 km (50
miles) away. Be sure to wear a jacket or
a sweater as it can be chilly on top of the
mountain.

**All aboard rail and sail:** The BC Rail
station, 1311 West 1st, is the start point
for a fun adventure aboard the historic
chugging **Royal Hudson Steamtrain**,
a popular one-day ride along the edge of
the North American continent overlooking beautiful Howe Sound, an ocean
fjord. After a stopover in scenic
**Squamish**, it's back to the city again as
the sun sets in the west. Alternatively,
you may choose to return home aboard
the *MV Britannia*, enjoying a fine sunset dinner cruise.

**Lynn Headwaters Park** has the du-
bious honour of being the city's most
lethal park. Perfectly safe with normal
precautions, young people seem to delight in standing too close to the edge of
the precipices. The best trail for a short
jaunt into the rainforest is over the
**Lynn Canyon suspension bridge** and
then make a left turn.

**Modern
native.**

# TOTEM POLE REVIVAL

Complicated and mysterious, bold and forceful, totem poles have become a powerful symbol for one of the world's great aboriginal arts. For centuries these massive columns, carved from western red cedar by skilled Pacific Northwest Coast native carvers, have been raised in tribute and as part of the potlatch ceremony in coastal villages.

A totem pole tells a story of a family's history and lineage, or recounts an historical event. Raven, Thunderbird, Bear, Whale or Frog are powerful beings often depicted on the poles. This custom can be traced to a time when it was thought that humans could transform into animals and vice versa. The right to use an animal's likeness was earned from an encounter, friendly or unfriendly, with the creature. The privilege was passed on to descendants.

From about 1910 to 1950, many totem poles fell down or rotted in abandoned native villages. Traditions and carving techniques were dying until their revival, largely due to the dedication of Kwakiutls Ellen Neel and master carver Mungo Martin. Martin selected a limited number of apprentices, the most famous being carver, jeweler and artist Bill Reid. "Bill found the dry bones of a great art and, shamanlike, shook off the layers of museum dust and brought it back to life," wrote art historian Bill Holm for a retrospective exhibit of Reid's work at the Vancouver Art Gallery in 1974.

Reid was born in Victoria in 1920, his mother a Haida from Skidegate in the Queen Charlotte Islands; his father a Scottish-German American. He began his career as a broadcaster, but while living in Toronto became inspired by a Haida pole at the Royal Ontario Museum. It originated in his grandmother's village of Tanu.

He enrolled in a jewellery-making course, and began incorporating Haida designs into his argillite, silver and gold jewellery. The big break came when he accepted an invitation from the University of British Columbia to recreate a traditional Haida village for the Museum of Anthropology, a project that lasted from 1958 to 1962.

His short experience in carving totem poles alongside master carver Mungo Martin earned Reed the right to call himself a carver. The pole on which they worked can be seen at the Peace Arch border crossing at Blaine, Washington. Martin, who died in 1962, was the last of the master carvers; he had worked on an early Museum of Anthropology restoration programme and also Thunderbird Park at the Royal British Columbia Museum in Victoria.

Reid was able to "indulge in a lifelong dream" when a totem pole he carved and donated was raised in 1978 in Skidegate. It was the first pole to be raised in his mother's village in more than a century, and it was Reid's way of offering thanks to the great Haida artists of the past.

He told author Edith Iglauer: "I've never felt I was doing something for my people, except what I could to bring the accomplishments of the old ones to the attention of the world. I think the Northwest Coast style of art is an absolutely unique product, one of the crowning achievements of the whole human experience. I just don't want the whole thing swept under the carpet without someone paying attention."

Extensive ceremonies were held when Reid passed away in 1998. ∎

**Carving out the past.**

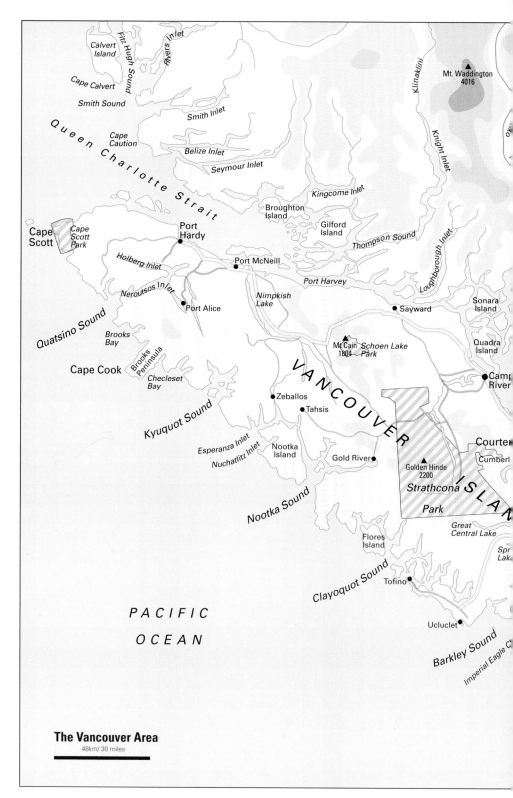

**The Vancouver Area**

48km/ 30 miles

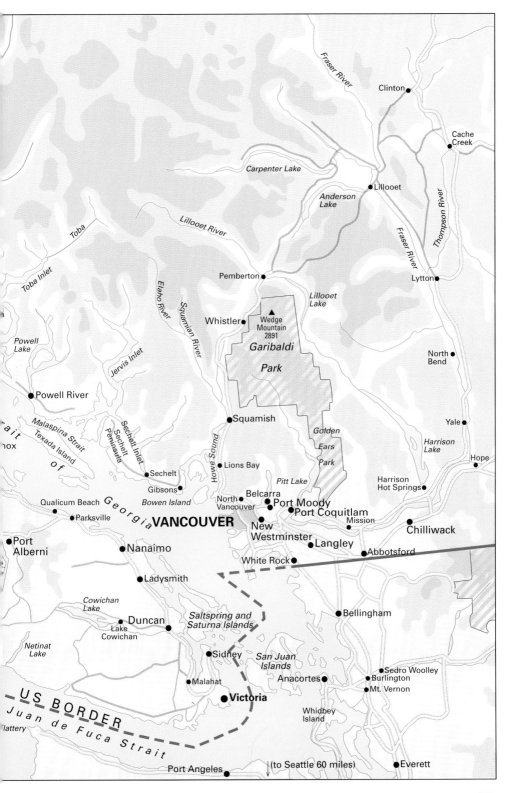

# VICTORIA

"To realise Victoria you must take all that the eye admires in Bournemouth, Torquay, the Isle of Wight, the Happy Valley at Hong Kong, the Doon, Sorrento and Camp's Bay – add reminiscences of the Thousand Islands and arrange the whole around the Bay of Naples with some Himalayas for background." – British author Rudyard Kipling recalling his visit to Victoria.

The largest island on the West Coast of North America, Vancouver Island lies to the west of its namesake city, with good ferry links between the two. Commonly called "the island," its principal city is Victoria, located so far to the south as to be nudged into a geographical corner with the United States mainland surrounding it on two sides. It is equidistant between Vancouver and the US city of Seattle, 183 km (114 miles) by ferry to either. Despite its proximity to its southern neighbour, Victoria is not only thoroughly Canadian, but more "British" in character than Vancouver. It's tea here, not coffee.

Known as the City of Gardens, Victoria is popular with visitors for its dazzling gardens, museums and castles; leisure time is also spent shopping on Government Street, and of course, taking afternoon tea.

Visitors can take the ferry, fly or take the bus from Vancouver; the return journey, plus sightseeing, can be accomplished in a long, action-packed day. But more pleasant is to emulate the leisurely pace of Vancouver Island and spend several days touring around.

**Capital city:** British Columbia's capital city, Victoria, like many other towns in Canada, began as a Hudson's Bay Company (HBC) fort. HBC's James Douglas chose the site as "a perfect Eden". By the turn of the 20th century it was clear to the city's boosters that, although the cash-strapped Canadian Pacific Railway (CPR) was not about to

connect Victoria to the mainland by bridge, regular ferry services would be a major enticement to visitors. "Built on gently undulating ground – such as is characteristic of old England – the very location of Victoria differs from that of American cities on the Sound," wrote Henry T. Finck in 1907. "Nor are the streets laid out with the geometrical regularity so universal in the United States. The ladies on horseback, the numerous churches, the animated streets on Saturday evening, the abundant beef markets, the pirated American novels in the bookstalls, the substantial appearance of the houses and many other things remind one of the fact that here we are in America indeed, but not in the United States."

Many of the earliest visitors were California prospectors who first touched down in Fort Victoria in 1858 on their way to search for gold along the Fraser River and later in the Cariboo mountains. The trip inland became slightly easier with the establishment of Francis Barnard's Express Company, the BX, a

Preceding pages: BC Ferry from Vancouver to Victoria; crossing Georgia Strait. Left, Provincial Parliament Buildings. Right, a touch of Britain in British Columbia.

The Elephant and Castle..

stagecoach line. Barnard's son George teamed up with riverboat captain J. W. Troup 30 years later to promote Victoria as a tourist destination. Barnard became a city councillor, then mayor, and along with his partner persuaded the CPR to build a fast ferry to link up with the mainland. In partnership with the city they constructed a luxury hotel, hiring as their architect the talented Francis Mawson Rattenbury, the man also responsible for the province's stunning **Parliament Buildings.**

Even after plans were finalised in 1904, it took years of work: dredging the harbour, filling in the mudflats, driving piles, before the 116-room **Empress Hotel** – costing $1.3 million – was ready. "Beautiful in its magnificent stateliness," one observer described it on opening day, 20 January 1908. It has dominated the city's harbour ever since. Resting on what its official biographer, Godfrey Holloway, describes as "a massive yellow crumpet" of clay, planking timber and concrete, the hotel was "not

so much a commercial enterprise as a civic development". Today, with 480 rooms and an international reputation (*see page 181*), it is probably Victoria's best-known local landmark.

The grand hotel lies at the centre of a tourist mecca. Tours to various parts of the city and Vancouver Island leave from outside the Empress. First, pick up a map or visit the helpful **Victoria InfoCentre** in the 1931 Art Deco building across from the hotel. Half a dozen principal tourist sites are located in or around the inner harbour area, the city's compact size lending itself well to do-it-yourself sightseeing.

**Acclaimed museum:** Organise your time to visit the **Royal British Columbia Museum**, 675 Belleville Street. There is usually a queue for the simulated **Under the Ocean trip**. In addition to periodic visiting exhibitions from around the world, the permanent collection includes floor-to-ceiling photographs, ancient and valuable totem poles, artefacts and old photographs of native

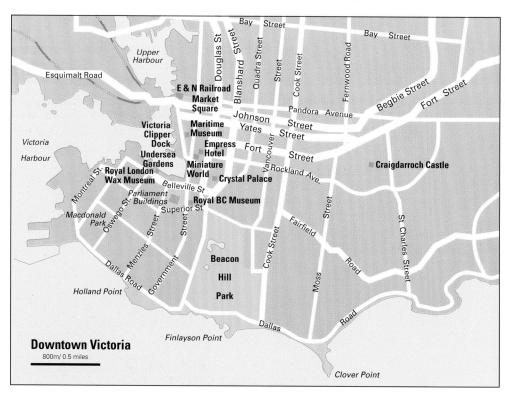

**Downtown Victoria**
800m/ 0.5 miles

tribes. There are lifesized dioramas of tidelands with ducks, wild fowl and stuffed seals basking on rocks, and it is possible to explore the cramped 18th-century charthouse of *HMS Discovery* to see how the captain lived. Outside, on the grounds are a totem pole park, **Thunderbird Park**, native plant gardens, and **Helmcken House**, the first Victoria doctor's residence and healing garden next to an original schoolhouse.

Proof of Victoria's love of gardens is within easy walking distance of the museum. The 74-hectare (184-acre) **Beacon Hill Park**, set aside as a reserve by James Douglas in 1852, is sprawling and green with duck ponds, colourful flower gardens, stone bridges, elegant trees, mini-lakes, a children's garden and benches overlooking the sea. The world's second tallest totem pole rises 39 metres (127 ft) above the grassy field, incorporating the 16 ancestral figures of the Kwakiutl Gee-Eskem clan. The broccoli-shaped tree, the **Garry Oak** (Oregon White Oak) is Victoria's

signature tree. Within the park, at the corner of Douglas Street and Dallas Road, is **Mile Zero** of the Trans-Canada highway, marking the beginning of the highway that links the country to St John's, Newfoundland, 7,820 km (4,860 miles) away.

Back on the waterfront, the **Provincial Parliament buildings** dominate the scene. In addition to showing the hidden outdoor spot where all 10 seals of Canada's provinces are displayed, free guided tours of the building's marble lined interior are ongoing. You can also catch a **horse-drawn carriage** here.

Also on the waterfront, at **Pacific Undersea Gardens**, window-lined corridors reveal rocky pools with shells and starfish, long, slender dogfish sharks and silvery salmon. In the theatre, a glassy wall separates you from scores of different species, including an elusive octopus named Armstrong.

**Wax works:** Occasionally in Victoria, you may find yourself confronted by a London bobby wheeling Queen Victo-

**Many of Victoria's sights are compactly arranged around its Inner Harbour.**

ria along the sidewalk. These recreated figures are a walking advertisement for the **Royal London Wax Museum**, another Rattenbury-designed building. The immobile characters inside include an array of figures from literature; Britain's royal family; sports legends like hockey player Gordie Howe; a group of inventors including Canada's Sir Frederick Banting, the discoverer of insulin; plus popular movie stars ranging from Ottawa-born Lorne Greene of *Bonanza* fame to America's Elvis Presley and Marilyn Monroe.

Behind the Empress, the **Crystal Garden** is yet another Rattenbury structure, a glass-roofed "tropical paradise", with an adjoining shopping mall. The building, which once boasted the largest salt water pool in the British Empire, today houses brightly-coloured birds, flamboyant flamingoes, timid turtles and miniature monkeys among plants and flowers, pools and a cascading waterfall. The popularity of afternoon tea at the Empress has been copied at many places around town, and this is one of them. Taking tea is a must while you are in Victoria.

Opposite the Crystal Palace, the **Collector Car Museum**, 813 Douglas Street, features a series of pseudo-workshops and gas stations, used as settings for obsolete Packards (last one manufactured in 1950), model-T Fords, DeLoreans, wood-paneled station wagons and a curious 1964 Amphicar which used 5 gallons of petrol an hour when travelling across water (never mass-produced).

**Teeny, weeny railway:** At the north side of the Empress Hotel is **Miniature World**, a collection of tiny tableaux including scenes from Dickens' novels, medieval England and the Old West, and a three-ring circus with animated acts. The highlight is the world's longest miniature railway, depicting the story of Canada's great railway building epoch. Squeezing 8,000 km (5,000 miles) of trans-continental track into a model only 34 metres (110 ft) long, with wooden figures and 10,000 trees pa-

**Reminders o a genteel age.**

178

tiently assembled branch by branch, took 12,000 man-hours and cost $100,000.

A stroll around the harbour's edge along Wharf Street to Fort Street leads to **Emily Carr Gallery**, 1107 Wharf Street, and its permanent exhibits. This Victoria-born artist who died in 1945 contributed greatly to the painting world of her day (*see page 147*). **Carr House**, Emily's childhood home at 207 Government Street, is also open to the public.

**Of architectural interest:** The **Maritime Museum of British Columbia** is located in Bastion Square, in a building that was once the Provincial Courthouse. Around **Bastion Square**, the site of Fort Victoria, are some of the city's most interesting architectural styles. In the square itself the 1887 **Burnes House** was once a luxury hotel. Samuel Maclure's **Temple Building** is now a bookstore and the **Bank of British Columbia** building, designed in 1883 by W. H. Williams, who was also responsible for the amazing Craigdarroch Castle, is now a year-round Christmas store.

On Johnson Street, between Store and Government, the old Milne Building (1891) and Strand Hotel (1892) form part of **Market Square**, today a busy shopping and leisure complex. Hardly mentioned is its unsavory past as the red light district. Be sure to catch the adjoining **Centennial Fountain** and its Elizabethan **Knott Garden**.

One block north, Fisgard at Government Street, **Fan Tan Alley**, a narrow street of artists' studios, anchors what was once a large **Chinatown**. Still rich in architectural treasures, the district's two stone chimeras, positioned at the **Gate of Harmonious Interest** at Fisgard and Government, are a gift from Suzhou, China. It is claimed they will come alive the day an honest politician walks between them. So far, no problem.

**Two great castle visits:** A little farther afield is **Craigdarroch Castle**, 1050 Joan Crescent, built by Scots-born Robert Dunsmuir to fulfil a promise made to his wife who expressed a dislike of her new country. Dunsmuir,

**The Empress Hotel, waterfront civility.**

sometimes seen as a classic robber baron, became rich from his Vancouver Coal Company. He died in 1889 before the castle was completed. It's a lengthy walk from the inner harbour but buses run along Fort Street.

On the way to this historic property, stop at the **Art Gallery of Greater Victoria**, 1040 Moss Street. In the vicinity too is **Government House**, 1401 Rockland Avenue, residence of the Lieutenant-Governor, provincial representative of the Crown. The well-groomed gardens behind include two rose gardens. Though the house is off-limits, the garden is open to the public.

A second castle, super-rich brother James Dunsmuir's creation, cost $11 milion in 1910. Its elaborate and extensive gardens remain intact and are free to the public. Well worth the effort to get there, **Hatley Castle a.k.a. Royal Roads University** is located at 2005 Sooke Road, west of Victoria.

West of town on Lampson street (take bus 24) is (spelled Ann here) **Ann**

**Hathaway's Cottage**, an authentic reproduction of her father's house in Shottery, England. It's part of a complex of Tudor-style buildings which includes an inn serving typically English fare and of course, afternoon tea. Another excellent adventure in tea taking, this time in the garden, is at **Point Ellice House**, 2616 Pleasant Street. An excellent way to arrive at this heritage property is via the tiny **Harbour Ferry** departing in front and below the Empress.

**World famous attraction:** A bit of a jaunt away, but a must-see, **The Butchart Gardens**, 21 km (13 miles) north of the city in Brentwood Bay, were transformed to their current splendour from an abandoned quarry. No sooner had Robert Pim Butchart established BC's first Portland Cement plant in 1904, than his ambitious wife Jenny began creating gardens within the limestone excavations. Winding paths lead past clumps of glorious colour, endless fragrant blossoms of honeysuckle and roses, green lawns, ponds and fountains. After sunset, night illuminations show off the plants and pathways.

Close to The Butchart at Keating crossroad is nature's own magic show, **Victoria Butterfly Gardens**. Thousands of butterflies, from showy orange to bright electric blue, flutter around in a brightly lit conservatory.

**Finest food:** If you have access to a vehicle, gourmet diners should not miss a chance to visit **Sooke Harbour House**, one of the best restaurants in the Pacific Northwest. The innovative chefs use fresh, local food to create exquisite dishes, specialising in local seafood with exotic flair. Try geoduck, scallops, periwinkles, or meat from the nearby farms. There is an inn attached to the restaurant so if you are an incurable romantic, or just too stuffed to move, you may want to stay overnight. To get there, follow Highway 1 north of Victoria to the Highway 1A underpass, which becomes Highway 14 leading west of Victoria. It's then 45 km (28 miles) to Sooke.

**The Butchart Gardens, sunken garden.**

# THE EMPRESS HOTEL

A misguided robber, it's said, once attempted to hold up the Empress Hotel only to be confronted by a defiant receptionist. "This sort of behavior is unacceptable here," spluttered the indignant employee. The baffled robber fled.

Apocryphal or not, the story would sound perfectly credible to anybody familiar with Victoria's best-known landmark which has been rated among the world's top hotels since it opened in 1908. With its elegant airs and strictly enforced dress codes ("no jeans, ever, ever, ever," the Bengal Room's hostess has told rejectees) the hotel can seem somewhat intimidating. Nevertheless, it is this formality that lies at the heart of the Empress's fame.

Named after Queen Victoria, Empress of India, the hotel was designed by English-born Francis Mawson Rattenbury. It was renovated in 1987 at a cost of $45 million.

Two decades earlier a similar overhaul had replaced heating and electrical systems, laid 6 km (4 miles) of new carpeting, booked special looms for the creation of hundreds of new bedspreads and checked for period authenticity the thousands of new (i.e. old) pieces of furniture for the additional rooms, which now total 480. The new pastry chef arrived with references from Buckingham Palace. The entire operation took place under the demure name of "Operation Teacup".

Antique oak furniture and teacups, of course, are major motifs of this harbourside hostelry, whose architectural style has been described as a cross between French chateau and Scottish baronial. Architect Rattenbury, already rich from successful gold prospecting in the north when he arrived in Victoria in 1892, promptly won a contest to design the city's Parliament Buildings, so his design for the Empress would not have come as a surprise.

Afternoon tea at the Empress has achieved "mythic proportions," according to one writer who reports that the hotel constantly receives enquiries from around the world about how to brew and serve tea correctly. Should the milk be poured into the cup before the tea, or only added afterwards? Guests reserve a table ahead in order to find out. Each person is served dainty, crustless sandwiches, honey-buttered crumpets, scones with clotted cream and jam, French pastries and, of course, tea — a blend of Darjeeling, China black and orange pekoe.

The visitors who come for tea, as well as the hotel's overnight guests, seem a conventionally decorous bunch these days, but in his official "biography" of the hotel Godfrey Holloway recalls wonderfully eccentric former guests, usually elderly ladies, who cooked aromatic liver and onions or made strawberry jam on hotplates in their rooms, wore threadbare tennis shoes with elegant gowns, and asked for pots of hot water in which to steep their own teabags, or came for a weekend and stayed 20 years.

In 1974 a dozen streakers tore through the elegant lobby past astonished tea-drinkers. "They went so fast and were shouting at the top of their lungs," gasped Dorothy Hart, operator of the lobby newsstand. "They must have had a car waiting; they made a quick getaway."

In deference to Empress traditions, the otherwise-naked streakers were reported to be wearing ties. ■

**Tea for two.**

# VANCOUVER ISLAND

Vancouver Island's climate is benign, the lifestyle slow-paced and friendly, and the scenery varied: it ranges from rugged snow-capped mountains and verdant forests to gentle farming areas and sun-drenched ocean beaches. To the west are craggy storm-battered coastlines with deep fjords and beaches, and on the east coast, peaceful country inns in sheltered bays. Stretching 453 km (282 miles) in length and spanning from 48 to 80 km (30 to 50 miles) across, the island is substantial and is best tackled by train, bus or car. The train passes mostly through forested areas, while hiring a car in Victoria gives access to the entire island including isolated western and northern coasts.

**North by train:** The **Esquimalt and Nanaimo Railroad**, known locally as the **E & N**, came into being through the efforts of industrialist Robert Dunsmuir. He needed an efficient transport system to move coal from his mines. In 1905 the Canadian Pacific Railway (CPR), later Viarail, paid $2.3 million for the line when it proved to be profitable. The deal included 600,000 hectares (1.5 million acres) of land, extending the E & N as far north as Courtenay where it ends today.

Although it has been many years since it carried coal or lumber, the 224-km (139-mile) single track from Victoria sees a solitary train traverse its route every day of the year. The **E&N Malahat Dayliner** leaves Victoria at 8.15 each morning, making 20-minute stops at Nanaimo and Courtenay before arriving back in Victoria at 5.45pm. Though the printed schedule draws attention to the sights en route, including a bridge over **Niagara Canyon** and the former mining town of **Cassidy**, unless you have sharp eyes you'll see very little of anything except endless forests. The pleasant rail excursion does offer the chance to study BC's major product

in its natural, living state. You will see sea-side arbutus trees, which shed their red bark every year and, perhaps, the twice-blooming dogwood, whose white flowers are BC's floral emblem. Those wanting to explore the island in depth should rent a vehicle.

Just north of Victoria is pastoral **Shawnigan Lake** with a busy schedule of summer festivities, lakeside resorts and plenty of campgrounds. **Cowichan Bay**, a busy harbour further north, is not on the railroad line but offers seafood restaurants, the **Glass Castle** and up island the whimsically named **Whippletree Junction**, a fun shopping area composed of reconstructed old buildings. This valley is world famous for its native-knitters and outdoor-lovers' favourite clothing – Cowichan sweaters.

**Malahat**, an Indian word meaning "plenty of bait," a reference to the fish-filled waters of the Saanich Inlet, is at the highest point of a 180-metre (600-ft) climb over a pass. Between here and

**Preceding pages:** powerboats make up at least half of BC's 35,000 vessels. **Left**, logging up time. **Right**, convoy of one.

Duncan, dairy farms line both sides of the track and skittish deer dart among the trees. Just before Duncan, the Cowichan River once flooded, necessitating the dramatic rescue of stranded train passengers by local natives in dugout canoes.

**City of totems:** At **Duncan**, an ambitious civic project has provided work for local and international aboriginal carvers from as far away as New Zealand. Over the past two decades they have produced more than 40 totem poles, half of which line the highway, with the remainder placed beside City Hall and the railroad station. Self-guided walking-tour maps are available. Visitors can pay a small fee to tour the riverside **Cowichan Native Centre** to watch totems being carved, hear stories, visit several big houses or attend a feast. According to legend, ocean-dwelling killer whale pods come to a special rock here to rub themselves and be transformed into wolves. Thus the packs continue to hunt on this land.

Just north of town on Highway 1 is the **British Columbia Forest Museum**. A little steam train chugs through the 40-hectare (100-acre) site viewing a turn-of-the-20th-century working sawmill, logging camp and blacksmith shop. There are films and demonstrations about forests and conservation. Beside the main building are a dozen fir trees, seeded from a mother tree 1,000 years old, and planted to celebrate Canada's 1967 centennial as a nation.

**The Little Town That Did:** Further north, the little town of **Chemainus**, reveling in its role as Canada's mural capital, proudly displays 30 enormous murals. The programme, begun in 1982 to revitalise a town whose sawmill had closed down, has brought it attention from all over the world. Each year hundreds of thousands of visitors stroll through **Waterwheel Park** and the downtown area, patronising gift galleries, restaurants and antique shops while admiring walls depicting local history, painted with ships, steam engines and ethnic

themes. One batch of murals can be spotted from the train as it stops briefly at Chemainus station, but for those seeking a closer look, a tourist trolley passes all of them. A special fund pays the original artists to return whenever the murals need touching up.

**Ladysmith,** named by its founder James Dunsmuir after a South African community that survived a siege in the Boer War, was one of BC's earliest boom towns. Dunsmuir, son of Scottish coal mine founder Robert Dunsmuir, created an instant town to house his miners here at the natural harbour, rather than at the site of his coal seams a few miles to the north (now a ghost town). He bought intact houses in Wellington, chopped them in half and shipped them on railway wagons. Reassembled on a scenic hillside, some of them still exist today.

The mines closed 60 years ago, the lumber business followed in the 1980s and the town's major industry today is tourism. Capitalising on its San Fran-

Chemainus has more than 30 murals depicting local history.

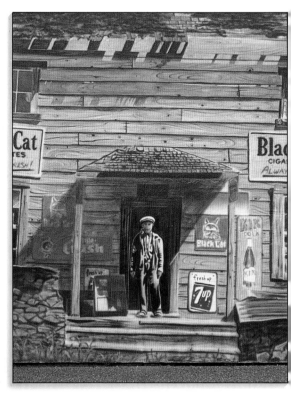

cisco style roller-coaster streets, Ladysmith has refurbished its historic heritage. The **Black Nugget Museum** houses a collection of memorabilia set around a splendidly restored western saloon-style bar dating from its 19th century days as a two-storey hotel. At the foot of Gatacre Street, George's Restaurant shares the **Comox Building** – once the headquarters of a giant logging company – with the **Ladysmith Railway Historical Society**'s exhibit of old locomotives. Nearby is a **seafaring museum** operated by the Tall Ships Society. Altogether, 17 of the town's buildings have been restored and another 27 upgraded, winning Ladysmith numerous awards and congratulations for its new-old look.

**Seaside Yellow Point:** The waterside **Inn of the Sea** on Yellow Point road north of Ladysmith is famous for its Murder Mystery Weekends. Not far away, in dense woods, is the equally attractive **Yellow Point Lodge**, an immense log cabin complete with an airy lounge and dining-room in which everybody shares the long tables.

**Tub city, hub city:** Just before Nanaimo, the train slows down and an elaborately fitted engine truck sprays high pressure steam into the foliage lining the tracks – the most efficient way, the company has discovered, to kill overgrown weeds without any polluting side-effects. **Nanaimo**, from the Indian phrase, *Sne-Ny-Mo*, meaning "where the big tribe dwells", is the largest community between Victoria and Courtenay. It was prosperous as far back as 1850 when natives digging for clams uncovered "a black rock that burned", the genesis of the coal-mining industry.

Once disembarked in Nanaimo, it's possible to walk the mile or so into town along the **Harbourside Walkway**, then the **Queen Elizabeth Promenade**, a trip that can also be made by taxi. Sometimes the not-so-sweet smell of cabbage will accompany your walk. It's the sign of a westerly wind bringing fumes from the pulp paper mill across the island.

**Swy-a-lana lagoon harbour, Nanaimo.**

The promenade winds around the edge of the **Maffeo-Sutton Park** and lagoon, ending at a hilltop. There the curiously-shaped octagonal **Bastion** features skirling bagpipes and a daily trooping of the guard. Built from squared logs fastened with wooden pegs, the canon-bearing Bastion was commissioned by the Hudson's Bay Company in 1852, and later turned into a city jail. Today it houses an **historic museum** and **tourist office**.

Adjoining the **Harbour Park Mall**, the **Nanaimo Centennial Museum** features an interesting 1900s main street and a mock-up of a coal mine, and visitors can take rubbings of **native petroglyphs**. Guided, eight-block strolls of the downtown area start from beside the museum twice each day.

It is a pleasantly unspoiled town today, apparently less dedicated than its neighbours to slicking itself up for tourists. Nanaimo makes headlines every July when it stages the hilarious and competitive Great Canadian Bathtub Race across the 58-km (36-mile) wide Georgia Strait.

Down in the harbour is the city's major attraction: 286-hectare (706-acre) **Newcastle Island**, created as a swanky resort by CPR early in the century but now a popular wilderness park with camp grounds, picnic sites, beaches, trails and bicycle paths. Wildlife abounds. On summer days, ferries run to the island every hour.

Some of the nicest places to eat are out of town, such as the lovely **Marble House Restaurant** on Cedar Road at Hemer, next door to the oldest road house bar in BC. English-style country pubs are scattered around – a particularly attractive one being the **Cow and Gate**, about 13 km (8 miles) southeast of town on Cedar Road off Island Highway. English pub grub – steak and kidney pudding, shepherd's pie – is served in a lovely bar or outdoor terrace in a village green-type setting.

**Major ferry link to mainland:** Regular BC Ferries ply from **Departure Bay** between two terminals at Nanaimo and the mainland, both to Tsawwassen, south of Vancouver near the US border, and to Horseshoe Bay on the North Shore 12 km (8 miles) from downtown Vancouver.

As the train climbs between Nanaimo and Wellington, the view eastwards is of **Long Lake**, noted for trout fishing, geese and ducks. In its heyday, **Wellington**, a busy coal shipping terminal, had a thriving vaudeville theatre and staged bicycle races. The rail track descends into **Pleasant Valley**, passing **Brannen Lake** and **Nanoose Bay** where clam diggers are often busy. A 319-metre (1,045-ft) trestle crosses **French Creek**, teeming with fish. Beside the **Big Qualicum River** is one of the hundreds of provincial salmon hatcheries. After splendid views of the Coast Mountains eastwards across **Comox Harbour** and the beautiful **Forbidden Plateau** to the west, the train arrives at **Courtenay**. The **Old House Restaurant** on Riverside Lane is a pleasant place to eat. The

Nanaimo's Great Canadian Bathtub Race.

main ski area, Forbidden Plateau in **Strathcona Provincial Park**, is about a 30-minute drive from town. Here the train turns south; anyone with a vehicle can continue up island or to Long Beach.

**Sidetrip to Long Beach:** Between Nanoose and Parksville, the junction to Highway 4 cuts west across the island to the open Pacific. Past **Englisman River Falls**, with its forested setting and deep gorge, is the old western-style town of **Coombs**, where goats graze on the roof of the local market. The **butterfly conservatory** and shops are interesting stops. **Little Qualicum River Falls** is a good place to stroll in a lush forest along a turbulent river gushing over cataracts. But the forest's giants are found in **Cathedral Grove**, a soaring old-growth forest of 800-year old Douglas firs. These are the awe-inspiring stands of trees that exhilarate humans, but are of little interest to wildlife, unmotivated by the dark forest floor devoid of food. Wildlife greatly prefers

the meadowy clearcuts found further along this highway – the very ones tourists find eyesores.

**Port Alberni** is the start point for the *MV Lady Rose,* a little working freight ship that services totally isolated villages among the Broken Islands. Visitors who book ahead are allowed the privilege of sailing with her. Continue onward around reflective **Sproat Lake**, home to a fleet of forest fire water bombers and then to **Ucluelet**, once a trading post for fur sealers. The white-capped ocean is the overriding attraction here. Storm watching takes on new meaning and in March thousands of Pacific grey whales from Baja, Mexico, migrate past this point.

Northward through **Pacific Rim National Park**'s long sandy beaches, wind-contorted trees, noisy gulls and darting shore birds accompany the sights, smells and sounds of crashing surf. The most popular stop is the **Wickaninnish Centre**, with its visitor displays and a glassed-in restaurant almost swallowed

**Dog paddling.**

up by the rolling waves. The town of **Tofino** offers the usual busy harbour and gift stores. Further explorations of forested wilderness areas originate here.

**Back on Island Highway 19: Qualicum Beach** is one of the most beautiful beachcombing spots on the island, while those with amateur spelunking ambitions can explore the accessible **Horne Lake caves**. There are numerous beaches and camping grounds between **Courtenay-Comox** and **Campbell River**, and winter brings large concentrations of shore birds including the renowned trumpeter swan.

Lovers of the wilderness delight in experiencing the sea and sunsets of the entire north island, though hikers in the **Forbidden Plateau** and **Mount Washington** area need to be extra-alert for cougars, wolves and bears.

Campbell River is famous for its tyee salmon, 30 lb giants that hide out in underwater depressions. Anyone can fish for $2 from the well-equipped public fishing pier.

The traffic thins out all the way north to **Port McNeil** and **Port Hardy**, and there are several intriguing sights. Everyone is fascinated by the quaint village-on-stilts boardwalk community of **Telegraph Cove**, part of a failed scheme to string a telegraph wire from New York to Paris via British Columbia and Russia. Think about it. After a stroll through this waterside village many take a day-long boat excursion to **Johnston Strait** to see pods of killer whales leaping and breeching in the wild.

**BC Ferries excursions:** BC Ferries operate trips to several offshore islands, the most popular being the native-inhabited **Alert Bay**, home to the tallest totem pole in the world and the Kwakiutl community's potlatch treasures. A 17-hour cruise up the **Inside Passage**, via the *Queen of the North* to Prince Rupert on the mainland, is a popular "poor man's" alternative.

<u>Right</u>, Vancouver Island's climate is both benign and beguiling.

# EAST, SOUTH, WEST AND THE GULF ISLANDS

East, south and west of Vancouver, the variety of landscape is spectacular. The fertile **Lower Fraser Valley** east of Greater Vancouver eventually gives way to grassland plateaux, basins and high alpine mountains. The level valley area is well-suited to agriculture, and, although development is continually encroaching on the lands around the city, fields of corn, berries, other fruits and vegetables, plus dairy farms offer pastoral vistas all the way to the optimistically named town of **Hope**. Fort Langley and New Westminster offer history in an accessible, cosy setting.

Southwest of Vancouver, between the mainland and Vancouver Island, the **Gulf Islands** (called the San Juan Islands south of the 49th parallel in the US) shelter marine life and provide delightful places to explore or relax as well as a tranquil lifestyle for their residents. Access is via several terminals, BC Ferries.

**East of Vancouver:** Two main highways head eastwards to the Fraser Valley and beyond: Trans-Canada Highway 1, euphemistically called "The Freeway," and the Lougheed Highway 7. The latter is a prettier route, but first we'll deal with **Highway 1**, crossing the **Fraser River** on the **Port Mann Bridge** bypassing Surrey, Cloverdale and Langley. Within the Greater Vancouver Regional District, a few attractions are worth noting. These can be explored before heading out on a longer route.

From Highway 1, take the Kensington Street exit, turn east on Canada Way and follow the signs to the **Burnaby Village Museum**, a living museum with staff in period costume (1890 through 1925), and more than 30 buildings and exhibits depicting typical village life. A blacksmith pounds out shoes for horses or oxen, a Chinese herbalist explains the traditional use for dried Canton lizard, and butter is churned. The guides are chatty and very well-informed. If it's near lunchtime, walk along Deer Lake Avenue to the Hart House Restaurant which serves country-style food emphasising fresh produce, herbs and local products. Past the Canada geese on the lawn behind the restaurant is **Deer Lake Park**, a serene and peaceful spot with a beach at one end.

Overlooking the park is the **Burnaby Art Gallery**, housed in an elegant 1909 mansion complete with fireplaces and lounges. Exhibits, changed frequently, include video and multi-media presentations. Behind the reputedly haunted gallery, the rhododendrons and Japanese maples of **Century Gardens** overlook a duck-filled lake. To get there by bus from Vancouver, catch the 120 New Westminster Station bus on Hastings Street between Burrard and Main.

**Elephants and all that:** The **Vancouver Zoological Centre** is further east, off Highway 1 on 264th Street in Aldergrove. Over 110 wildlife species (ever seen a nilgai or guanaco?) can be seen roaming in large paddocks on this 50-hectare (120-acre) farm. The flat land between the Vedder Canal and Abbotsford was reclaimed from marshland by drainage of Sumas Lake and an ingenious network of canals, dykes and dams. Completed in 1924, the project created an additional 13,000 hectares (29,000 acres) of fertile farmland.

In Abbotsford in alternate years in August see the biggest air show in North America. It's often one of the warmest weekends of the year, but that doesn't stop hundreds of thousands of spectators from joining the highway crawl to the **Abbotsford International Airshow**. There are stunts, drills, aerobatics, antique and war planes. World-class demonstrations have included the Canadian Snowbirds, USAF Thunderbirds, US Angels and the Soviet MiG-29.

**Lougheed east:** The scenery is more absorbing along Lougheed Highway 7. First stop is the **Riverview arboretum**, 405 hectares (1,000 acres) of land once set aside as a place for mental patients to regain their sanity. The Riverview sanitarium buildings are mostly empty, but the century-old trees from every corner of the globe stand in glorious fullness. A wonderfully silent experience, enter at 500 Lougheed Highway, Coquitlam, and follow the signs to the kiosk and free maps.

If one starts from **Broadway** and follows the north bank of the Fraser River through Coquitlam and Port Coquitlam, the landscape begins to open up at **Pitt Meadows** and **Maple Ridge**. Blending in with commercial and residential development are Holstein cows grazing in lush fields, horse riding stables and boarding ranches, fruit and berry farms, sloughs and creeks, dykes and farms.

**Renewing BC forests:** A rewarding place to learn about forestry practices is at the **UBC Research Forest**. Spread over a network of walking trails in varying stages of growth are demonstrations of reforestation, tree-planting, and the effects of clearcut logging. An arboretum here has 120 tree species from around the world. The easy-walking research

forest (open daily) is between **Alouette Lake** and the scenic **Pitt Lake** a.k.a. **Grant Narrows Regional Park** recreational areas, 8 km (5 miles) north of Highway 7 on 232nd Street.

A fascinating exercise is to view personally a portion of the 370 million seedlings replanted and hardened each year for BC's immense forests *(see pages 102 and 103)*. A quick phone call and the largest tree replenishment nursery in North America, **Pelton Reforestation Ltd**, 203rd Street in Maple Ridge, is open for your own private tour.

In **Golden Ears Provincial Park**, wryly named after the twin peaks that glow at dusk, there is a pleasant walk around **Mike Lake.** The **Alouette Lake** area on the park's east boundary was used by the Coast Salish and Interior Salish Indians for hunting and fishing, but in the 1920s the timber was cleared and traces of early railway logging still remain among the second-growth forest of Douglas fir, western hemlock, and western red cedar. A lucky hiker might catch glimpses of deer, beavers, mountain goats, or black bears in the park.

**HBC fur-trading post:** The **Albion Ferry** will carry you at no cost across the Fraser River from the south end of 240th Street to the historic and fun-loving town of **Fort Langley**, a Hudson's Bay Company (HBC) supply post originally built in 1827 as a fur trading-post. It was here that British Columbia was declared as a British Crown colony and where in 1828 the company's chief trader, Archibald McDonald, first began processing salmon for export. Despite the discovery that the Fraser River wasn't a navigable route to the interior, agriculture and fish-processing kept the trading-post in operation until 1866. It was restored in 1955 as a **National Historic Park**.

The only original building is the storehouse but the others are authentic representations of the 1850s. Staff in period dress, called historic animators, demonstrate such tasks as barrel-making and blacksmithing.

**An historic animator at Fort Langley brings the past to life.**

Fort Langley can also be easily reached via Highway 1 or you may view it from the deck of an 1800s paddle-wheeler boat. The **Fraser River Connection** leaves from **Westminster Quay** in New Westminster and arrives two hours later at Fort Langley. The entire cruise takes about six hours, depending on the current.

**Early capital:** The easiest way to get to the Westminster waterfront is via Sky-Train. **New Westminster** was established in 1859 by Governor James Douglas as the capital of BC and was named The Royal City by Queen Victoria. Nine years later Victoria was chosen by the Legislative Council as the province's capital. More of the area's history can be seen at the **Irving House Historic Centre** in the 14-room home built in 1865 for the riverboat king, Captain William Irving. The parlour and master bedroom contain original furniture imported from England.

Continuing east on Highway 7, on the low flood plain area of **Hatzic Lake** is the town of **Mission**, the tranquil home to Benedictine monks at **Westminster Abbey**, completed in 1982 after 28 years of construction. Its impressive bell tower rises 180 metres (600 ft) above the valley and 64 colourful stained-glass windows decorate the lower portion below the dome. Visitors are welcome most weekday afternoons; head north on Dewdney Trunk Road and you should see the abbey.

The **Kilby General Store Museum** near Harrison Mills is a two-storey general store and nine-bedroom rooming house built by Thomas Kilby in 1904. Three bedrooms, the dining-room, sitting-room, pantry, and post office look pretty much as they did when prospectors, railwaymen and loggers passed through this small community at the junction of the Harrison and Fraser rivers. The store is staffed with informative, entertaining historic animators as well as being fully stocked with goods from the 1920s and '30s – tins of coffee and tea, candy sticks in

Morning showers gather over Pitt Lake near Golden Ears and the UBC research forests.

jars, galvanised pails, hand tools, brooms, sock and glove stretchers for shrinkable woollens. On hot summer days, you might get a sample of home-made ice cream in the dairy and every day is fine for tea and home baked pies.

Nearby **Kilby Provincial Park**, with its sandy beach, picnic and camping facilities, is a good place from which to spot trumpeter swans and bald eagles (in the winter months of January and February only, alas.)

**Home of the Big Foot:** At Agassiz, Highway 9 north leads to the town of **Harrison Hot Springs**, a year-round resort spot at the southern tip of **Harrison Lake**. During the gold rush in the 1850s, the lake was awash with wild-eyed optimists en route to the gold mines of the Cariboo. The landmark Harrison Hotel has been a resort since 1926. Supplied by two sulphur-potash springs, a large pool near the grand hotel is open to all.

There have been reported sightings of the legendary Bigfoot or Sasquatch – the Salish word for "hairy men" or "wild

men". Visitors are unlikely to see this supposedly smelly creature in **Sasquatch Provincial Park**, but who knows? Keep your eye out for gigantic footprints and a loping ape-like creature about twice the size of a man.

**Sensational show garden:** Between Harrison and Highway 1, with Mount Cheam in the background, the award-winning **Minter Gardens** at Bridal Veil Falls comprise several separate gardens interspersed with jade green lawns, babbling creeks and graceful trees. Roses, ferns and rhododendrons have their own special spots and to complete the plan are meadow, formal and fragrance themes. There are also three aviaries and the largest collection of miniature **Penjing rocks** outside China. These are yin/yang arrangements of coral and unusual rocks. The gardens are open April through October, 9am until dusk. Allow three hours for a visit.

Three major mountain highways branch out from the town of Hope, gateway to BC's interior, 154 km (96 miles) from Vancouver. The Trans-Canada Highway 1 cuts through the Fraser Canyon to **Cache Creek** and then to the far away Rockies.

The newer Coquihalla Highway 5 is the fastest, four-lane toll highway to **Kamloops**. The Hope-Princeton Highway 3 passes right through **Manning Park,** and on to the **Okanagan.**

**Hope springs eternal:** Set on the east bank of the Fraser River and ringed by mountains, **Hope** is a beautiful place with many accommodation options. At the **Rainbow Junction** of Highways 1 and 3, stop for tea and homemade pie at the restored **Canadian National Railway Station**, built in 1916 by the Great Northern Railway. Moved from its original site at Hudson Bay Street and Fifth Avenue, it is now a tea house and arts centre. The **Hope Museum** next to the **Travel InfoCentre** has displays on the fur trade, mining, logging and native culture. Next to it is **Friendship Garden**, a Japanese garden dedicated by internees from World War II.

The Abbotsford International Airshow attracts performers from many nations.

A walk through the deep, dark **Othello Quintette Tunnels** is especially fascinating. The Kettle Valley Railway blasted five tunnels through the solid granite walls of the **Coquihalla Canyon**, linking the Kootenays with the coast. It was an extraordinary and costly effort – one particular mile cost $300,000 back in 1914. The line operated until 1959. To reach the dramatic walk-through tunnels, take the Kawkawa Lake Road off Highway 5 or off 6th Avenue in Hope to Othello Road. The tunnels are open in the summer only.

**Day-trip circle tour:** The Coquihalla Highway makes a long, steady ascent to **Coquihalla Summit,** which slopes up to 1,247 metres (4,092 ft). The landscape is gentler, with a more subtle beauty than the awesome **Fraser Canyon**. Notice, however, the avalanche paths where rubble collects and trees remain bent and crippled. In winter, be prepared to get caught crawling along behind a snowplough in a blinding snowstorm; in summer it's usual to see cars

**A sign to heed.**

stopped on the shoulder with overheated radiators. Stop at **Coldwater River Provincial Park** for a cooling stroll along the river. Trees become sparser, mountains smooth out and around Merritt it's dry, hilly, ranching country. To return via the Fraser Canyon, Highway 8 through the Nicola Valley to Spences Bridge and Lytton leads to the junction. The circular tour, starting and returning at Hope, is 150 km (93 miles) – 320 km (199 miles) from Vancouver.

**River-rafting:** There are two small provincial parks in the area, Goldpan, just south of Spences Bridge, and Skihist, just east of Lytton. Open May through October, both offer overnight camping. River-rafting is a favourite activity near **Lytton** where the Fraser and Thompson rivers meet. Lytton was once an interior Salish town called Camchin, meaning "great forks".

The **Stein River Valley**, between the Lillooet River Valley on the west and the Fraser River Valley on the east, can be reached from Lytton. The valley is

sacred to the Lillooet people and the Nlaka'pamux people who have hunted, fished, gathered plants and held spiritual ceremonies here for centuries. From the headwaters at 2,900 metres (9,700 ft), to the valley at 130 metres (430 ft), the geography, climate and vegetation are more diverse than in any park in BC. It encompasses two climatic zones, three small glacier systems, and four major lakes. Within its confines are arid plains, cedar glades and pine forests, nearly motionless swamps and rushing rapids. Wildlife includes grizzly and black bears, mountain goats, wolves, cougar, deer and marmots.

**Yale**, 63 km (39 miles) north of Hope, began as a Hudson's Bay Company fur post in 1848 and boomed with the gold rush, becoming a terminus of one of the largest sternwheeler operations on the West Coast. By 1868 the feverish days when a saloon might take in $10,000 in a day were over. The CPR construction activity that followed was short-lived; Yale, with a population of only 500) is now a small forestry and service town.

The **Historic Yale Museum** colourfully depicts the 1858 gold rush as well as the building of the CPR; other exhibits include Indian artefacts and baskets and a national monument which commemorates the work of the Chinese construction workers on the railway. Their daily pay of 50¢ was half that of a white worker, and poor living conditions caused the death of hundreds from illness or accidents.

**Deep narrow gorge:** The **Hell's Gate Airtram** that zips 153 metres (502 ft) across the river offers spectacular views of the rapids and narrow gorge below, as well as both the CN and CP railway tracks. The fish-ladders, built as a cooperative effort between the US and Canadian governments, were designed to help salmon over debris from a 1913 rock slide that obstructed the channel. This disaster caused huge losses to the salmon trade. Tasty salmon dishes can be sampled at the Salmon House Res-

**Mountain-climbing.**

taurant, which serves a delicious, hearty salmon chowder.

Most of the mountain highway routes in BC are subject to landslides, avalanches and flooding and the Hope-Princeton Highway 3 is no exception. In 1965, a small tremor triggered the release of 46 million cubic metres (60 million cubic yds) of rock, snow and debris from Johnson's Peak. It swept three vehicles and four passengers off the highway, dumping 60 metres (200 ft) of fill in the Nicolum Creek valley. The **Hope Slide** viewpoint plaque just east of Hope gives all the details.

**Wildflower heaven:** A sprawling and diverse region in the North Cascades, **Manning Park**, 225 km (140 miles) east of Vancouver, offers some of the most accessible alpine splendour to be found. **Rhododendron Flats** is best in June when this indigenous evergreen shrub is covered with deep pink flowers. It's possible to drive as high as the **sub-alpine meadows** along Blackwall Road; in July and August the area is profuse with towhead babies and flowers like lupins and yellow snow lilies. There is an extensive trail system and skiing in winter. Information, maps and brochures are available at the Park Headquarters and **Visitor Centre**, half a mile east of the **Manning Park Lodge**. The trailhead to the 3,780-km (2,350-mile) **Pacific Crest Trail** is east of the park headquarters. Six months put aside is recommended for this awesome trek through the wilderness, which leads right to the Mexican border.

The **Skagit Valley Provincial Recreation Area** can be reached from trails within Manning Park or by following the Silver Skagit Road, 32 km (20 miles) southeast of Hope. The area is noted for its wide range of mammals such as deer, black bear, cougar, bobcat, beaver, coyote, mink, squirrels, hares and chipmunks. Over 200 species of birds have been recorded and more than 50 species of waterfowl. The **Skagit River** is famous for fly fishing. As with any other area in BC, get a licence and check the

**Fraser Canyon.**

local regulations – it's catch and release fishing here.

**Back south of Vancouver:** Between Vancouver and the United States border, there are a number of attractions off the main artery, Highway 99. After the George Massey Tunnel, exit right (west) on to the Steveston Highway, turn left on No. 2 Road, then south to Moncton Street. First stop will be the historic **fishing village of Steveston**, a great place to browse through shops, sample the fish and chips, then wander down to the wharves where the day's catch of salmon, rock cod, snapper, prawns, crab, shrimp, sole, and herring is sold right off the boat.

Japanese fishermen were attracted to the area in the past by the huge catches of salmon. They were evacuated by the federal government during World War II, but eventually returned and their influence is evident today. One of the largest canneries on the lower Fraser, the **Gulf of Georgia Cannery**, was built here in 1894.

**Major migration route:** The **George C. Reifel Waterfowl Refuge** on **Westham Island** at the mouth of the Fraser River supports the largest wintering population of waterfowl in Canada. The 340-hectare (850-acre) habitat and estuarine marsh serves as a sanctuary to more than 240 species of birds. In November, vast flocks of migrating snow geese stop here on their flight from their breeding grounds in the Arctic to the Sacramento River Valley in California.

Pathways and covered shelters with peeking windows allow visitors to observe without disturbing the birds, which include barn swallows, song sparrows, mallard ducks, Canada geese and the less common black-crowned night heron, spotted redshank and gyrfalcon. The refuge can be tricky to find: follow River Road for 3 km (2 miles) south of **Ladner**. Turn right on to Westham Island Road, then cross a one-lane bridge and continue, following the signs.

Another good place to go birdwatching is at **Boundary Bay**, where you'll find salt marshes, mud flats, dykes and dunes. Look for eagles, gulls, herons, terns and ducks along the sandy tidal beaches. Go south on Highway 17, left (east) at 56th Street and left (east) again at 12th Avenue to Boundary Bay Road.

**Beaches and benches:** On the eastern side of Boundary Bay are some of the lower mainland's best beaches. Follow Highway 99 south to Canada's southernmost mainland community, **White Rock**, on Semiahmoo Bay.

**Crescent Beach** and **Blackie's Spit** are the most popular beaches in the area, where strong-armed bathers can fantasise about swimming to another country. **White Rock** is an artistic seaside community where the work of local artists can be seen at the **Station Art Centre** in a restored Great Northern Railway Station, built in 1913. **White Rock Pier** extends 469 metres (1,538 ft) out into Semiahmoo Bay.

**The Gulf Islands:** Southwest of Vancouver and sheltered from Pacific Ocean storms by Vancouver Island, are about

Noisy Canada geese.

200 enticing islands and islets in the Strait of Georgia. Most have dry woodlands, abundant marine life, sandy beaches and rocky outcrops. The beautiful scenery is complemented by the drier, mild climate. Residents on the few inhabited islands lead a simpler, more natural life (made easier by the electronic cottage) and, except for the developers, most wish the gates could be closed after they arrive.

A visit to any one of the islands is a refreshing respite from the Lower Mainland's gnarly traffic and relentless city strain. For those who can spare more than a day, the islands not only have a multitude of cosy bed and breakfast places, but most also offer camping facilities. Many of the larger islands can be reached easily by ferry from both **Tsawwassen ferry terminal**, 30 km (20 miles) south of Vancouver, and **Swartz Bay ferry terminal**, 32 km north of Victoria on Vancouver Island.

**Artists' paradise: Saltspring Island** is the most populated, developed and largest of the five major Gulf Islands. The first permanent settlers were black immigrants, arriving from the US almost half a century ago. They began one of the earliest agricultural communities in the region and the island is still known for its sheep, fruit and dairy products.

The modern seaside town of **Ganges** is the largest community in the Gulf Islands and here you'll find all the usual shops and services. There's a pricey hotel, Hastings House, whose meals, theme rooms (the sealoft overlooks the ocean) and perfect setting once earned it the title of Canadian country house of the year by a widely-circulated travel newsletter.

At the other end of the accommodation scale, there is camping at **Ruckle Provincial Park**, where rocky headlands and coves along the shore can be explored. Also part of the local landscape is the sheep farm, and its original buildings, that has been run by the Ruckle family since 1872. The best view of Fulford Harbour, Vancouver Island and

**Retreat Cove, Galiano Island.**

the other Gulf Islands is from Baynes Peak on **Mount Maxwell**.

**Outdoor recreation island: Galiano Island**, long and narrow, was named for Dionisio Galiano, a Spanish navy commander who explored the area in 1792, although it was undoubtedly inhabited by the Salish Indians for thousands of years before he arrived. Archaeological surveys have found ancient Coast Salish sites and huge *midden* deposits in the area.

It is the driest island of the group, receiving only 46 cm (18 inches) of annual rainfall. BC's oldest marine park is on this island; **Montague Harbour Provincial Marine Park** offers well-protected anchorage for boaters, sandy beaches and the opportunity to do some clam digging or fishing. A tidal lagoon is the most likely place to see great blue herons. Birders can also watch for oystercatchers, pelagic cormorants and bald eagles. There are 40 campsites in this very popular park and some excellent restaurants on the island itself including

a local favourite, the Pink Geranium, plus another called La Berengerie; and one pub, the Hummingbird Inn.

**Miner's Bay** on **Mayne Island** became a major stopping point between Vancouver Island and the mainland during the 1858 gold rush. Its central location and the development of hotels and lodges have made it a favourite retreat since 1900. Mayne is much quieter and more peaceful than it was when the jailhouse, built in 1896, was needed. This jailhouse now serves as the **Mayne Island Museum**. The island itself is tiny and can easily be seen in a day. Reserve ahead if you plan to stay anywhere on the island overnight.

**Coves and beaches: North** and **South Pender Islands**, best known for their many small coves and numerous beaches, are joined by a one-lane bridge between Bedwell and Browning Harbours. **Bedwell Harbour Resort** on South Pender is a Canadian port of entry from the United States. There is a waterfront pub here, the Whale Pod, and one at Port Browning Marina on North Pender, the Sh-qu-ala or "watering hole".

**Saturna Island** is the most remote southern Gulf Island and is less visited than the others since it requires a ferry transfer. It's a good day trip, or a longer destination for those who like to travel off the beaten track. Note, however, that **Saturna Beach** is the scene of the Gulf Island's biggest annual event – a "lamb bake" for Canada Day, which is held on the first day of July.

The **East Point Lighthouse**, built in 1888, is a must for lovers of scenic locations; the same visitors will also appreciate the sculptural sandstone formations, kelp beds and a shell and gravel beach at the end of a short, steep lane. Killer whales are often spotted from here in summer, but more common are seals, sea-lions, and sea birds such as cormorants, sandpipers and herons. **Winter Cove Provincial Marine Park** has mud and sand beaches and can be reached by land or water. Accommodation on Saturna is limited, and there is no camping.

**Left**, tidal pools. **Right**, Saturna Island's sculptural sandstone formations.

# NORTH TO WHISTLER

Preceding pages: snowfall at lower elevations, sticky and wet. Left, Horseshoe Bay is at the westernmost edge of Northern America. Right, ice maiden.

"When people say they love Vancouver I suspect it's not so much the city they love but the setting," architect Arthur Erickson once said of his home city. And it's true – the setting *is* the best thing about Vancouver. The ocean, rugged mountains, lush vegetation, clear water lakes, rivers and abundant wildlife, all within minutes of downtown, make it a paradise for those who appreciate the outdoors. And amongst all this scenic overload, what is the favourite valhalla? The hands-down winner is the year-round recreational mountain village, Whistler, only 75 minutes from Vancouver on the Sea-to-Sky highway. But first let's divert our attention to the Sunshine Coast, a worthy weekend jaunt away from the roar of city life.

**Sunshine Coast sidetrip:** Highway 99 to Horseshoe Bay and beyond is the only road leading directly north of Vancouver. From **Horseshoe Bay ferry termi-** nal, incurable island enthusiasts can make the 20-minute ferry crossing to Snug Cove on tiny **Bowen Island** in Howe Sound or to the Sunshine Coast, a peninsula isolated from Vancouver by both Howe Sound and the Coast Mountains.

Though part of the mainland, the **Sunshine Coast** has a kind of *laissez-faire* island-feeling that comes from its isolation and the 45-minute ferry ride required to access it. Typical residents include artists, writers, loggers, fishermen and reclusive types, all of whom appreciate the 2,400 hours of annual sunshine and low level of precipitation.

The only land link north along the Sunshine Coast is Highway 101 extending for about 150 km (93 miles) to its northern terminus at the small fishing village of **Lund**. Scuba diving in the so-called Emerald Sea, fishing, cycling, hiking, kayaking, skiing, beachcombing, sunbathing and gazing at the spectacular seaside scenery are among the favourite activities.

Follow lower Marine Drive to Molly's Reach Café in the fishing village of **Gibsons**. Excellent fish and chips are served at the Gibsons Fish Market near the grocery market. The **Elphinstone Pioneer Museum** has a tremendous shell collection, as well as pioneer and Coast Salish displays. The first of several provincial parks is at **Roberts Creek**, 14 km (9 miles) northwest of Gibsons. Picnic or camp in the second-growth fir and cedar forest or walk down to the pebble beach. Low-tide marine life includes starfish, mussels, and oysters. There is saltwater fishing here, but the rugged coastline requires good navigation skills. There's a better beach for swimming at **Wilson Creek/Davis Bay** further up on Highway 101.

As one enters the town of **Sechelt**, the impressive Sechelt Nation's **House of Hehiwus** or House of Chiefs is hard to miss. The band's office is here, as well as a small museum, native arts and crafts, a theatre and gift store. Not far away is a unique totem grouping called "Stonehenge". Faceless figures represent the

tribe's status before they became a self-governing entity more than a decade ago. Sechelt itself is a busy service centre with access to scuba diving, fishing and boating, but it has surprisingly little character. **Porpoise Bay Provincial Park** is a good spot for cyclists to camp and for canoers and kayakers to paddle around the **Sechelt Inlets Marine Recreation Area**.

**Reversing tidal narrows:** Further up the **Sechelt Peninsula** is a must-see: the West Coast's largest reversing saltwater rapids. It's a beautiful drive past the peaceful **Pender Harbour** area to **Skookumchuck Narrows Provincial Park** on the northeast tip of the peninsula, east of Egmont. Skoo-kumchuck, or "strong waters", refers to the rapids created as ebbing and flowing water is constricted in the narrow channel. The churning action of billions of gallons of water forced through a channel narrows is awesome to watch.

Check the tide tables (usually posted at the trailhead or in the local papers).

Allow enough time and bring refreshments to watch the hours-long transition from calm to seething water. The greatest action off **North Point** occurs on the outgoing tide and on the incoming tide off **Roland Point**. At low tide extraordinary specimens of giant barnacles, sea urchins, sea anemones, and molluscs can be observed. Extreme caution is advised for boaters or paddlers. It's a one-hour hike to Roland Point from the parking lot.

The highway continues to **Earls Cove** BC ferry terminal, 16 km (10 miles) beyond Madeira Park, where a BC ferry makes a 50-minute crossing of Jervis Inlet. **Powell River** is a popular summer resort location and the scuba-diving capital of Canada. Here in the so-called Emerald Sea, several sunken ships attract octopi, wolf eels and lingcod. One of the world's largest pulp and paper plants is the mainstay of the economy. Another BC ferry links Powell River to Comox on Vancouver Island.

**Sea-to-Sky to Whistler:** Now let's turn our attention to the year-round alpine village of Whistler. Twisting and winding along steep cliffs and mountains above **Howe Sound**, Highway 99 from Vancouver, the Sea-to-Sky highway to Whistler, is the most scenic drive immediately out of the city. It's moody and dramatic when great grey banks of clouds hover low on the slopes, and arbutus and fir trees drip with captured rain. Change to sunshine and it all becomes a sparkling vista. If you'd rather not drive, you can access Whistler by bus or BC Rail train any day of the year.

In summer only, the Howe Sound (not Whistler) portion of the trip is accessible by means of a popular day trip aboard the **Royal Hudson Steam Train** to Squamish and back again on board the cruise ship *Britannia* (*see Travel Tips section*). The day long rail-boat adventure allows for time to see Shannon Falls or to take an optional flight over mountain glaciers.

Along Highway 99 at the residential community of **Lions Bay**, 11 km (7

**Eat and sleep like a king.**

miles) north of Horseshoe Bay, beautifully designed homes perch precariously on the steep slopes below the western cirque of **The Lions**, the two prominent rock summits that highlight Vancouver's skyline.

**Porteau Cove** offers easy access for scuba divers, kayakers, windsurfers and anglers. This provincial park, only 39 km (24 miles) north of Vancouver, features camping by the ocean, boat launching facilities and picnic areas. The highway continues up and along another rise, then winds down to **Britannia Beach**, a former mining town. The mine was once the largest copper processor in the British Empire, separating 7,000 tons of ore daily at its operating peak in the late 1920s and early 1930s. Underground tours are available at the **BC Mining Museum**, now a National Historic Site. The museum is filled with artefacts and working displays of widow-makers, slushers, muckers, drills and one of the world's last remaining gravity-fed concentrators. Building the plant

**Sechelt on the Sunshine Coast.**

on a 45-degree slope conserved vital power in the processing operation.

Further along, **Shannon Falls**, thundering 340 metres (1,110 ft) down a granite bluff, is a spectacular sight. Squamish natives claim it was formed when a huge sea monster crashed into the coast in the futile pursuit of a giant eagle. A short, easy walk through the forest gives you a close-up view of this, BC's third highest waterfall. The Klahanie Restaurant across the highway serves delicious butter tarts for those who have forgotten to bring a picnic lunch, or if – as too often happens – it's raining.

The **Stawamus Chief**, a 650-metre (2,140-ft) granite monolith, geologically comparable to the rock of Gibraltar, towers over the town of Squamish, 61 km (38 miles) north of Vancouver, and attracts climbers from around the world. Most days when it's not raining, colourful ropes can be seen trailing down route lines and tiny dots move with deliberation up the rock face. These are the peer-

less rock-face climbers. Ambitious non-climbers can hike up the back trail to any of the Chief's three summits.

**Logging and bald eagles: Squamish**, a small but growing logging town, has shops and pleasant restaurants (good espresso at Quinn's) as well as places to stay. Shortly after Europeans settled the valley around 1873, logging the giant cedar and fir trees became the leading industry. Recreational tourism is growing rapidly with the area's reputation as a premier rock-climbing and wind-surfing destination. Still, the town is proud of its logging heritage and in August holds a **loggers' sports show** with competitive events such as springboard chop and power-saw bucking.

Squamish means "mother of the wind" in Coast Salish and some of the best windsurfing in Canada is here. A good place to view bald eagles, especially from November to February, is the viewpoint further north along Highway 99, in a protected wilderness identified by the **Brackendale Art Gallery**. They nest here and feast on spawned-out salmon in the Squamish River.

**Serious hikes:** The largest and most visited provincial park in the Lower Mainland, **Garibaldi Park** covers 197,187 hectares (487,260 acres) on the east side of Highway 99, beginning just north of Squamish and extending past Whistler. It offers incredible alpine beauty and numerous day-hiking options. The glacier-fed, clear blue **Garibaldi Lake** with the granitic **Panorama Ridge** beyond is a breathtaking sight. A very popular hike is to the top of the stark black volcanic plug, **Black Tusk**, which ends in a scramble up a 99-metre (325 ft) chimney.

For the less sure-footed, the surrounding meadows, especially when covered in alpine flowers in late summer, are more than satisfying. Allow six hours for a return hike to **Garibaldi Lake** or Black Tusk from the trailhead. The park has 196 wilderness walk-in campsites at five locations, four overnight alpine shelters and six day-use shelters.

Chateau Whistler, BC's premier ski resort.

**Whistler alpine village:** It's hard to believe today, but before 1960, **Whistler mountain** and **Blackcomb mountain**, as well as the **Alta Lake Valley**, were a remote destination home to only a few hundred hard-core outdoor recreationists and loggers. Since then, a fast-growing but nonetheless carefully designed town development, with cobbled streets, quality shops, gift galleries and restaurants, has sprung up to complement the two adjoining world-class ski mountains.

Blackcomb, the mile-high mountain with its year-round ski area called **7th Heaven and the Horstman Glacier**, and Whistler mountains are both equipped with ultra-modern express lifts moving millions of downhill enthusiasts to scores of runs. Rising directly above the village, they offer more skiable terrain than any other ski area in North America. Now rated by top ski and snowboard magazines, celebrities, professional skiers and amateurs – and even England's two young princes – as among the best in the world, the ski facilities and the aprés ski alpine village are popular both winter and summer.

Summer? Yes, skiing is not all there is to Whistler: there's a golf course created by Arnold Palmer plus five lakes and lots of year-round recreational possibilities. In summer, thousands ride the lifts to the meadowy mountain tops, with or without a mountain bike in tow, hike the meadows (listening for marmots whistling) or check the dates when the Vancouver Symphony Orchestra performs on the mountain top. There's windsurfing, boating, horseback riding, hiking, fishing, paragliding, kayaking, swimming, canoeing and whitewater rafting. Play tennis, go for a nature tour, charter a helicopter or hire an adventure guide to see some backcountry.

To sort out this plethora of activities, head for the anchor tenant of the village, the impressive **Chateau Whistler Hotel.** There, an activity desk is staffed with helpful people to get you started.

**Whistler has a mile-long vertical drop down.**

And for aprés-recreation-in-the-mountains, there are whirlpools, saunas, steamrooms and health clubs with juice bars and massage therapists.

For those with a more laid back attitude, Whistler is a favourite among gourmet power-grazers (local talk for non-stop healthy snack food nibblers). The coffee houses, gift shops, eateries and curiosities in Whistler village itself are enough for a full day of people-watching from an outdoor café. The resort picks up where the mountains leave off.

If you have a vehicle handy, you might want to wander around Whistler's outlying subdivisions. Some condominium owners can literally live on their skis, popping out their chalet doors onto the ski-hill to pick up a lift to the mountain top. Cool, rushing **Fitzsimmons Creek** traverses the lower slopes of Blackcomb mountain. It too is the setting for various cliffhugging phases of multi-dwelling projects as well as neighbourhoods of enormous alpine chalets. Each

seems the perfect place to nestle into the spectacular setting. Poking around the various districts with innovative names like Pinnacle Ridge, Cedar Hollow or Snowy Creek is a dreamy adventure in itself.

**Impressive falls and seed potatoes:** North of Whistler by 32 km (20 miles), a pleasant half-hour walk along the Green River leads to **Nairn Falls**. Although not particularly high, its powerful tumble is loud and impressive.

Highway 99 traffic thins out towards the farming and logging town of **Pemberton**, seed potato capital of BC. East 64 km (40 miles) is the whispered-about **Meager Creek Hot Springs**, a popular spot for weary skiers and hikers. Access is via the **Lillooet Forest Road** northwest of the town, then left up an unpaved logging road marked M24. The springs are the largest in BC, but it is an undeveloped site with no tourist facilities, no changing area, and a few primitive tenting spots. In winter, in addition to intrepid adventurers, lizards and snakes cluster here for warmth.

**Into the wilderness:** Throughout British Columbia, beyond Vancouver's beaches, scattered along an otherwise rugged shoreline, the **Coast Mountains**, along with nine other forested mountain ranges, extend from the lowlands of the Fraser River north to the **Yukon** territory. They form an unbroken chain of glaciated peaks, deep valleys, fjords and coastal rainforest. If you decide to venture into this vast wilderness, make sure you are properly equipped and go with proper respect. Many hikers have lost their way barely beyond Vancouver's back yard. And don't expect to see everything in one visit. Some local explorers lose themselves in remote mountain regions for weeks on end, claiming to find something new at every turn.

Of course, there are options other than adventurous outdoor activity. Relaxation is a natural complement to adventure. And while you are in Vancouver, that's an unofficial command.

**Left** and **right**, the old man and the tree.

43F-11E

**HECETA HEAD LIGHTHOUSE - OREGON COAST**
This lighthouse beams its light 21 miles out to sea through its spectacular first order Fresnel lens (insert photo). The light is 205 feet above the ocean.

*Photos by Michael Anderson*

**ANOTHER**

*André*

**ORIGINAL ®**

0 42545 00001 5

HECETA HEAD

LIGHTHOUSE

*Oregon Coast*

# INSIGHT GUIDES

# TRAVEL TIPS

Insight Guides *portray destinations in depth, providing the complete picture and the top photography*

*Insight Pocket Guides focus on the best choices for places to see and things to do and include large fold-out maps*

*Insight Compact Guides' portability makes them the perfect books to carry with you for on-the-spot reference*

# Three types of guide for all types of travel

**INSIGHT GUIDES** Different people need different kinds of information. Some want *background information* to help them prepare for the trip. Others seek *personal recommendations* from someone who knows the destination well. And others look for *compactly presented data* for on-the-spot reference. With three carefully designed series, Insight Guides offer readers the perfect choice. Insight Guides will turn your visit into an experience.

**The world's largest collection of visual travel guides**

# CONTENTS

# Getting Acquainted

**Cities:** Vancouver, Victoria, Whistler (village or resort).
**Province:** British Columbia (BC).
**Population:** Greater Vancouver: 1.9 million; Victoria: 335,000; Whistler: 7,500.
**Language:** English.
**Time Zone:** Pacific Standard Time (GMT minus eight hours). In April, the clocks are advanced by one hour and Daylight Saving Time comes into effect. Clocks revert back one hour the last Sunday in October.
**Weights and Measures:** metric.
**Electricity:** 120 volts, identical to the United States.
**North America Dialling Code:** (1).
**International Dialling Code:** (011).
**Local Dialling Codes:** (604) for Vancouver and surroundings; (250) for Victoria, Vancouver Island and elsewhere.

## Climate

There are lots of jokes about the BC weather. British Columbia has been dubbed "The Wet Coast" and its inhabitants have adopted a nonchalant attitude. Even if it has been drizzling steadily for several days it doesn't stop Vancouverites from hiking, jogging, camping, fishing, picnicking or drinking lattés in outdoor cafés. "You don't tan in Vancouver," they say. "You rust."

The climate is generally moderate. The average temperature in January is a mild 2°C (36°F) and in July an equally mild 17°C (63°F), although by the beaches temperatures can be higher. The wettest season is during the winter, with an average precipitation of 117 cm (47 inches). During the winter there is snow at higher elevations

and rare snowfalls at ground level. At the first hint of a sunny day Vancouverites head for Stanley Park for a brisk walk around the sea wall. In this climate, a variety of sports can be enjoyed from January to December.

Summer temperatures are pleasant, sometimes hot enough to risk a sunburn, but always cool and comfortable in the evenings. The mild climate makes Vancouver a popular vacation and retirement centre, attracting people from other parts of Canada. There are some advantages to the rain. It washes away the pollution and keeps the air clear and fresh.

For updated weather forecasts for the Greater Vancouver area, tel: 299-9000 and extension 3501 and for British Columbia, extension 3500. Additionally you may call Weather Information, tel: 664-9010.

The average daily highs in Vancouver are:

| Month | °C | °F |
|---|---|---|
| January | 5 | 41 |
| February | 7 | 44 |
| March | 10 | 50 |
| April | 14 | 58 |
| May | 18 | 64 |
| June | 21 | 69 |
| July | 23 | 74 |
| August | 23 | 73 |
| September | 18 | 65 |
| October | 14 | 57 |
| November | 9 | 48 |
| December | 6 | 43 |

## Government

Like most Canadian towns and cities, Vancouver, Victoria and Whistler are self-governing. The City Council consists of a mayor and aldermen who are elected by the citizens for two-year terms. The mayor is chairman of the City Council and acts as the city's chief law enforcement officer. The mayor also brings matters of interest and importance concerning the community before the City Council. The City Council is responsible for governing the city, operating hospitals, and the school system,

overseeing law enforcement agencies, regulating building development, maintaining municipal parks and administrating certain social programmes. Councils operate under a council-committee system with a series of boards and commissions.

The region generally called "Vancouver" actually consists of the City of Vancouver and several outlying municipalities. Each of these municipalities has its own mayor and council and runs its own hospitals and school systems, etc. In Greater Vancouver these municipalities are: Burnaby, Coquitlam, North Vancouver, West Vancouver, Richmond, Delta, New Westminster, Port Coquiltlam, Port Moody, Maple Ridge and Langley.

The Greater Vancouver Regional District (GVRD) Board consists of 24 members appointed by the surrounding municipalities. It oversees the water supply, regulates the supply of land taken away from forests or agriculture for human inhabitation, and runs several large regional parks of interest to visitors.

Greater Victoria consists not only of Victoria proper but also the municipalities of Sidney, Saanich, Langford, Sooke and Mill Bay.

## Business Hours

Most **offices** in Vancouver, Victoria and Whistler conduct business during the hours of 9am–5pm and are usually open from Monday through until Friday. Government offices, including post offices, usually close by 4.30pm.

**Retail stores** have an option of staying open seven days a week. There are varying hours on certain days. In addition to regular hours from 9am–6pm Monday–Wednesday, on Thursday and Friday many stores open all day and in the evening to 9pm, and also open Sundays from noon–5pm. Retail stores in the major shopping centres are usually open on holidays but smaller businesses may close.

**Post offices** are hard to find. Instead check pharmacy windows for red Canada Post signs and mail letters or packages there. Hours are 8.30am–4.30pm Monday–Friday; they're closed on weekends but you can buy stamps.

**Grocery stores** are open daily, many until 10pm or midnight. Safeway supermarkets are open 8am–midnight. There are also all-night convenience stores such as 7-11 and Macs.

**Pharmacies** usually close by 9pm; however, there are some that offer late-night service.

## Public Holidays

Government agencies, banks and businesses close for statutory holidays and schools are dismissed. More than one traveller has been disappointed by not taking these holidays into account. These are the statutory holidays observed in British Columbia:

**New Year's Day** – 1 January
**Good Friday and Easter Monday** – date varies according to first full moon after Spring equinox. Not all businesses close Easter Monday.
**Victoria Day** – third Monday in May
**Canada Day** – 1 July
**BC Day** – first Monday in August
**Labour Day** – first Monday in September
**Thanksgiving** – second Monday in October
**Remembrance Day** – 11 November
**Christmas Day** – 25 December
**Boxing Day** – 26 December

# Planning the Trip

**Note:** Telephone numbers beginning with 1-800 or 1-888 are toll-free if dialled in North America. All prices quoted are in Canadian dollars.

## Visas and Passports

**Identification, all citizens except Americans:** All foreign travellers entering Canada are required to show a valid passport or an alternative legal travel document. Some people may require a visa to enter Canada. Before leaving your home country, inquire at the Canadian Embassy. Foreign visitors coming into Canada via the US should check with the US Immigration and Naturalisation Service to make sure they have all the necessary papers to get back into that country.

**Identification, citizens of the United States:** Citizens or permanent residents of the US do not require passports or visas; however they should carry proof of citizenship such as a birth certificate or driver's licence. Naturalised US citizens need a naturalisation certificate or proof of citizenship. Residents of the US who are not citizens are advised to carry their Alien Registration Receipt Card.

**Intention to Work:** Foreign persons may not be employed or work in Canada, however casually, without a work permit. Note: This includes foreign tour guides passing through with groups. For more information contact Human Resources Canada, tel: (604) 687-7803, Employment Canada, tel: 775-7015, or Immigration Canada, tel: (604) 666-2171.

## Customs

All goods must be declared., but clothes and **personal effects** for use by visitors while in the country are admitted free of duty.

**Alcohol and Tobacco:** Visitors 19 years old and over will be allowed to bring in, duty-free, 50 cigars, 200 cigarettes and 1 kg (2.2 lbs) of tobacco duty-free; and either 1.14 litres (40 oz) of liquor or wine; or 355 ml (12 oz) cans or bottles of beer, ale or equivalent.

Canada Customs officers are authorised to conduct thorough **searches** of persons they suspect of carrying contraband materials. Trained dogs and other modern surveillance equipment are in use at all points of entry.

Revolvers, pistols and fully automatic **firearms** are prohibited entry into Canada. All weapons, i.e. hunting rifles, shotguns, must be declared. Canada has strict gun possession laws and there are strict regulations prohibiting the entry of firearms into the country.

**Agriculture:** Many foods may be brought into Canada for personal use but bulbs, plant cuttings and seeds are prohibited to prevent plant pests from entering and causing damage to Canada's crops and forests. All plant material will be inspected by an Agriculture Canada inspector when you enter the country; for further information tel: (604) 666-8750.

For additional information, contact Revenue Canada, Customs and Excise, tel: (604) 666-0545 or toll free: 800-461-9999. For precise information, write to the Public Inquiries Unit, Canada Customs and Excise, 333 Dunsmuir Street, Vancouver, BC, V6B 5R4. For general recorded information on Canada Customs, tel: (604) 299-9000 and extension 3487.

### *Departing from Canada*
When you are leaving Canada, keep a list of all purchases you have made, keep sales receipts and invoices and pack your purchases separately for the convenience of customs inspection in your own

country. If you are re-entering the US you will require proof of the right to re-enter. US residents returning from Canada to the US after more than 48 hours are allowed to take back, duty free, $400 worth of articles for personal use. Families travelling together may combine their personal exemptions. Included in the duty-free exemption are cigars (up to 100 non-Cuban); one litre of alcoholic beverage and 200 cigarettes (one carton) per person. Gifts may be sent to friends and relatives in the US duty and tax-free if the retail value doesn't exceed $50.

## Money Matters

**Canadian dollars make sense:** The Canadian money system is based on dollars and cents. For several decades the Canadian dollar has been generally weak against foreign currencies, making travel to Canada quite a bargain. In recent years the exchange rate has fluctuated in the following range: US $1 = Canadian

## Animal Know-How

● **Entry of pets into Canada:** If you want to bring your older than 3 month pet into Canada, all dogs and cats must be accompanied by a certificate issued by a licensed veterinarian which clearly identifies the animal and certifies that it has been vaccinated against rabies during the preceding 36-month period; for further information tel: 666-8750.
● **Acceptance of pets:** If you are planning to camp in BC notice the regulations regarding animals in campgrounds. Some parks do not permit dogs or other pets. Animals are not permitted on public transport or in most taxis. Some but not all accommodations will accept pets. Ask before booking. Other services for pets including boarding kennels and veterinarians can be found in the *Yellow Pages* telephone directory.

$1.30 to $1.45; British £1 = Canadian $ 2.10 to $2.30.

**Changing your money:** Vendors will usually accept American money at an approximated exchange rate. For the best rate, currency should be exchanged for Canadian dollars at any bank or credit union, or exchange booth at the airport or border crossing points. It's a good idea to have some Canadian funds with you when you arrive, in case the exchange booths or banks are closed. Traveller's cheques are the safest way to carry money and are universally accepted by banks and major commercial establishments, but proof of identification may be required. Most major credit cards and bank cards are honoured throughout British Columbia. Banking hours vary but are usually 9am–5pm Monday–Friday. Some banks have extended hours Friday night and many are open for limited times on Saturday.

### Currency Exchanges

There are several currency exchanges in Vancouver and Victoria. Consult the *Metro Vancouver* phone book white pages under the specific names below for numerous other locations. Most downtown branches of banks have foreign exchange departments. There are 25 foreign banks in Vancouver. Check the *Yellow Pages* telephone directory.

**Thomas Cook Group (Canada) Ltd:** Foreign Exchange, 130–999 Canada Place, Vancouver, tel: (604) 641-1229, fax: 641-1219. Monday–Saturday 9am–5pm.

**International Securities Exchange Ltd.**, 1169 Robson Street, Vancouver, tel: (604) 683-9666; and 1036 Robson Street, tel: (604) 683-4686. Daily 9am–9pm.

### Sales and Goods Taxes

In most provinces of Canada, a provincial sales tax is added to purchases of retail goods with the exception of groceries, books and magazines. In British Columbia the sales tax is 7 percent. In addition, the Canadian government has added a Goods and Services Tax

(GST). This 7 percent tax is applied to almost everything you purchase except groceries. It's an unpopular and confusing tax, and the two taxes compound this, managing to add up to 15 percent.

**GST rebate for visitors:** If you're a visitor to Canada it is possible to apply for a rebate on certain purchased items (not food or services) adding up to $200 or more in value, as long as they are for use outside Canada and are removed from Canada within 60 days of purchase. To claim a GST rebate (7 percent only) you must obtain a form. Tourism Vancouver or Tourism Victoria will have one. Fill it out and mail it to Revenue Canada, Customs and Excise (the address is given on the form), including your receipts. If you have goods shipped out of Canada by the seller, you won't have to pay the GST and won't be eligible for a rebate. For GST tax rebate information inside Canada, tel: 1-800-668-4748, and outside Canada (902) 432-5608.

## What to Wear

Come prepared for the rain when you visit Vancouver but don't expect a monsoon. It's more of a Scottish mist. Vancouverites are used to getting around in it, even without an umbrella, but if you come it's advisable to bring an umbrella, as well as a light raincoat or waterproof jacket that you can tuck away into your bag when the sun shines. Additionally, you may want to bring slacks year round, and from November to March, boots, gloves and warm clothing are recommended.

Vancouver is a cosmopolitan city and any fashion is acceptable. Sports clothing and casual dress are worn most of the time. During the evening hours, many people dress up and a few establishments do have a dress code.

Comfortable walking shoes are a must if you plan to enjoy the many scenic walks around the city. For serious mountain hiking, proper equipment and know-how as well as proper footwear is advised.

Vancouver is a city of beaches

and there are many lakes in the nearby recreational areas, so bring your bathing suit. You'll need a sweater or jacket for the cool evenings from May to September, medium- to heavy-weight apparel for the autumn months.

Although Vancouver doesn't get much snow, during the winter you'll need a warm coat and waterproof boots. If you plan to visit the ski slopes in winter, bring proper clothing. Shops at the ski resorts are usually pricey. If you are unable to bring your own skis and boots or snowboards, rentals are available. Snowboard fastening stance is North American style. It is also possible to rent hiking equipment.

## Information Centres

Tourism information centres, called **BC Travel InfoCentres**, will book accommodation, make tour reservations, help you with your tour plans, arrange car rental or make restaurant reservations for you. You can contact them before you leave home or after you arrive. You can get free maps, brochures, BC Transit tickets and schedules from Travel InfoCentres.

Travel InfoCentres are operated by the provincial government. There are 140 of them throughout the province of BC. When you see one, be certain to stop in and visit. Summer opening hours are 8am–6pm daily, May–September; winter hours: Monday–Saturday 9am–5pm.

**Written Information from Canada and the USA:** Tourism British Columbia, PO Box 9830, Stn Provincial Govt, Victoria, BC, Canada, V8W 9W5.
**Written Information from England:** Tourism British Columbia, 1 Regent Street, London , England, SW1Y 4NS.
**Information by phone from North America :** have a pencil handy and phone toll free: 1-800-663-6000.
**Information by phone from overseas:** have a pencil handy and tel: (250) 387-1642.
**Information by phone from**

## Talking to the Travel InfoCentre

● **Handy terms to know:** When talking about BC and requesting free tourism literature, it pays to know **Southwestern BC** or the **Vancouver Coast** includes the city of Vancouver, Whistler and the Sunshine Coast, while Victoria and Long Beach are located on **Vancouver Island.**
● **Useful mailout requests:** When contacting any Travel InfoCentre,

**Vancouver:** have a pencil handy and tel: 663-6000.

For details of a particular area or specifics about something in this Insight Guide contact the relevant Travel InfoCentre in the province (see Practical Tips: BC Travel InfoCentres).

## Websites

**British Columbia tourism:** http://www.travel.bc.ca
**Vancouver tourism:** http://www.bancouver-bc.com
**Victoria and Vancouver Island tourism:** http://www.victoriabc.com
**Whistler tourism:** http://www.dualmountain.co
**Beautiful British Columbia:** www.beautifulbc.com
**Adventure travel BC:** http://travel.bc.ca.
**Rocky Mountains and BC by rail:** www.rkymtnrail.com
**BC by rail:** www.bcrail.com/bcrpass
**BC Ferries:** www.bcferries.bc.ca
**BC Forests:** www.forestalliance.org

## Getting There

For more information on regional travel, see Getting Around and Attractions.

### BY AIR

**Vancouver International Airport** is one of the largest airports in Canada; this privately owned facility is the Canadian gateway to the Pacific Rim countries. Many millions of passengers a year use two side by side main terminals, one domestic, one international.

among the most useful free publications to request are: the BC Accommodations Guide; a BC map; booklets outlining specific cities or towns you intend to visit; and BC special interest publications on skiing, sports-fishing, hunting, camping, adventure travel, guest ranches, winter sports, boating, etc.

**International carriers** include Air New Zealand, British Airways, Air China, Cathay Pacific, Japan Airlines, KLM Royal Dutch Airlines, Lufthansa, Qantas, and Singapore airlines. **Carriers from the US** include Alaska, Airlines, American Airlines, Continental, Delta Airlines, Horizon Airlines and United Airlines. In all there are over 325,000 take-offs and landings a year.

The **principal airport** is situated on Lulu island at the mouth of the Fraser River in Richmond, 13km (8 miles) from downtown Vancouver. In addition to the main airport, a smaller **South terminal** services regional airlines and private planes. Float plane services originate from various waterways. If you need transportation between two terminals, connecting airlines will arrange this.

**Airport Assistance and Services** Information booths can be found on levels one and two. The Vancouver International Airport has a "Green Coat" service to assist travellers. Tel: (604) 276-6101 from any public phone if you need additional help. For airport Lost and Found, tel: (604) 276-6104.

There are many other services in the airport including duty-free shops, gift shops, a coffee shop and restaurant/bar, post office, bookstore, bank machines, barber shops, newsstand, flower shop, credit card fax machines, video games room and an interfaith chapel. The money exchange bureaux are on each level. On levels one and two you will find hotel courtesy phones. You can make hotel reservations from the airport and also rent cars.

## Airport Departure Fees

Be sure to save some Canadian money for departing from the Vancouver International Airport. Like many airports worldwide, Vancouver charges an Airport Improvement Fee (AIF) to all departing passengers. The rate is $5 per person travelling within BC; $10 per person for points in North America including Hawaii; and $15 per person for points outside North America. Both ticket machines and passenger service booths will accept Canadian or American dollars (at a punitive rate), or credit cards.

## BY SEA

Vancouver is Canada's busiest port. In addition to serving as the main centre of distribution for bulk goods shipped between Canada, the United States and Asia, the port is also visited by some of the world's top **cruise lines**. Each year from May until October hundreds of thousands of cruise passengers arrive in Vancouver, usually on their way to Alaska. Some of the cruise lines are: Costa Cruise Lines, Crystal Cruises, Cunard Line, Holland America Line, Princess Cruises, Regency Cruises, Royal Caribbean Cruises, Royal Cruise Line, Royal Viking Line, Salen Lindblad Cruising, Seven Seas Cruise Line, World Explorer Cruises.

For more information about Vancouver as part of an Alaska cruising itnerary contact any travel agency in your locale.

If you arrive in Vancouver by cruise ship your vessel will be berthed at either the Canada Place Cruise Ship Terminal or Ballantyne Terminal. The **Canada Place Terminal** is located on the waterfront in downtown Vancouver. The berth is next to the Vancouver Trade and Convention Centre and the Pan Pacific Hotel, close to city buses, the SkyTrain and the SeaBus. Shops and theatres are within walking distance as are

## By Air to Victoria

Victoria is also serviced by an international airport, though it is not as large or as busy as Vancouver's. The fastest way to travel from Vancouver to Victoria is by (surprisingly inexpensive) float-plane. They take off from the harbour in the centre of Vancouver just below Canada Place, and land in Victoria's Inner Harbour. (See *Getting Around* for more information.)

● **Air BC:** tel: 688-5515, toll free in BC: 1-800-663-3721.

● **Harbour Air:** tel: 278-3478, or toll free 1-800-663-4267.

**Note:** Whistler is accessible by helicopter.

several sightseeing attractions including Gastown and Stanley Park.

The **Ballantyne Terminal** is located a short distance east of Canada Place, about a 10-minute taxi ride from the downtown area.

The cruise ship terminals are a 25-minute taxi ride from the Vancouver International Airport. A complimentary shuttle runs to and from the terminals at Ballantyne or Canada Place.

## Car Storage While You Cruise

There is car storage at Canada Place Parking, tel: (604) 681-7311, or CruisePark, 9260 Oak Street, tel: (604) 266-4243. It is recommended you allow two overnights (one full day) in addition to your cruise stopover times to see the basic sights in Vancouver.

## Port Tours

For public viewing of port loading operations contact the Vancouver Port Corporation, 1300 Stewart Street, Vancouver, BC, tel: (604) 666-6129 (9am–5pm).

## *By Ferry to Victoria*

Hundreds of thousands of visitors take an international (or national) flight to Seattle in the USA, then travel to various ports in the state of Washington just south of British

Columbia and approach Victoria, BC via the water. There are several services for this purpose. All passengers must pass through both Canada and US Customs and Immigration. Of course, all the ferry services go both ways.

**Princess Marguerite:** Vehicle/passenger service between Seattle and Victoria, mid-May to mid-September, tel: (206) 448-500, toll free: 1-800-888-2535.

**Victoria Clipper:** passenger service from Seattle to Victoria, year round, tel: (250) 382-8100 or (206) 448-500, toll free: 1-800-888-2535.

**Victoria and San Juan Cruises:** passenger service from Bellingham, Washington to Victoria, May to October, tel: (360) 738-8099, toll free: 1-800-443-4552.

**Victoria Express:** Passenger service from Port Angeles, Washington to Victoria, May to October, tel: (360) 452-8088.

**Black Ball Transport:** Vehicle/passenger service from Port Angeles, Washington to Victoria, tel: (250) 386-2202.

## BY BUS

The Greyhound Bus connects Vancouver with the rest of Canada and the United States. Contact the **Greyhound Canada Transportation Corp.**, tel 662-3222, toll free: 1-800-661-8747.

Overseas visitors who wish to enjoy the scenic beauties of Canada are reminded that North America is vast and distances are much greater than in other parts of the world. For instance, the distance from Montreal to Vancouver is 4,800 km (2,980 miles) and from Toronto it is 4,490 km (2,790 miles).

Long-haul buses are made for comfort with lounge seats and toilet facilities. Some even have videos to watch during night travel. They make frequent stops, provide good service and a smoke-free journey. If you have time, it's a good way to see the country. The express bus from Eastern Canada takes three days and three nights.

To access Vancouver from the

nearest major city in the US is much faster. From Seattle, Washington the trip is approximately four hours. If you enter Canada by bus from the US there is a Canada Customs and Immigration office at the Douglas crossing, Blaine, Washington. American passengers will require adequate identification. Foreign visitors need valid passports and/or visas.

### Vancouver Bus Depot

The new Vancouver Bus Depot is located at Pacific Central Station, 1150 Station Street, corner of Station and Main streets near the heart of downtown Vancouver. There is a coffee shop, magazine and gift shops and a left luggage depot or lockers. You can catch city buses (BC Transit) or a taxi right outside the front door, or the SkyTrain rapid transit is across the street at the Main Street Station.

## BY TRAIN

Transcontinental rail service in Canada was cut back (not discontinued as widely reported) several years ago with the two major railways amalgamating their services into VIA Rail Canada Inc.

If you want to make a cross-Canada train trip, see the VIA website: http://www.viarail.ca. Arrivals and departures are three times a week from the Canadian National Railway Station at Main and Station streets in Vancouver. For information about cross-Canada trains, tel: (604) 640-3741, or in Canada toll free 1-800-561-8630. For arrival and departure times, tel: 1-800-835-3037.

For information and ticketing connecting with AMTRAK, US rail travel, tel: (604) 585-4848.

## BY CAR OR CAMPER

Trans-Canada **Highway 1** crosses Canada and is the major land route into Vancouver from the east. The main Vancouver corridor system includes the Vancouver freeway system, passing through east Vancouver, across the Second Narrows Bridge to the North Shore,

and ending at Horseshoe Bay ferry terminal. To get into downtown Vancouver watch for the freeway exit signs and proceed west.

**Highway 99** is the main route from the United States border, crossing the south arm of the Fraser River via the George Massey Tunnel. The US border is about an hour's drive from downtown Vancouver. Watch for the signs indicating traffic into the city centre. Just past the George Massey Tunnel the highway branches off into Highway 17 to the Tsawwassen ferry terminal and ferries sailing for Victoria, Nanaimo and the Gulf Islands. Highway 99 then runs north to the ferry terminal at Horseshoe Bay, then on to Squamish and points north. This is the highway you take to get to Whistler ski resort.

**Highway 91** is another route from the US border into the eastern municipalities of Greater Vancouver.

There are no toll charges on the highways or bridges entering Vancouver. The highways are well maintained and policed so be aware of the speed limits and traffic indicators posted on the right-hand side of the road.

### Vehicle Rental

Cars are rented at the Vancouver International Airport from the concession area on level two or at depots throughout the city. All major car rental companies are represented. Campers and recreational vehicles (RV) are available for weekly rentals. Many visitors revel in the myriads of wonderfully situated, inexpensive campgrounds in BC's rainforests and along its ocean fronts. **Go West Campers International**, 1577 Lloyd Avenue, North Vancouver, BC, V7P 3K8, tel: (604) 987-5288, fax: (604) 987-9620. **Westcoast Mountain Campers**, #150, 118 Voyageur Way, Richmond, BC, V6X 3N8, tel: (604) 279-0550, fax: (604) 279-0527, website: http://www.jumppoint.com/westcoast **Note:** Telephone numbers beginning with 1-800 or 1-888 are toll-free if dialled in North America.

# Practical Tips

All telephone numbers are preceded by the area code (604). All prices quoted are in Canadian dollars.

## Media

### Newspapers

Vancouver has two major daily newspapers, the *Vancouver Sun* and *The Province*. "The Sun" publishes every afternoon except Sunday. The Thursday edition contains complete entertainment listings in the What's Happening section and the Friday edition has the weekly *TV Times*. *The Province* is a tabloid-style newspaper and is published every morning except Saturday. The entertainment and TV listings are published on Friday.

Canada's national newspaper *The Globe and Mail*, published in Toronto, is also available daily from coin boxes and news vendors.

*The Georgia Straight* is an enter-

## News from Home

If you are lonely for news from home these free services may help a bit. Tel: 299-9000. **International news:** extension 3121 **American news:** extension 3123 **Canadian news:** extension 3120 **Off-beat news:** extension 3116

tainment weekly published on Thursday. *Business in Vancouver* is a weekly tabloid published on Friday. *BC Bookworld* is a weekly literary newspaper available at most book stores.

Vancouver also has a number of ethnic newspapers. *The Chinese Times* is the oldest Chinese daily newspaper in North America. There is also a First Nations publication called *Kahtou*. A list of all the local newspapers, including those published in other languages, is available in the *Yellow Pages*.

### Newsstands
The best selection of out-of-town and international newspapers can be found at Mayfair News in the Royal Centre mall at Burrard and Georgia streets.

### Radio
Vancouver has at least 30 AM and FM radio stations broadcasting in English, French and multilingual. Radio listings usually appear once a week in the newspapers.

### Television
There are numerous television channels to choose from. These include local, national and US networks in addition to Pay TV. Consult a daily newspaper or television guide for your choice of channels.

Depending on the service your provider is paying for, your location in the city, and the cable service's latest innovations, more than 60 major US and Canadian TV channels are present on most TV dials. In addition many hotels and motels have a special TV station piped into their rooms informing guests about visitor services.

In addition to weather and road reports, certain channels broadcast airline departures and arrival information and ferry schedules.

## Telecommunications

### Telegrams
Unitel provides a worldwide telegram service, tel: 681-4231. American Telegram offers a 24-hour service, toll free: 1-800-343-7363. Also, Canadian National Canadian Pacific (CNCP) offers a telex, telegram and fax service via the CNCP office at 175 West Cordova, tel: 681-4231, or 200 Granville Square, tel: 662-1262; fax: 662-1002; telex: 04-508834.

### Fax
Most major hotels have a business

centre where visitors can access a fax machine.

### Telephone
**Direct dial calls:** You can make a phone call from any public telephone or from hotels. To call within BC, Canada and the USA, dial 1 + area code + number. For international calls dial 011 + the country code + city routing code + local number.
**Credit card calls:** Dial 0 + the number; wait for the prompt and enter identification numbers.
**Collect calls or other operator assisted calls:** Dial 0 + the number; wait for the prompt and press 0.

The telephone directory white pages list some charges for long-distance calls. If you're in doubt you can request time and charges from the operator.

### Phone Directory Listings
The *Metro Vancouver White Pages* list various services available at the front of the book. The *Yellow Pages* directory lists businesses and public services. Community services are listed in a special section in the front. There you will find city transit maps, a map of Stanley Park, bus, ferry and airport information, a map of the University of BC, weather information and news.

## Postal Services

There are postal sub-stations throughout the city, and the times they are open may vary. Many postal outlets are located in pharmacies and convenience stores. Most post offices are closed weekends unless they are located in pharmacies or shopping malls. The main post office is open Monday–Friday from 8am–5.30pm. The Bay and Eaton's downtown stores have postal services. Postage stamps may also be purchased from newsstands and automatic vending machines located in most hotel lobbies, railway stations, airports and bus terminals.

In addition to regular mail, Canada Post offers special services such as Special Letter, Registered Mail, Security Mail and Priority Courier.

The **main post office** in Vancouver is: Main Post Office, 349 West Georgia Street, V6B 1Z1, tel: 662-5725. Visitors may have mail sent to them c/o "General Delivery" which is the same as the international *Poste Restante*. Use the name of the post office in the location where you will be staying. Mail must be picked up by the addressee in person within 15 days and you must show adequate identification.

## BC Travel InfoCentres

**Vancouver Travel InfoCentre,** Plaza Level, 200 Burrard Street, tel: (604) 683-2000, fax: (604) 682-6839.
**North Vancouver Travel Info-Centre,** 131 East Second Street, tel: 987-4488, fax: 987-8272.
**New Westminster Travel InfoCentre,** New Westminster Quay Public Market, 810 Quayside Drive, tel: 526-1905.
**Sunshine Coast Travel Infocentre** (for attractions, accomodations and BC ferry access to the entire Sunshine Coast): **Southwestern BC Tourism,** #204, 1755 West

Broadway, Vancouver, V6J 4S5, tel: 739-9011, toll free: 1-800-667-3306, fax: 739-3306.
**Tourism Association of Vancouver Island (also covers Gulf Islands),** #304, 45 Bastion Square, Victoria, tel: (250) 382-3551, fax: (250) 382-3523.
**Victoria Travel InfoCentre,** 812 Wharf Street, tel: (250) 953-2033, fax: (250) 382-6539, reservations: (250) 953-2022, toll free: 1-800-663-3883.
**Whistler Travel Infocentre,** 2097 Lake Placid Road, tel: 932-5528, fax: 932-3755.

## Consulates

There are 40 consulates in Vancouver, but no embassies. If you need to contact your country's Consulate General, the *Yellow Pages* directory lists consulate and foreign representatives. Here are a few:
**Australia**, tel: 684-117.
**Britain**, tel: 683-4421
**France**, tel: 681-2301
**Germany**, tel: 684-8377
**Hong Kong**, Hong Kong Trade and Development Council, tel: 685-0883
**India**, tel: 801-5101
**Ireland**, tel: 683-9233
**Italy**, tel: 684-7288
**Japan**, tel: 684-5868
**Mexico**, tel: 684-3547
**Monaco**, tel: 682-4633
**Philippines**, tel: 685-7645
**Singapore**, tel: 669-5115
**South Africa**, tel: 609-3090
**United States**, tel: 685-4311

## Disabled Travellers

New building codes in Canada address the needs of people with disabilities, providing accessible parking, entrances, interiors and washrooms of public buildings.

BC Transit offers a custom transit service **HandyDART**, which is fully accessible to people with disabilities, tel: 540-3400. Call 48 hours in advance. Some transit buses in Vancouver and Victoria are equipped with lifts for wheelchairs and all vehicles have reserved seating for the disabled and elderly. The SkyTrain and SeaBus services, except for the Granville Street Station, are fully accessible.

For a complete guide to Vancouver for people with disabilities, the **BC Coalition of People with Disabilities'** *Accessible Vancouver* can be obtained from their office at #204, 456 West Broadway, Vancouver V5Y 1R3, tel: 875-0188; fax: 875-9227.

Other service agencies for persons with disabilities include:
**Western Institute for Deaf and Hard of Hearing**, tel: 736-7391 and 24-hour message relay centre, tel: 1-800-855-0511 .

**Canadian National Institute for the Blind**, tel: 321-2311.
**BC Paraplegic Association**, tel: 324-3611.

## Gay Travellers

For information on both events and entertainment in and around Vancouver contact: The **Gay and Lesbian Centre**, 2, 1170 Bute Street, tel: 684-6869 or 222-7807. This organisation promotes events for lesbians and gay men including the annual Stonewall Festival commemorating police persecution of gays in Greenwich Village, NY. There are also several theatre groups, choirs and sports events for gay people. Annually in August there is the Gay and Lesbian Pride Festival at Sunset Beach.

## Religious Services

There are hundreds of churches of every religious belief and faith in Vancouver. You can find listings in the *Yellow Pages* directory. Some of Vancouver's churches are historic buildings and others are worth going to see for their cultural uniqueness.
**St James Anglican**, Cordova and Gore streets. This church was built in 1935, inspired by the Gothic Revival. The interior is Byzantine-style.
**Vancouver Buddhist Church**, 220 Jackson Avenue. Built in 1906 with traditional gable and corner tower.
**St Francis Xavier Chinese Catholic Church**, 579 East Pender Street. This imposing brick-faced church was built in 1910. It was the first Swedish Evangelical Lutheran Church, then St Stephen's Greek Catholic, then St Mary's Ukrainian Greek Catholic; now it has a congregation of Chinese Canadians.
**Our Lady of the Holy Rosary Cathedral**, Dunsmuir and Richards streets. This impressive, Gothic-styled church was built in 1899–1900 and has served as a cathedral since 1916.
**Christ Church Cathedral**, Georgia and Burrard streets. This Anglican church, built in 1889–95, is the oldest surviving church in

## Tipping

To show your gratitude for service at hotels and restaurants it is usual to give a tip. Applicable service charges and taxes are added to your bills. In Canada, tips are not added to your bills. In general, a restaurant tip is calculated on the generous side of 15 percent of the food and beverage total before taxes. Exceptional service rates a higher amount. Only in the case of the most abysmal experience is it proper to withold a tip. Normal glitches or delays do not merit penalty. Service providers are, in most cases, paid minimum wage and depend on tips for a living.

The tip is left discreetly under the edge of a plate or inside the provided bill-folder.

Tipping also applies to barbers, hairdressers and taxi drivers. Bellhops, doormen, and porters at hotels, airports and railway stations are usually paid $1 per item of luggage. You do not need to tip in self-serve cafeterias or fast-food outlets.

Vancouver and was recently restored. It is located in the heart of downtown Vancouver. Next to the church is a little park in Cathedral Square.
**St Andrew's-Wesley United Church**, 1012 Nelson Street. The rich stained-glass window in this church was made by Gabriele Loire of Chartres, France in 1969. The church itself was built 1931–33.
**Sikh Temple**, 8000 Ross Street, South Vancouver. This is the main temple of Vancouver's large Sikh population, designed in the geometric form of India with religious symbols and designs.
**St George's Greek Orthodox Church**, Arbutus Street and Valley Drive. The original St George's church is now the Kitsilano Neighbourhood House hall at Seventh Avenue and Vine Street. The present church serves most of Vancouver's large community of

Greeks who reside in this area. **St Paul's Catholic Church**, Esplanade, North Vancouver (walking distance from Lonsdale Quay). This is the oldest surviving mission church in the Vancouver area, built in 1884 on the Mission Reserve. Chief Snat, a renowned Squamish leader assisted by the Oblate missionaries, built the first church on this site in 1868. It is a designated historic site of Canada. Extensive restoration was done in 1979–83. Nearby is a monument honouring all First Nations servicemen who fought in World War I, World War II, Cyprus and Vietnam, which reads *Kwetsi – Wit Na Nam Xeyx*, "Those who went to war."

## Medical Treatment

British Columbia has a fine health care system. But although medical costs are not as extreme as in the United States, it can be very expensive for visitors who require hospital care. Before leaving home, it is advisable for visitors to Canada to obtain special travel insurance to cover medical expenses and emergency care. Visitors taking prescription medicines should bring a copy of their prescription(s) for verification by a doctor here.

### Hospitals

For an emergency ambulance, tel: 911. All hospitals are listed in the *Yellow Pages*. General (non-specialty) hospitals are open to the public through the Emergency Department. Staff doctors are on duty 24 hours.
**Lions Gate Hospital**, 231 East 15th Street, North Vancouver, tel: 988-3131.
**St Paul's Hospital**, 1081 Burrard Street, Vancouver, tel: 682-2344.

Victoria has several hospitals. Whistler has an emergency clinic, doctors and no hospital. Severe injuries are evacuated to Vancouver.

Be aware: Due to the many remote areas in British Columbia, it is possible for hikers and other outdoor sports participants to be injured far from medical help. Today's smart hikers carry cell phones and global positioning devices. Medical evacuations take many hours, and in the case of bad weather several days. Be responsible. You (or your heirs) are likely to be billed thousands of dollars for your rescue and evacuation.

### Medical and Dental Clinics

Clinics staffed with registered doctors for which no appointment is necessary are listed under "clinics" in the *Yellow Pages*.
**Medicentre**, 1055 West Dunsmuir, tel: 683-8138.
**Dentacentre**, 1055 West Dunsmuir, tel: 669-6700.
Both the above are located on the lower level of the Bentall Centre, Dunsmuir and Burrard streets.
**Dental Help**, Dentist Referral, College of Dental Surgeons, tel: 736-3621.
**Dentures,** Academy of Dentistry Denture Clinic, 750 West Broadway, tel: 876-7311.

### Opticians

**Granville Mall Optical**, 807 Granville Street. tel: 683-4716.
**Contact Lens Centre**, 815 West Hastings Street, tel: 681-9488.

### Pharmacies

Non-prescription drugs can be purchased off the shelves but certain drugs are available only with a valid prescription issued by a recognised doctor. You can find a complete list of pharmacies in the *Yellow Pages* directory. These are some that are located near the downtown area:
**London Drugs**, 1187 Robson Street, tel: 872-0396; Pharmacy, tel: 669-7474.
**Pharmasave**, Harbour Centre, 555 West Hastings, tel: 669-6906.
**Shoppers Drug Mart**, 1125 Davie, tel: 669-2424. Open 24-hours, 7 days a week.
**Supermarkets:** Some large supermarket chains have pharmacy departments. Check out foodstores, especially Safeway and Save-On Foods.

## Crisis Numbers

See also the Community Services section at the front of each city's White Pages telephone book.
**General Emergency:** tel: 911
**Vancouver Crisis Centre Distress Lines:** 24 hours, tel: 872-3311
**Aids Information Line:** 24 hours, taped, tel: 872-6652
**Sexual Assault Crisis Line Vancouver:** 24 hours, Rape Crisis Centre, tel: 255-6344 or 872-8212
**Sexually Transmitted Diseases Clinic:** tel: 660-6161
**Lawyer Referral** (Canadian Bar Association): tel: 687-3221
**Legal Aid:** Vancouver, tel: 687-1831; Burnaby/New West, tel: 437-4432; Surrey, tel: 584-8535

## Security & Crime

Although Vancouver, Victoria and Whistler rank as generally safe travel destinations, as in all big cities and tourist meccas there are problems. Purse snatching, muggings and car break-ins are common occurrences. Never leave your belongings unattended. Never leave the slightest item, not even an old jacket or crumpled papers in your car. Lock all items in the truck. It is advisable to carry with you only the cash you need. Traveller's cheques are preferable and use credit cards whenever possible. If you lose your traveller's cheques or credit cards, report the loss immediately to a bank and to the police. At hotels leave your valuables with hotel security.

At night, it is not sensible to walk alone in dark areas. Of the three, Whistler is probably the safest place to walk at night. Be sure to keep to the well-lit streets where there are other pedestrians. Use your street-sense and avoid places where your comfort-zone is challenged. When walking in parks, women should not venture off the main trails unescorted. Under no circumstances should children be left alone in parks or playground areas.

**Hitchhiking** is illegal on the freeways, and picking up hitchhikers is also illegal. Note to women: hookers in the Greater Vancouver area use hitchhiking as a means of soliciting business. If you want to avoid the hassles involved in this practice, don't do it.

**Jaywalking** (crossing mid-street or not observing pedestrian "stop" signs) is an offence and if caught you will be fined.

### Littering
It is illegal to dispose of trash on the roadsides and streets, and under the Litter Act, offenders are penalised; in some cases the fines for littering start at $500. Littering is a big deal in BC, so don't do it.

### Lost and Found
If you lose something on BC Transit, go to the Lost Property Office located at the Stadium SkyTrain station, Vancouver. Open: Monday–Friday 9.30am–5pm, tel: 682-7887. If you lose something of value anywhere in Vancouver, contact the city police Lost Property Room, tel: 665-2232.

## Drink, Drugs & Sex

### Liquor
The law in BC prohibits the sale of alcoholic beverages to persons under the age of 19. You are not allowed to drink alcohol in public places such as beaches and parks. In some, not all, eating establishments, you must order food in order to buy drinks. Liquor establishments stop serving at 1am. Depending on regulations, some may stop earlier.

### Smoking
Smoking continues to meet with more and more restrictions. In Vancouver, many restaurants and eateries ban smoking altogether, including smoking in the outdoor portions of their facilities. Smoking is prohibited in many pubs as well. In Victoria and Whistler, smoking is similarly restricted. Always check signs before lighting up. On the other hand, certain restaurants encourage (expensive) cigar smoking.

### STDs
Vancouver has one of the highest incidences of AIDS in North America. Incidences of other sexually-transmitted diseases are similiarly high.

### Illegal Drugs
Like all the world's port cities, there is an active sector dealing in illegal drugs. The United States is particularly vigilant in stopping illegal drugs entering its borders from British Columbia.

### Police
**Emergency**, tel: 911.
**Vancouver City Police**, tel: 665-3321.
**Royal Canadian Mounted Police (RCMP)**, tel: 264-3111. The RCMP are in charge of communicating urgent messages to anyone on vacation. Watch for messages posted in newspapers and at campground bulletin boards.

## Etiquette

Canadians are similar to the British in many of their customs and etiquette. It is usual to queue for service in stores, banks and while waiting for public transportation, such as buses and ferries. It is courteous to express your thanks when someone has given you help. Littering is treated as a crime; this include cigarette ends. Residents are generally friendly and helpful except in the cases of smokers. Smoking anywhere in public may attract unfavourable comment. To enjoy your holiday without being chastised, be exceptionally considerate in this regard.

# Getting Around

## On Arrival

### Orientation
Here's a quick guide to geographical Vancouver, written in the local lingo. Vancouver is also known as Van (as in North Van).
**Bee Cee:** The common designation for the province of British Columbia (i.e. BC).
**Lower Mainland:** Means the southwest corner of British Columbia, the area where Greater Vancouver is located. Also simply called the Mainland when contrasted with Vancouver Island.
**Marine Drive:** This is the Lower Level, the road that runs along the shoreline of West Van from the Lions Gate Bridge to Horseshoe Bay. Don't confuse it with SW and NW Marine Drive in the Point Grey university area of Vancouver.
**New West:** New Westminster is a city, east of Vancouver on the shore of the Fraser River, part of Greater Vancouver. It is one of many Van suburbs.
**Saltchuck:** The Pacific ocean offshore; the chuck refers to any body of water – "It's over by the chuck."
**Second Narrows:** The second of only two bridges crossing Burrard Inlet, the name actually refers to the waters underneath the bridge.
**The Bay:** This isn't a body of water at all, but the venerable Hudson's Bay Company department store.
**The Bridge:** This can refer to any of the ten bridges in metropolitan Vancouver, but it usually means the Lions Gate Bridge. Also, the Lions Gate is annoyingly called First Narrows.
**The Ferry:** "Taking the ferry" means you're going on one of the BC

Ferries from either terminal at Horseshoe Bay or Tsawwassen.

**The Island:** There are hundreds of islands off the coast of BC, the largest being Vancouver Island. Usually if you're heading for Victoria or Nanaimo, you are going to The Island.

**The Lions:** The twin mountain peaks visible beyond North Van were once known as the Two Sisters. They were renamed because of their resemblance to a pair of lions. The Bridge was named after them, as was Vancouver's football team, The BC Lions, usually just referred to as The Lions.

**The North Shore:** Meaning the north shore of Burrard Inlet, location of the municipalities of North Vancouver and West Vancouver.

**The Valley:** The rural areas of the Lower Mainland along the Fraser River.

**Sunshine Coast:** The Sechelt Peninsula, a few kilometres northwest of Vancouver, has more sunshine than the mainland. Hence its name.

**Upper Levels:** Highway 1 on the north shore between Second Narrows and Horseshoe Bay.

**Whistler:** The world-class ski resort north of Vancouver.

### From the Airport
**By Taxi**
The taxi ride to downtown Vancouver will cost about $25. Vancouver's taxi fares are high, so be warned.

**By Limousine**
Airport Limousine has a 24-hour service between the airport and downtown locations. Tel: 273-1331 for bookings.

**By Bus**
A cheaper option is to take the Vancouver Airporter, tel: 946-8866. It leaves downtown every 30 minutes from major hotels and from the airport at the second level for trips into town.

Public transit buses run from the airport, but if you have large pieces of luggage this may not be a convenient means of travel. If you take the bus from Vancouver to the airport, take the #20 Granville south to 70th Avenue and transfer to the #100 Airport bus. Going from the airport, take the #100 Port Coquitlam/New Westminster Station and transfer at 70th Avenue to the #20 Victoria.

### Rental Cars
You can pick up rental cars at the airport from concessions on level two. There is a large parking area in front of the airport terminal and a free shuttle bus that transports you from pickup spots in the lot. Valet parking is available on levels two and three. Drop-off rented cars in the main lot are at the end closest to the terminal.

### Arriving or Departing Seattle
The **Quick Shuttle** (tel: 940-4428, toll free: 1-800 665-2122, email reservations: rez@quickcoach.com) operates between downtown Vancouver (Sandman Inn, 180 West Georgia) and downtown Seattle in the United States (Eighth and Blanchard), as well as Seattle's SeaTac airport, every two hours between 6.45am and 8.30pm, a trip taking 3 hours and costing about $25 each way.

## Recommended Maps

To help you find your way around the Greater Vancouver, Victoria and Whistler areas, there are a number of good tourist maps and pamphlets available from:

**Vancouver Travel InfoCentre**, Plaza Level, 200 Burrard Street, tel: 683-2000, fax: 682-6839.

**World Wide Books and Maps**, 736A Granville Street (across from Eaton's), Vancouver, downstairs. Tel: 687-3320, fax: 687-5925. For detailed maps, terrain and hiking maps.

**British Columbia Automobile Association (BCAA)**, 999 West Broadway, tel: 268-5600; Travel Agency, tel: 268-5622. Maps and books here are priced slightly higher if you are not a member of an Automobile Association.

**Victoria Travel InfoCentre**, 812 Wharf Street, tel: (250) 953-2033 or toll free: 1-800-663-3883, fax: (250) 382-6539.

## Local Public Transport

### By BC Transit
The Vancouver Regional Transit System, BC Transit, operates a 1,000-bus fleet throughout Greater Vancouver and Victoria. Transit requires exact coin fares, pre-purchased tickets or passes. The fares are the same on city buses, **SkyTrain** and **SeaBus**; you can transfer to and from all three without extra charge.

The BC Transit system offers regular service on downtown routes from 5am to midnight, then a scant late night "owl" service until 4am. The single transit system attempts to cover 2,849 square km (1,100 square miles), which is why many opt to rent a car in spite of parking costs.

## To Market, to Market

A low-cost mini-adventure, and a great way to see much of Vancouver by transit, is to start at Waterfront Station. Board the bus to **Lonsdale Quay** in North Vancouver. Have a quick lunch, skipping dessert. Still on the same 90-minute-valid transfer, recross the Inlet on Seabus, then transfer to Skytrain for the 28-minute ride to **Westminster Quay** for dessert. Buy a new ticket and return to the downtown. For just two transit tickets, it's a lot of fun and great grazing too (local slang for healthy snacking).

### Zones and Fares
The Vancouver transit system is divided into three zones and your fare depends on the number of zones you cross. Regular cross-zone fares are in effect Monday–Friday from 5am until 6.30pm. After 6.30pm discount fares are in effect. Transit operators do not sell tickets, so when you board a bus you must have the correct change or a ticket, a pass or valid transfer. Transfers

between journeys are good for 90 minutes and can be used in any direction.

## Transit Passes
Tickets and passes are sold through retail outlets displaying a blue and red "Faredealer" sign, such as 7–11 stores. They can also be purchased from vending machines at the SkyTrain or SeaBus depots. A Daypass is available.

## Special Summer Bus
From April until October there is a special bus service around Stanley Park. Many Vancouver bus routes such as this one are scenic and provide a cheap and interesting way to see the city and the outlying areas.

## Skytrain
Vancouver's rapid transit system runs on an elevated track every three to five minutes for a distance of 28km (17 miles) from Surrey to Canada Place downtown, at a speed of 80 kph (50 mph). The single line trip takes 39 minutes one way. Trains are run by computers but security officers patrol the trains and stations. You will be fined severely if you are caught riding without a valid ticket or transfer. Because most of the SkyTrain route is on an elevated track it is one of the best ways to see the city.

## SeaBus
SkyTrain connects with the SeaBus at Waterfront Station. It is a waterborne public transit bus that crosses Burrard Inlet every 15 minutes during the day, connecting Vancouver with North Vancouver. The 12-minute trip is a great way to see Vancouver's impressive harbour.

### By Train to the Countryside
Early morning and late afternoon only, along a 65-minute route from downtown Vancouver to Mission in the Fraser Valley, a speedy local train with beverages, cuppuccino and snacks aboard, connects Vancouver with outlying countryside areas. Each car provides space for at least two bicycles and there are

bike lockers at most of the stations. It's easy to create a do-it-yourself adventure, particularly recommended on Sundays. The **West Coast Express** departs from Waterfront Station at the edge of Gastown.

## The Essential Guide

If you intend to travel Vancouver and Victoria by public transit try to obtain a copy of the *Discover Vancouver on Transit Guidebook* ($2) before you arrive. It describes all transit routes and transfers to points of interest around metropolitan Vancouver and (in spite of its title) Victoria areas. Write to: BC Transit Customer Information & Marketing, 13401-108 Avenue, Surrey, BC, V5T 5T4, or tel: 540-3040 (Monday–Friday, 9am–4pm).

### Schedules
Detailed transit schedules are available at all 7–11 stores, public libraries, municipal halls, information and community centres, SeaBus and SkyTrain terminals and ticket outlets. BC Transit operators are very friendly and helpful, so you shouldn't have any trouble finding your way around the city.

### Public Transit Numbers
**BC Transit** (including Skytrain and SeaBus information), tel: 521-0400 or 299-9000 and extension 2233. North Shore's **West Vancouver Transit**, tel: 985-7777.
**West Coast Express train**, tel: 689-3641; website: www.wcxpress.com.
**HandyDart Custom Transit Service for Disabled Persons**, Vancouver, tel: 540-3400. Call 48 hours in advance of travel.
**Victoria transit**, tel: (250) 385-2551.
Note: there is no Whistler transit system.

## Regional Trains

One of the best ways to see the scenic beauty of British Columbia is to take the train. One operator, BC

Rail, travels BC mainland routes and another, Viarail's E&N, Malahat, services Vancouver Island (Victoria, Duncan, Nanaimo, Qualicum Beach, Courtenay and other waypoints).

Contact **BC Rail** at: 1311 West 1st Avenue, North Vancouver, tel: 631-5500 or 299-9000 and extension 7245; website: www.bcrail.com/bcrpass.

For **Viarail (E&N)**, phone (from overseas) Leisure Rail Cambridge: 01-733-33-55-99, fax: 01-733-505-451; or in Britain phone Air Savers Scotland: 0141-303-0100, fax: 0141-303-0306; or from anywhere, tel: (506) 857-9830 in Canada, toll-free: 1-800-561-8630.

### Sightseeing Train Trips
You can make a day trip from Vancouver to Lillooet with a 2-hour stopover for lunch and sightseeing. The BC Rail train leaves every day in summer at 7.30am for the 253-km (157-mile) journey northeast via **Horseshoe Bay**, **Squamish** and **Whistler**. The train arrives back in North Vancouver at 8.35pm. There is also a popular sightseeing day-tour on the *Royal Hudson* steam train as well as a romantic evening dinner aboard the *Pacific Starlight Express*.

### Regular Service to BC Interior
BC Rail has a daily service from North Vancouver to points north of Vancouver, such as the **Cariboo Explorer route** to Squamish, Whistler, Pemberton, Lillooet and Prince George. There is a service three days a week to Clinton, 100 Mile House, Quesnel, Williams Lake, Prince George and other waypoints.

## BC Ferries

The nature of travel in this Pacific West Coast region necessitates the catching of ferries. The BC Ferries system rates from good to excellent and moves over 10 million passengers each year. Most vessels carry vehicles and accommodate foot passengers, bus passengers and vehicles; a few are passenger-only. Fares are based on three seasons, days of the week and if appropriate, the length of the vehicle.

Lineups are common in the summer, but foot passengers can always walk onto the next ferry. Motorcoach passengers have prioity over other vehicle passengers, who should listen to radio updates for lineup wait times. A "one sailing wait" implies a wait of 1½ to 2 hours. A "two sailing wait" is double that time. All passengers should report to the terminals at least 40 minutes before scheduled sailing times.

To sort out routing and the various boarding terminals, and for general information, it is recommended visitors contact in advance: **BC Ferries Information and Reservations**, 1112 Fort Street, Victoria, BC, V8V 4V2, tel: (250) 386-3431, toll free: 1-888 223-3779, fax (250) 388-7754. Also for general information, tel: 299-9000 and extension 7444. For car reservations to Vancouver Island, tel: 1-888-724-5223, or for reservations out of the province, tel: (604) 444-4890. The BC Ferry Corporation website is at: www.bcferries.bc.ca/ferries.

**On the Ferries:** Each ferry has a restaurant, snack bar, newsstand and ship-to-shore telephones. Most have newsstands and video game rooms. No smoking is allowed on any vessels and pets must remain on the car deck. All the ferries are wheelchair accessible and have lifts for passengers who are unable to walk up the stairs.

### Vancouver to Victoria
Separated by an ocean channel, this journey involves a 95-minute sea crossing: from **Tsawassen** terminal to **Swartz Bay** near Victoria; or from **Horseshoe Bay** terminal to **Nanaimo** plus a 2-hour drive south to Victoria. Additionally the Mid-Island Express ferry goes from Tsawassen to Nanaimo.

### Sunshine Coast
Access this area from Horseshoe Bay terminal to **Langdale terminal**, via a 45-minute ferry crossing.

### Gulf Islands
There are several access points from the mainland, from Vancouver Island and between islands. You will need a map to sort them all out.

### Services and Schedules
To sort out the myriad of services provided, including access to the Gulf Islands and several fjord-isolated communities, it is best to obtain a routing map. These are available through Travel Infocentres and on dedicated television stations. For 24-hour recorded information on Mainland/Vancouver Island routes, phone toll free in BC: 1-888-BCFERRY.

### Ferry/Motorcoach Combinations
Motorcoaches are the first vehicles in line to board the ferry. Passengers get off the bus once it is on the ferry, then reboard to disembark from the vessel. From Vancouver to Victoria, you can travel from the downtown bus terminal in Vancouver to the central bus terminal in Victoria. Buses depart every two hours during the day and the trip takes approximately three hours. **Pacific Coach lines** pick up at designated stops along the way. Phone at least an hour before the bus leaves the terminal, tel: 662-8074. You don't need a reservation to ride this bus.

Alternately, on the Mainland/Vancouver Island routes, foot passengers can board the ferry and at an onboard desk buy a bus ticket to continue the journey onward by coach.

To access the Nanaimo ferry terminal by motorcoach, call **Maverick Coach lines**, tel: 255-1171. These buses usually leave every two hours.

**BC Transit** services both Tsawwassen and Horseshoe Bay terminals, tel: 299-9000 and extension 2233, or 521-0400.

## Private Transport

### By Taxi
You can hail a taxi in downtown Vancouver or you can go to any large hotel to call one. Taxi fares are regulated, with the meter price starting at around $2.60. GST tax is added, making taxis a rather expensive means of transportation. Taxis do not carry animals and many of them are non-smoking cars. Ask before you light up.
**Black Top & Checker Cabs**, tel: 731-1111, 681-3201. If you want to go in style, request a Checker car. **Vancouver Taxi**, tel: 871-1111. This cab has space for wheelchairs and oversize items.
**Yellow Cab Company**, tel: 681-1111.

### Driving
If you have a valid driver's licence from Canada or the US or an International Driver's Licence you may drive in British Columbia. Note that fuels in BC are expensive by Amerian standards, and are sold by the litre: 4.5 litres = 1 British gallon; 3.78 litres = 1 American gallon.

## Help from BCAA

If you belong to an automobile club affiliated with the British Columbia Automobile Association (BCAA) you can get 24-hour emergency road service by calling 293-2222. The BCAA will also help you with questions and provide road maps. Their main office is at 999 West Broadway, tel: 732-3911.

### Distances
If you are travelling from the US on highway 99, the distance from Seattle to Vancouver is 225km (140 miles). The distance from the US border to Vancouver is 50km (30 miles). To drive from Vancouver to Victoria is 69km (43 miles), not counting the 1½ hour ferry trip from Tsawwassen. If you are in Victoria and wish to drive up the east coast of Vancouver Island to Campbell River, it is 225km (140 miles).

### Park and Ride
To combat traffic congestion and pollution from exhaust fumes, a "Park and Ride" system is in place. Large parking lots, owned by BC

## Rules of the Road

**BC buckles up:** The use of vehicle safety belts, front and back seat, are mandatory at all times
**Helmets when riding:** Bicycle helmets or motorcycle helmets are mandatory at all times.
**Speed limits:** The speed limit on the highways is 100 or 110 kph (65 or 70 mph). Limits on rural two-lane highways are 80 or 90 kph (50 or 55 mph). On most urban streets the limit is 50 kph (30 mph). All speed limits are posted in kilometres on signs at the right-hand side of the road.

**Drinking and driving:** It is a criminal offence to operate a motor vehicle, water vessel or aircraft while impaired by alcohol or a drug, or to have more than 80 milligrams of alcohol in 100 mililitres of blood (0.08 percent).It is an offence to refuse to provide a breath or blood sample when a demand is made by a police officer.
**Reporting accidents:** It is usual to report all vehicle accidents to the police, and accidents involving damage or injury must be reported by law.

Transit, are located at various areas throughout metropolitan Vancouver and near some SkyTrain or West Coast Express stations.

### Vehicle Accidents
All visitors should contact their insurers in the event of an accident. Before leaving home, US residents should obtain a "Canadian Non-resident Interprovincial Motor Vehicle Liability Insurance Card" from their insurance company. Other visitors should seek an International Drivers Licence.

### Highway Conditions
For up-to-the-hour reports contact one of the following before setting out on any long journey:
Ministry of Transportation recording, tel: 660-8200, or toll free: 1-900-451-4997.
BC Highway Road Conditions, tel: 299-9000 and extension 7623.

## Transport Mentioned in the Essays

**E&N Viarail:** in "Vancouver Island" essay. See *Regional Trains*.
*Royal Hudson* **steamtrain and optional boat trip:** in "Stanley Park and North Vancouver" and "North to Whistler" essays. Reservations, tel: 688-7246 or 984-5246, toll free: 1-800-663-1500 or 1-800-663-8238.
**Buses to Whistler resort:** in "North to Whistler" essay. Pacific Coach Lines, tel: 662-8074; Perimeter

Transportation, tel: 261-2299.
**Granville Island mini-ferries:** in "West Side Story" essay. Aquabus Ferries Ltd., tel: 689-5858, fax: 251-1468.
**Albion Ferry:** in "East, South, West and Gulf" essay. Enquiries, tel: 660-2421.
*MV Lady Rose* or the *MV Frances Barkley,* working boat adventure to remote locations: in "Vancouver Island" essay. Reservations, tel: (250) 723-8313.
*Queen of the North,* poor man's cruise from Port Hardy to Prince Rupert: mentioned in "Vancouver Island" essay. BC Ferries, tel: (250)-386-3431, toll free: 1-888 223-3779, fax: (250) 388-7754. Reservations are mandatory.
**Charter boats, yachts and dinner cruises from Granville Island and elsewhere:** in "West Side Story" essay. Contact Vancouver Tourism InfoCentre for a complete list, tel: 683-2000.
**Champagne Cruises:** in "West Side Story" essay, #100, 1676 Duranleau Street, Granville Island, tel: 688-6625.
**Starline Tours,** Surrey: in "East, South, West and Gulf" essay. Runs several Fraser River tours, tel: 584-5117, fax: 930-0556.

# Where to Stay

## Choosing Accommodation

Throughout BC a blue "Approved Accommodation" sign is awarded to accommodations that have met basic Ministry of Tourism standards. The term "resort' is used in a rather broad way throughout British Columbia. It can mean anything from budget accommodation in a motel, e.g. AAA Beachside Resort, to a recreation complex, e.g. ABC Golf and Play Awhile Resort, to a whole mountain village with its own mayor, council and many services, e.g. Whistler resort.

Before you leave home, or immediately upon arrival, ask for a copy of the free *BC Accomodation Guide* or *Camping Guide* available from any BC Tourism InfoCentre. It gives details of all properties. The following associations provide accommodations listings throughout British Columbia. Ask them for free promotional materials:
**BC Bed & Breakfast Association,** #101, 1001 West Broadway, Box 593, Vancouver, BC, V6H 4E4, tel: 734-3486.
**Western Canada Bed & Breakfast Association,** 2803 West 4th Avenue, Box 74534, Vancouver, BC, V6K 4P4, tel: 255-9199.
**Hostelling International Canada,** BC Region, #402, 134 Abbott Street, Vancouver, BC, V6B 2K4, tel: 684-7111, toll free: 1-800-661-0020, website: http://www.hihostels.bc.ca
**BC Fishing Resorts & Outfitters Association,** Box 3301, Kamloops, BC, V2C 6B9, tel: (250) 374-6836.
**BC Motels, Campgrounds & Resorts Association,** #209, 3003 St Johns Street, Port Moody, BC, V3H 2C4, tel: 945-7676.

If you want to stay in Vancouver for more than one week, a furnished condominium may be more economical than paying hotel rates. Book properties through **WestWay Accommodation Registry**, tel: 273-8293.

Most hotels offer Corporate, Family Plan and off-season rates. Reservations are usually made in advance with a deposit of the daily room rate to hold the accommodation. When making a reservation you should ask for the cancellation of deposit and refund policy applicable to the establishment. Most hotels accept all major credit cards and will cash traveller's cheques.

**Room tax:** An 8 percent provincial hotel and motel room tax and the 7 percent Goods and Services Tax (GST) is added to the quoted price of rooms. In some cases an additional 2 percent tax is levied by the local municipal government.

## Vancouver

### HOTELS

Greater Vancouver has many hotels in the expensive (**$$$**) category and fewer in the other ranges. Between May and late September, for any category, reservations are mandatory.

#### Near International Airport
**Delta Vancouver Airport Hotel & Marina**, 3500 Cessna Drive, Richmond V7B 1C7, tel: 278-1241 or toll-free 1-800 268-1133, fax: 278-0969. Airport limo service, hotel marina, swimming-pool,, wheelchair access, full service. **$$$**

#### Downtown Vancouver
**Barclay Hotel**, 1348 Robson Street, Vancouver V6E 1C5, tel: 688-8850, fax: 688-2534. A small heritage hotel in the heart of downtown near Stanley Park and English Bay. Parking facilities, restaurant, lounge. European style. **$$**

**Best Western Chateau Granville Hotel**, 1100 Granville Street, Vancouver V6Z ZB6, tel: 669-7070,

toll-free: 1-800 663-0575, fax: 669-4928. Located in the heart of downtown though slightly towards the seedy part, 20 minutes from the airport, five minutes cab ride from cruise ship terminal and convenient to public transport. Comfortable rooms with a city view, underground parking. Wheelchair access. **$$**

**Buchan Hotel**, 1906 Haro Street, Vancouver V6G 1H7, tel: 685-5354, toll free: 1-800-668-6654, fax: 685-5367. One of Vancouver's lovely old apartment-hotels located close to Stanley Park in a residential setting. Quiet, comfortable non-smoking rooms. **$**

## Price Guide

Price in Canadian dollars for a double room per night, excluding breakfast and taxes:

| | |
|---|---|
| **$$$** | Over $230 |
| **$$** | $100–230 |
| **$** | $60–100 |

● Accommodation in the **$$$** range is luxurious, with valet service, swimming-pools, fitness rooms and other amenities. The **$** accommodation is simple, with plain, clean rooms and basic facilities.

**Dominion Hotel**, 210 Abbott Street, (Gastown), Vancouver V6B 2K8, tel: 681-6666. One of Vancouver's oldest historic buildings in the heart of Gastown. The Lamplighter Pub downstairs was the first establishment in Vancouver to acquire a beer licence in 1925 and the first bar to serve ladies in Vancouver. Comfortable rooms, casual atmosphere, good dining, dancing and entertainment. Ski packages. **$**

**Holiday Inn Hotel & Suites – Vancouver Downtown**, 1110 Howe Street, Vancouver V6Z 1R2, tel: 684-2151, toll-free: 1-800 465-4329, fax: 684-4736; website: www.iwg.com.atlific. Comfortable guest rooms and suites for business and vacation travellers. Wheelchair access. Disabled rooms available. Indoor pool. **$$**.

**Hotel Georgia (Crown Plaza Hotel)** (mentioned in the essays section), 801 West Georgia Street, Vancouver V6C 1P7, tel: 682-5566 or toll-free 1-800 663-1111, fax: 682-5579. This is one of Vancouver's most charming old hotels, built in 1927 and consistently renovated. Close to the Vancouver Art Gallery, BC Place Stadium and downtown shopping. Excellent restaurant and pub. Covered parking. Full service. **$$$**

**Hotel Vancouver** (mentioned in the essays section), 900 West Georgia Street, Vancouver V6C 2W6, tel: 684-313, toll-free: 1-800 268-9411, fax: 662-1929. Vancouver's grand old Canadian Pacific (CPR) hotel in the heart of Vancouver. Executive class facilities and meeting rooms. Indoor pool and health club. Full service, wheelchair access. **$$$** (very expensive)

**Kingston Hotel Bed & Breakfast**, 757 Richards Street, Vancouver V6B 3A6, tel: 684-9024, toll free: 1-888-713-3304, fax: 684-9917. European-style hotel with Continental breakfast. Seniors discounts. Close to BC Place Stadium, theatres, restaurants. **$**

**Pan Pacific Hotel Vancouver** (mentioned in the essays section), 300–999 Canada Place, Vancouver V6C 3B5, tel: 662-8111, or toll-free: 1-800 937-1515, fax: 685-8690; website: ww.ppacific@panpacific.hotel.com. One of the most beautiful hotels in Vancouver, located by the spectacular Canada Place Convention Centre and cruise ship docks. The Five Sails Restaurant is an award-winning seafood restaurant. Racquet courts, health club and spa, indoor running track. Outstanding views of the harbour and mountains. **$$$**

**Shato Inn Hotel at Stanley Park**, 1825 Comox Street, Vancouver V6G 1P9, tel: 681-8920. Sleeping and housekeeping units, free indoor parking, two blocks to beach and Stanley Park. Off-season rates. **$**

**Sylvia Hotel**, 1154 Gilford Street, Vancouver V6G 2P6, tel: 681-9321. A gracious old hotel on English Bay, covered parking, restaurant, lounge,

Family Plan, pets. Kitchens available. **$**
**YMCA Hotel/Residence**, 733 Beatty Street, Vancouver, V6B 2M4, tel: 895-5830, toll free: 1-800-663-1424, fax: 681-2550; website: www.ywcavanhotel@bcsympatico.ca. New property for men and women; comfortable. **$**

## MOTELS AND MOTOR INNS

Most motels and motor inns charge moderate or very reasonable rates and are conveniently located on or near major motorways entering the city, or in the suburbs. In Vancouver you will find many motels along Kingsway.

### Near International Airport

**Best Western Abercorn Inn**, 9260 Bridgeport Road, Richmond V6X 1S1, tel: 270-7576,toll free: 1-800 663-0085, fax: 270-0001. Seven minutes from airport; courtesy shuttle service. Twenty minutes from downtown Vancouver. Just off highway 99 linking to US Interstate 5. Twenty minutes from Victoria ferry. European-style country inn. Spacious rooms with jacuzzis. Dining room and lounge. Wheelchair access. **$$**
**Howard Johnson Hotel (Vancouver Airport)**, 9020 Bridgeport Road, Richmond V6X 1S1, tel: 270-6030, toll free:1-800-663-2337. Located between Highway 99, Oak Street Bridge and the airport entrance. Thirty minutes from US border; 10 minutes from downtown Vancouver; six minutes from airport. Tasteful rooms, kitchens, restaurant and lounge. Sauna and outdoor jacuzzi. Free airport transportation. **$$**
**Quality Inn Airport**, 725 Southeast Marine Drive, Vancouver V5X 2T9, tel: 321-6611, toll free: 1-800-663-6715, fax: 327-3570; website: www.qualityinn.com. Free shuttle service to airport. Free parking for extended periods. Comfortable air-conditioned rooms. Restaurant, lounge. Full service, Family Plan, wheelchair access. **$$**
**Stay'n Save Motor Inn – Vancouver Airport**, 10551 St Edwards Drive, Richmond, V6X 3L8, tel: 273-3311,

fax: 273-9522, toll free 1-800-663-0298; website: www.staysave.com. Beauty rest, mattresses, kitchens, 206 units, air conditioned, complimentary coffee, hot tub, free airport shuttle. **$**

### Downtown Vancouver

**Sandman Hotel Vancouver**, 180 West Georgia Street, Vancouver V6B 4P4, tel: 681-2211, toll-free: 1-800 726-3626, fax: 681-8009. Located in downtown Vancouver across from the bus depot. Near shopping and easy access to public transit for sightseeing. Buses to connect with Amtrak and Greyhounds from the US stop here. Comfortable rooms, swimming-pool, restaurants. Discounts for seniors over 55 years. **$$**
**Tropicana Motor Inn**, 1361 Robson Street, Vancouver V6E 1C6, tel: 687-6631, fax: 687-5724. Situated in downtown Vancouver with easy access to shopping and sightseeing. Suites with kitchenettes, free parking. Indoor pool and sauna. **$$**

## BED AND BREAKFAST

Many bed and breakfast inns are located in heritage houses. Most accept children, some are wheelchair accessible and allow pets. Some meals in addition to breakfast may be available. Most take major credit cards and discounts are available for long stays. See *Choosing Accommodation* for a list of Bed and Breakfast BC registries. Additional registries representing B&B homes in Vancouver and area are:
**Beachside Bed and Breakfast Registry**, 4208 Evergreen Avenue, West Vancouver, BC, V7H 1H1, tel: 933-7773, fax: 926-8073.
**Canada-West Accommodations**, PO Box 86607, North Vancouver BC, V7L 4L2, tel: 929-1424.
**Old English Bed and Breakfast Registry**, 1221 Silverwood Crescent, North Vancouver, V7P 1J3, tel: 986-5069, fax: 986-8810.
**Town & Country Bed and Breakfast**, Hotel Accommodation Guide, PO Box 74542 RPO Kitsilano, tel: 731-5942.

## BUDGET ACCOMMODATION

Some BC hostels are members of the International Youth Hostel Federation. Annual membership cards are available from the Canadian Hostelling Association. The cards can be used at any hostel in Canada. Purchase an International Youth Hostel card before you leave home.
**Hostelling International Canada**, BC Region,#402, 134 Abbott Street, Vancouver, BC, V6B 2K4, tel: 684-7111, toll free: 1-800-661-0020.
**Simon Fraser University**, Room 212 McTaggart-Cowan Hall, SFU, Burnaby BC, V5A 1S6, tel: 291-4503. Residences available from May to August. No catering service but meals are available from cafeteria on campus. Kitchen facilities, laundry rooms, TV lounge and parking. Wheelchair access. Twenty kilometres (12 miles) east of downtown. Near public transit.
**UBC Housing**, 5961 Student Union Blvd, Vancouver, tel: 822-1010, fax: 822-1001; website: www,conferences,ubc.ca. Located 16km (10 miles) west of downtown on the UBC campus. Free visitor parking, meals available at SUB across the street. Limited rooms in fall and winter for which reservations are necessary.

## Victoria

### HOTELS

Victoria is popular from May through the end of September. Reservations during this time are mandatory. The high season is September. The *BC Accommodation Guide* has complete listings of all properties.

### Downtown Victoria

**Canadian Pacific Hotels – The Empress** (mentioned in the essays section), 721 Government Street, Victoria V8W 1W5, tel: (250) 384-8111, toll free: 1-800-441-1414, fax: (250) 381-4334. Victoria's grandest old hotel; overlooking Inner Harbour, Parliament Buildings. Across from Royal BC

Museum and US Ferries. Wheel-chair access. **$$$**

**Dashwood Manor**, 1 Cook Street, Victoria V8V 3W6, tel: (250) 385-5517, toll free: 1-800-667-5517, no fax. Heritage tudor 1912 mansion overlooking harbour and Beacon Hill Park. Suites, fully equipped kitchens, laundry. **$$**

**James Bay Inn**, 270 Government Street, Victoria V8V 2L2, tel: (250) 384-7151, toll free: 1-800-836-2649, fax: (250) 385-2311. Historic hotel in oldest residential area of Victoria. European-style guest house. Some shared baths; pub; near downtown and Beacon Hill Park. Off-season rates. **$**

**Queen Victoria Inn**, 655 Douglas Street, Victoria V8V 2P9, tel: (250) 386-1312, fax: (250) 381-4312, e-mail: info@queenvictoriainn. Downtown hotel with family suites, kitchens, penthouses with jacuzzis and fireplaces. Full service; free parking. Near Royal BC Museum and Thunderbird Park. Wheelchair access. **$$**

**Strathcona Hotel**, 919 Douglas Street, Victoria V8W 2C2, tel: (250) 383-7137, toll free: (250) 1-800-663-7476, fax: (250) 383-6893. Old hotel but recently redecorated, well located near Inner Harbour, British pub and restaurant; near tourist attractions. **$**

**Swans Hotel**, 506 Pandora Avenue, Victoria V8W 1N6, tel: (250) 361-3310, toll free: (250)1-800-668-7926, no fax. Located in heritage building on Inner Harbour. Spacious suites; Continental breakfast. **$$**

### *Country Inns: Victoria Area*

**Olde England Inn** (mentioned in conjuction with Anne Hathaway's cottage in essays section), 429 Lampson Street, Victoria V9A 5Y9, tel: 388-4353. A bit of Olde England. Tudor mansion in English Village; Anne Hathaway's Cottage; Shakespeare connections. Units furnished with 17th- and 18th-century antiques. English dining-room. Wheelchair access. **$$**

**Sooke Harbour House** (mentioned in the the essays section), 1528 Whiffen Spit Rd, RR#4, Sooke VOS 1NO, tel: 642-3421. Well-known

hotel outside town with a restaurant worth travelling for. Ocean view units. Antique furnishings. **$$$**

## MOTELS

Most motels are located on Douglas Street north. For budget-minded travellers, motels are usually reasonably priced and conveniently located. Here are some in the downtown Victoria area and outside the city.

### *Victoria Airport*

**Victoria Airport Travelodge**, 2280 Beacon Avenue, Sidney V8L 1X1, tel: (250) 656-1176, toll free: 1-800-578-7878, fax: (250) 656-7344. Near airport and ferries. Some king-size units; pool; licensed dining and pub. Wheelchair access. **$**

### *Downtown Victoria and Area*

**Embassy Motor Inn**, 520 Menzies Street, Victoria V8V 2H4, tel: (250) 382-8161. Quiet location. Sleeping and housekeeping units and suites. Sauna and pool. Close to Inner Harbour, Parliament Buildings and US ferries. Wheelchair access. **$**

**Mount Douglas Park Resort**, 4550 Cordova Bay Road, Victoria V8X

## Price Guide

Price in Canadian dollars for a double room per night, excluding breakfast and taxes:

| | |
|---|---|
| **$$$** | Over $230 |
| **$$** | $100–230 |
| **$** | $60–100 |

● Accommodation in the **$$$** range is luxurious, with valet service, swimming-pools, fitness rooms and other amenities. The **$** accommodation is simple, with plain, clean rooms and basic facilities.

3V5, tel: (250) 658-2171. Surrounded by 203 hectares (500 acres) of parkland. European style; kitchenettes, honeymoon suites; ocean or park views. Jacuzzi, sauna, barbecue, play area. Continental breakfast. Wheelchair access. **$**

**Shamrock Motel**, 675 Superior Street, Victoria V8V 1V1, tel: (250) 385-8768, toll free: 1-800-663-7476, fax: (250) 383-6893. By Beacon Hill Park; family housekeeping units. Near shopping and sightseeing. Off-season rates. **$**

## BED AND BREAKFAST

A registry of the numerous quaint, historial and delightful B&Bs in Victoria and area is available through the **All Seasons Bed & Breakfast Agency**, Box 5511, Station B, Victoria BC V8R 6S4, tel: (250) 595-BEDS.

Here are a few of the many wonderful properties available: **Abigail's Hotel**, 906 McClure Street, Victoria V8V 3E7, tel: (250) 388-5363, toll free: 1-800-561-6565, fax: (250) 388-7787; website: www.abigailshotel.com. Heritage tudor mansion. Adult oriented. Near Inner Harbour and Beacon Hill Park.

**Beaconsfield Inn**, 998 Humboldt Street, Victoria V8V 2Z8, tel: (250) 384-4044, toll free: 1-888-884-4044, fax: (250) 384-4025. Heritage English mansion with elegant rooms. Near Beacon Hill Park and Inner Harbour.

**Crow's Nest**, 71 Linden Avenue, tel: (250) 383-4492. Close to seafront. French spoken.

**Joan Brown's Bed & Breakfast Inn**, 729 Pemberton Road, tel: (250) 592-5929. An elegant mansion dating from 1883.

**Prior House Bed and Breakfast Inn**, 620 St Charles Street, Victoria V8S 3N7, tel: (250) 924-8847. Elegant English mansion near East Inner Harbour. Full breakfast and afternoon tea. Off-season rates, credit cards.

**Ryans Bed and Breakfast**, 224 Superior Street, Victoria V8V 1T3, tel: (250) 389-0012. Heritage home in residential area. Large lounge with piano and harp. Visa, MasterCard.

## BUDGET ACCOMMODATION

**Hostelling International – Victoria**, 516 Yates Street, Victoria V8W 1K8, tel: (250) 385-4511, fax: (250) 385-3232. The Victoria

International Hostel was recently renovated and reopened. It is situated in a turn-of-the-century building accommodating up to 104 persons. Kitchen and laundry facilities, games room, TV room and family rooms. Open daily 7.30am–midnight.

**Selkirk Guest House,** 934 Selkirk Avenue, Victoria BC, V9A 2V1, tel: (250) 389-1213, toll free: 1-800-974-6638, fax: (250) 389-1313. Beautiful historic home on Gorge Waterway. Fifteen minutes by bus to downtown Victoria. Non-smoking. Couples and families welcome.

**University of Victoria,** Housing and Conference Services, Sinclair at Finnerty Road, Box 1700, Victoria V8W 2Y2, tel: (250) 721-8396. Furnished single and twin rooms with shared baths available May to August. Breakfast included. Wheelchair access.

**Victoria YM-YWCA Women's Residence,** 880 Courtney Street, Victoria V8W 1C4, tel: (250) 386-7511. Sleeping units; shared bath. Women only. Near tourist attractions.

## Vancouver Island

### Chemainus
**Laughing Gull Guest House,** 9836 Willow Street, Chemainus, tel: (250) 246-4068, fax: (250) 246-4067. Bed and breakfast home, 2 spacious units. **$–$$**

### Yellow Point/Ladysmith
**Yellow Point Lodge** (mentioned in the essays section), RR3, 4130 Yellow Point Road, Ladysmith, V0R 2E0, tel: (250) 245-7422, no fax. Log lodge, rustic cabins on 72 hectares (178 acres) of oceanfront parkland, adult retreat. **$**

**Inn of the Sea Resort,** 3600 Yellow Point Road, RR3, Ladysmith, V0R 2E0, tel: (250) 245-1011. **$$**

### Nanaimo
**Coast Bastion Inn,** 11 Bastion Street, Nanaimo, V9R 2Z9, tel: (250) 753-6601, toll free: 1-800-663-1144, fax: (250) 753-4155. Dowtown waterfront location,

restraunt, lounge, pub, exercise room. **$$**

### Qualicum Beach
**Qualicum College Inn,** College Road, tel: (250) 752-9262; fax: (250) 752-5144. Historic landmark overlooking ocean, landscaped grounds. Murder mystery packages. **$**

### Courtenay
**Beach House Bed and Breakfast,** 3614 South Island Highway, RR 6, Site 688, Comp 28, Courtenay, V9N 8H9, tel: (250) 338-8990, fax: (250) 338-5651. Oceanfront cedar home, shared baths, pool table, piano, 4 units. **$**

### Campbell River
**Painters Lodge and Fishing Resort,** 1625 MacDonald Road, Box 560, Dept 2, Campbell River, V9W 5C1, (250) 286-1102, toll free: 1-800-663-7090, fax: (250) 598-1361. Famed oceanfront resort, private baths, hot tubs, pool, lounge, adventure tours, fishing guides and equipment. **$$–$$$**

### Parksville
**Tigh-Na-Mara,** 1095 East Island Highway, Parksvile, V9P 2E5, tel: (250) 248-2072, 299-900 and extension 7373, toll free: 1-800-663-7373, fax: (250) 248-4140; website: www.island.net/~tnm. Authentic log cottages and oceanview condos on sandy Rathtrevor Beach. Pools, saunas, forest setting. **$$**

### Ucluelet/Long Beach
**Canadian Princess Resort,** Peninsula Road, Box 939, Ucluelet, V0R 3A0, tel: (250) 726-7771, toll free: 1-800-663-7090, fax: (250) 598-1361. Historic West Coast steamship permanently moored and made into tiny but wonderfully polished state rooms. Whale watching and fishing packages. **$$**

### Tofino/LongBeach
**Hot Springs Lodge,** Hot Springs Cove, Box 200, Tofino,V0R 2Z0, 65 km (40 miles) north of Tofino by water taxi, phone for reservations: (250) 670-1106. Remote facility,

double and queen beds, kitchens, no phones. **$–$$**

**Wickaninnish Inn and Restaurant** (mentioned in the essays section) Osprey Lane at Chesterton Beach, Box 250, Tofino, V0R 2Z0, tel: (250) 725-3100, toll free: 1-800-333-4604, fax: (250) 725-3110. Situated on a rocky promontory overlooking the crashing surf, panoramic ocean views, storm watching, soaker tubs, 46 units. **$$–$$$**

### Port Hardy
**North Shore Inn,** 7370 Market Street, Box 1888, Port Hardy, V0N 2P0, tel: (250) 949-8500, fax: (250) 949-8516. All ocean view units with balconies, fishing charters arranged. Useful for the night before departing on the *Queen of the North.* **$**

## Gulf Islands

Reservations are mandatory for accommodation on the Gulf Islands; phone the **Gulf Island Bed and Breakfast Registry,** tel: (250) 539-5390. Accommodation on most islands is limited. It is also worth contacting the **Tourism Association of Vancouver Island** (which also covers the Gulf Islands), #304, 45 Bastion Square, Victoria, tel: (250) 382-3551, fax: (250) 382-3523. Ask for the *BC Accommodation Guide* and BC Ferries diagrams to determine access points to the islands.

## Whistler Village

The resort town of Whistler has well over 1,000 units including 60 hotels, lodges, B&Bs and condominiums for rent. The Whistler Accommodation Centre reservation agency will find the right priced place for you to stay awhile.

**Whistler Accomodation Centre,** 4227 Village Stroll, Whistler, V0N 1B0, tel: 932-6500, toll free: 1-888-242-7205, fax: 932-3268.

The following agencies will help you find activities, provide maps or locate appropriate accommodation: **Whistler Resort Association,** Box 1400, Whistler, BC, V0N 1B0, tel:

## Camping

About 85 percent of BC is forested, with much of the recreation management handled by the Forest Service. There are six enormous **national parks** and four **national historic park sites** in BC in addition to more than 300 **provincial parks** and 16 **regional parks** operated by the Greater Vancouver Regional District. For BC parks information, ask at any TravelInfo Centre or write to: BC Parks, Parliament Buildings, Victoria BC, V8V 1X5. Remember, some provincial parks are as big as the nation of Switzerland.

There are campsites in most national and provincial parks, maintained by the forestry or parks services. There is a small fee for staying and in some parks your stay may be limited to 7 days.

For camper and recreational vehicle rentals, see *Planning the Trip: Getting There*.

In general **BC Provincial Campgrounds** are as good as or better than private campgrounds. Conact Tourism BC, Sixth Floor, 612 View Street, Victoria BC, or have a pencil handy and tel: 663-6000, (250) 382-2160, toll free: 1-800-663-6000.

For information on private campgrounds, contact **BC Motels, Campgrounds & Resorts Association**, #209, 3003 St Johns Street, Port Moody, BC, V3H 2C4, tel: 945-7676. Ask for listings.

932-4222, from Vancouver toll free: 685-3650, from the US toll free: 1-800-663-8668. This association has information on properties for rent, all sorts of outdoor activities, shopping, golf, river rafting, heliskiing, special events and more. **Whistler Visitor InfoCentre**, 2097 Lake Placid Road, Box 181, Whistler, V0N 1B0, tel: 932-5528, fax: 932-3755. This is your best source for a number of quaint Bed and Breakfast accommodations.

**Canadian Pacific Chateau Whistler Resort** (mentioned in the essays section), Whistler Village, base of Blackcomb Mountain, Whistler, V0N 1B0, tel: 938 8000, toll free from Ontario, Quebec: 1-800-268-9420, from the rest of Canada: 1-800-268-9411, from the USA: 1-800-828-7447. Lavish deluxe resort attracts skiiers and landscape-lovers from all over the world, at all times of the year, to its elegant surroundings. **$$$**
**Whistler Hostel**, PO Box 128, Whistler, BC, V0N 1B0, tel: 932-5492. Reservations recommended; advance deposit required. **$**

## Sunshine Coast

### Gibsons
**Cedars Inn**, 895 Sunshine Highway 101, Box 739, Gibsons V0N 1V0, tel: 886-3008, fax : 886-3046. Five km (3 miles) north of Langdale ferry terminal on Highway 101. Queen beds, air-conditioned, pool, pub, wheelchair access. **$**

### Sechelt
**Driftwood Inn**, 5454 Trail Avenue, Box 829, Sechelt V0N 3A0, tel: 885-5811, fax: 885-5836. Near beach, housekeeping and sleeping units, restaurant. Swimming, fishing, golf, horseback riding. **$**

### Powell River
**Beach Gardens Resort Hotel**, 7074 Westminster Avenue, Powell River, V8A 1C5, tel: 485-6267, toll free: 1-800-663-7070, fax: 485-2343. Waterfront units overlooking Malaspina Strait; cottages too. Tennis, pool, sauna. **$**

# Where to Eat

## Vancouver

Vancouver's multicultural nature is well represented in almost 2,000 restaurants. Many chefs are internationally experienced. Listed here are a few restaurants, chosen for their popularity, reputation or interesting fare.

### *Restaurants With a View*
**Cloud 9 Revolving Restaurant**, 1400 Robson Street, the 42nd floor of the Empire Landmark Hotel, tel: 687 0511. All credit cards. **$$$**
**Top of Vancouver**, 555 West Hastings Street, tel: 669-2220. Dining atop the Harbour Centre. Seafood and Sunday buffet. All credit cards. **$$$**
**Grouse Nest Restaurant**, 6400 Nancy Greene Way, North Vancouver, tel: 984-0661. Elegant dining atop Grouse Mountain. **$$**
**Horizons on Burnaby Mountain**, 100 Centennial Way, Burnaby, tel: 299-1155. Excellent seafood. **$$**
**The Roof Restaurant and Lounge**, 900 West Georgia Street, tel: 684-3131. In the Hotel Vancouver. Formal dining. Ballroom dancing. **$$$**

### *Outdoor Dining*
**Park Royal Hotel**, Tudor Room, 540 Clyde Avenue, West Vancouver, tel: 926-5511. Luxury inn. All credit cards. **$$$**
**Athene's**, 3618 West Broadway, tel: 731-4135. MasterCard, Visa, Amex. **$**
**Bridges Restaurant**, 1696 Duranleau Street, Granville Island, tel: 687-4400. **$$**

### *Seafood With a Sea View*
**Ship of the Seven Seas**, anchored at the foot of Lonsdale, North

Vancouver, next to the SeaBus, tel: 987-3344. Sparkly nightime view, fresh fish buffet, all-you-can-eat. **$$**

**The Prow Restaurant**, #100, 999 Canada Place, tel: 684-1339. Excellent view of the city from water level, fresh fish a specialty. **$$**

**The Cannery Seafood Restaurant**, 2205 Commissioner Street, tel: 254-9606. Cosy, with a harbour view, quickly prepared *à la carte* seafood specialities. **$$**

**Salmon House on the Hill**, 2229

## Price Guide

Restaurant prices are in Canadian dollars, based on a three-course meal per person, excluding alcohol, taxes and tips.

| | |
|---|---|
| **$$$** | Over $20 |
| **$$** | $10–20 |
| **$** | $10 or less |

Folkestone Way, West Vancouver, tel: 926-3212; fax: 926-8539. Excellent seafood; panoramic view of downtown and ships in the harbour. MasterCard, Visa, Amex. **$$**

**Monk McQueens Fresh Seafood & Oyster Bar**, 601 Stamps Landing, tel: 877-1351. Mountains and the sea along with fun and fish. **$$**

### *Dining in the Parks*

**The Prospect Point Café**, 2099 Beach Avenue, Prospect Point, Stanley Park, tel: 669 2737. Romantic harbour view. Dine on the deck in nice weather. **$$**

**The Teahouse Restaurant**, Ferguson Point, Stanley Park, tel: 669-3281. Quiet, romantic dining in the park. **$$**

**Seasons in the Park**, Cambie Street at 33rd Avenue, tel: 874-8008. Fine dining in Queen Elizabeth Park. City view. **$$**

### *Late Night Fill-up*

**Fresgo Inn**, 1138 Davie Street, tel: 689-1332. Large servings at reasonable prices. Open: Monday–Saturday 8am–3am, Sundays and holidays 9am–midnight. **$$**

**The Bread Garden**, 1880 West First Avenue, tel: 738-6684; 812 Bute Street, tel: 688-3213. Deli food; good breakfasts; muffins and cakes. Open: 24 hours. **$–$$**

### *Gastown*

**Umberto Al Porto Restaurant**, 321 Water Street, tel: 683-8376. Exquisite Italian cuisine. **$$$**

**Old Spaghetti Factory**, 53 Water Street, tel: 684-1288. Informal, turn-of-the-century atmosphere. Family oriented. Reserve for parties over six. MasterCard, Visa, Amex. **$**

### *West End*

**English Bay Cafe**, 1795 Beach Avenue, tel: 669-2225. Dine on the Bay. Excellent food, good reputation. **$$**

**Fogg 'n' Suds Restaurant Robson**, 202–1323 Robson Street, tel: 683-2337. Informal pub fare. No reservations necessary. **$**

### *Granville Island/False Creek*

**Mulvaney's**, 9 Creek House, Johnston Street, Granville Island, tel: 685-6571. Cajun-style food. **$$**

### *Kitsilano/Fourth Avenue*

**Las Margaritas Restaurante y Cantina**, 1999 West 4th Avenue, tel: 734-7717. Mexican food and a fiesta atmosphere. **$**

**Milestones – 4th Avenue**, 2966 West 4th avenue, tel: 291-7393. California style fresh food. **$**

## Dining Notes

● The standard tip is 15 percent or more based on the cost of the food and beverages before taxes.

● A 10 percent sales tax is added to alcohol and the GST of 7 percent is applied to the cost of meals.

● Most restaurants recommend reservations. As a courtesy, if you are unable to keep the reservation or will arrive late, please phone the restaurant so your table can be given to other diners.

## *Asian Cuisines*

### Chinese

**Pink Pearl Chinese Seafood**, 1132 East Hastings Street, tel: 253-4316. *Dim sum*; Cantonese and Szechuan cuisine. **$$**.

**Ming's Restaurant**, 147 East Pender Street, tel: 683-4722. Excellent *dim sum* served 10am–2pm. Credit cards. **$**

**Imperial Chinese Seafood Restaurant**, 355 Burrard Street, tel: 688-8191. Fine Cantonese-style food with a beautiful view. **$$$**

### Indian

**Heaven & Earth India Curry House**, 1754 West 4th Avenue, tel: 732-5313. Curries and sitar music. **$$–$$$**

### Japanese

**Kobe Japanese Steak House**, 1042 Alberni Street, tel: 684-2451. Hibachi-style cooking. **$$–$$$**

**Naniwa-Ya Japanese Seafood Restaurant**, 745 Thurlow Street, tel: 681-7307. Good Japanese fare in a simple setting. **$$**

**Taiko International Noodle Restaurant-Parkhill Hotel**, 1160 Davie Street, tel: 685-1311. Lots of noodles for filling up. **$**

### Thai, Vietnamese, Cambodian

**Thai House Restaurant**, 1116 Robson Street, tel: 683-3383; 1766 West Seventh Avenue, tel: 737-0088; 129–4940 No. 3 Road, Richmond, tel: 278-7373. Bangkok trained chefs. **$**

**Phnom Penh Restaurant**, 244 East Georgia Street, tel: 682-5777. Authentic Vietnamese atmosphere. **$**

**Seoul House Garden Korean Restaurant**, 36 East Broadway, tel: 874-4131. Japanese and Korean food; tatami rooms. Reserve for parties over six. **$**

### *First Nations Flavours*

**Liliget Feast House**, 1724 Davie Street, tel: 681-7044. First Nations owners, specialises in First Peoples foods adapted to modern tastes. **$$**

**hiwus Feasthouse**, atop Grouse Mountain, 6400 Nancy Greene Way, North Vancouver, tel: 980-9311. First Peoples longhouse dining with

## The Whistler Eating Experince

● **Après-ski or Anytime:** Bistros, eateries, coffee houses and pubs are scattered throughout Whistler village, all within walking distance of the two entrances to the ski lifts. Village food is considered healthy cuisine, and ranges from good to excellent.

● **Lunch on a Glacier:** From an airport near Whistler, take off for the ultimate experience, landing on a glacier for a sumptuous lunch. Expensive (**$$$**) but worth it. Contact **Alpine Adventure Tours**, Squamish, tel: 683-02209, 898-9016.

traditional native dancers performing after dinner. **$$–$$$**

### French
**Hermitage Restaurant**, 115–1025 Robson Street, tel: 689-3237. Lovely outdoor patio. **$$$**

### Greek
**Greek Characters Restaurant**, #1 Alexander Street, tel: 681-6581. Greek food with flair. **$$**

### Italian
**Bacchus Ristorante & Lounge**, 845 Hornby Street at the Wedgewood Hotel, tel: 608-5319. Romantic European setting. **$$$**
**La Piazza Dario's Ristorante**, 3075 Slocan Street (at the Italian Cultural Centre), tel: 430-2195. Authentic Italian cuisine. **$$**

### Vegetarian
**Bodhi Vegetarian Cuisine**, 5701 Granville, tel: 261-3388; fax: 266-6661. Casual. Buddhist vegetarian food. **$**
**Naam Restaurant**, 2724 West Fourth Avenue, tel: 738-7151. Established vegetarian restaurant with wood fireplace, live music at lunch and dinner. Licensed. Open: 24 hours. **$**

### West Coast Cuisine
**Raincity Grill**, 1193 Denman Street, tel: 685-7337. Excellent chefs prepare evolving West Coast style cuisine and serve with fine local wines. **$$$**

## Victoria

### Afternoon Tea
**The Olde England Inn**, 429 Lampson Street, tel: (250) 388-2831. Tudor setting for taking a full afternoon tea.
**James Bay Tearoom**, 311 Menzies Street, tel: (250) 382-8282. Traditional resting place for sipping tea and eating cakes.

### British
**The Elephant and Castle**, Government and View street, tel: 383-5858, steak and kidney pie, hearty soups, seafood and traditional desserts. **$**
**The Sticky Wicket Pub & Restaurant**, 919 Douglas Street in the Strathcona Hotel, tel: (250) 383-7137. Victoria-era setting for English pub fare and family dining. **$**

## Price Guide

Restaurant prices are in Canadian dollars, based on a three-course meal per person, excluding alcohol, taxes and tips.

| | |
|---|---|
| **$$$** | Over $20 |
| **$$** | $10–20 |
| **$** | $10 or less |

### Fish n' Chips
**Haultain Fish and Chips**, 1127 Haultain, tel: (250) 383-8332. Fresh fish, clam strips, prawns and calamari plus a warm welcome. **$**

### Greek
**Periklis**, 531 Yates Street, tel: (250) 386-3313. Relaxed atmosphere, belly dancers on the weekends, taverna-style dining. **$**

### Indian
**Taj Mahal Restaurant**, 679 Herald Street, tel: (250) 383-4662. Tandoori, tikka and curries. **$$**
**Spice Jammer Restaurant**, 852 Fort Street downtown, tel: (250) 480-1055. Spices from warm to fiery; tandoori ovens. **$**

### Japanese
**Tomoe Japanese Restaurant**, 726 Johnston Street, a short walk from the Inner Harbour, tel: (250) 381-0223. Shogun dinners for two in tatami mat rooms. **$$**

### Mexican
**Cafe Mexico**, in Market Square, tel: (250) 386-1425. Adobe-style interior and sizzling *fajitas*. **$**

### Outdoor Dining
**Wharfside**, 1208 Wharf Street, tel: (250) 360-1808. Indoor and outdoor balconies, stunning views and excellent fresh seafood, wines and local draught beers. **$$**

### Seafood
**Blue Crab Bar & Grill**, 146 Kingston Street overlooking the harbour, tel: 480-1999. Everything guaranteed fresh, and creative service makes it the best. **$$**
**Six Mile Pub**, 494 Island Highway. A great excuse for a 15-minute drive. Established in 1855, its the place for pub fare in a fireside room. Try the fresh herbs. **$–$$**
**Spinnakers Brewpub Restaurant**, 308 Catherine Street, tel: (250) 386-BREW. Taproom with pub fare and West Coast cuisines. **$$**

### West Coast Cuisine
**McMorrans Beachside Restaurant**, 5109 Cordova Bay Road, tel: 658-5527. Stormy days are best at this split level restaurant with West Coast munchies. **$**

### Countryside Inn
**Sooke House**, 1528 Whiffen Spit Rd, RR#4 Sooke, V0S 1N0, tel: 642-3421. Worth the trip out of town to Sooke Harbour. Known for its country-fresh ingredients and innovative recipes. **$$$**

# Attractions

**Vancouver**

## TOP DOZEN ATTRACTIONS

### Stanley Park
At the foot of Georgia Street, Stanley Park incorporates the **Vancouver Aquarium**, tel: 268-9000, a 1,000-acre forested park, outdoor totem poles, stops of interest, picnic areas, the SeaWall for biking or walking, beaches and nature. Children will enjoy the **petting zoo** and a ride on the **miniature railway**, tel: 257-8400, or the heated **Second Beach pool**. In addition to an exhibit of aquatic wildlife, the Vancouver Aquarium includes an Arctic Canada exhibit featuring Beluga whales and an Amazon jungle gallery with rare plants, birds and monkeys. Aquarium website: http://www.vancouver-aquarium.org Also in the park is **Stanley Park Horse Drawn Tours**, 1-hour tours of Stanley Park, tel: 681-5115. No reservation required. Website: http://www.stanleyparktours.com.

### Granville Island
Located on Duranleau and Johnson streets, Granville Island, tel: 666-5784, features a **Public Market**, restaurants, art studios, glass makers and craft vendors as well as theatres and continuous street entertainment. Two popular stops are **Kids World** and the **Granville Island Brewing Co. Ltd**; tel: 687-2739 for tours of the microbrewery. Visit the **Granville Island Sport Fishing Museum**, 1502 Duranleau Street, tel: 683-1939; website: http://www.netminder.com/gisfm. The best way to arrive is via the little blue electric ferries, **False Creek Ferries**, tel: 684-7781.

### Canada Place and IMAX
Canada Place, located at the foot of Burrard Street, 999 Canada Place, is an impressive complex, resembling an enormous ship with billowing sails, housing the **CN IMAX theatre**, tel: 682-2384, Vancouver Trade and Convention Centre, a cruise ship docking terminal, the Vancouver Board of Trade, the World Trade Centre, restaurants, and the **Pan Pacific Hotel**. The theatre (cinema) presents a rich odyssey of 2- and 3-dimensional films on a huge screen.

### Gastown
Gastown is along Water Street, and features the **Gastown Steam Clock** powered entirely by waste steam, on the corner of Cambie and Water streets. Gastown is an historic area of shops and restaurants ending at the amusing **statue of Gassy Jack**.

### The Lookout
The Lookout at **Harbour Centre**, 555 West Hastings, tel: 689-0421, offers 360° views of the Lower Mainland whatever the weather. Accessible by glass SkyLift elevators, tickets are valid all Many visitors come back again f look at Vancouver by night. Website: http://www.harbour-centre-tower.com.

### Chinatown
This district is along East and West Pender streets, extending to the **Dr Sun Yat-Sen Classical Chinese Garden**, 578 Carrall Street, tel: 689-7133, 662-3207, the only formal Ming Dynasty Chinese scholar's garden outside China. Garden website: http://www.discovervancouver.com/su Chinatown also features an active Asian community market area.The new **Chinese Cultural Centre**, 50 East Pender, tel: 687-0729, and its art exhibits are open to the public. On Fridays and Saturday evenings vendors descend for a special street market session.

### Science World
Science World and the OMNIMAX **theatre**, 1455 Quebec Street, tel: 268-6363, together in one building feature a hands-on exhibit centre exploring themes of biology, physics and natural history. OMNIMAX has one of the world's largest dome screens. Website: http://www.scienceworld.bc.ca

### Totem Museum and Garden
**UBC Museum of Anthropology** (6393 NW Marine Drive, tel: 822-3825; Website: http://www.moa.ubc.ca) and nearby **Nitobe Memorial Gardens** combine an impressive collection of Northwest Coast First Nations art and totem poles in a dramatic building with an adjacent authentic Japan-

## Vancouver & Area: What's Up

Begin your trip to Vancouver with a stop at the **Vancouver Travel InfoCentre**, Plaza Level, 200 Burrard Street, tel: 683-2000, fax: 682-6839. For a quick update on what's happening use your telephone. Dial the following basic number and add any of these extensions for up-to-the-minute information.

| | | | |
|---|---|---|---|
| Basic number: 299-9000 | | 3210 | Van Aquarium |
| 2233 | BC Transit | 5055 | Bloedel Conservatory |
| 3232 | Festivals | 6500 | Burnaby Village |
| 3213 | IMAX theatre | 6825 | Greater Van Zoo |
| 4431 | Van Museum | 7722 | Gulf Cannery |
| 2212 | Maritime Museum | 7191 | Minter Garden |
| 3214 | Planetarium | 9666 | Botanical Gardens |
| 2626 | Harbour Centre | 7194 | VanDusen Garden |
| 3211 | Science World | 8047 | Lynn Canyon |
| 3825 | MOA | | |

...anquillity and
...n to explore
...and see the
...village.

### QE Park and Conservatory
**Queen Elizabeth Park Quarry Gardens**, the **hillside arboretum** and the **Bloedel Floral Conservatory**, 33rd Avenue and Cambie, tel: 257-8570, combine a converted gravel quarry, a show garden, a city overlook and a triodetic dome filled with tropical plants and maccaws.

### Vanier Museum Complex
The complex of museums at **Vanier Park**, 1100 Chestnut Street, includes the **H. R. MacMillan Planetarium** and the **Pacific Space Centre,** tel: 738-STAR, along with the **Vancouver Museum** (tel: 736-3656; website: http://www.vanmuseum.bc.ca) and the **Vancouver Maritime Museum**, 1905 Ogden Avenue, tel: 257-8300, website at http://www.vmm.bc.ca. The planetarium features programmes on astronomy and space science with special children's presentations. The museum covers First People in Vancouver as well as its early history and the Maritime Museum houses the historic *St. Roch*, first boat to circumnavigate the legendary Northwest Passage (yes, it was icebound for a year) and the horn of South America. Additionally, the small domed building beside the museum/planetarium complex is the **Gordon Macmillan Southam Observatory**, tel: 738-2855, offering free star gazing on rare cloudless nights. Always phone ahead to check if it will be open. Behind the observatory are the **Vancouver City Archives**, tel: 736-8561, with free displays of photographs of Vancouver's early history.

### Harbour Tours
Vancouver Harbour Tours, #1, north foot of Denman Street, tel: 688-7246, 1-800-663-1500, offers 75-minute fully narrated tours of the working Port of Vancouver aboard the paddlewheeler *MPV Constitution*. Also offers Indian Arm luncheon cruises or the boat portion of the boat/train daytrip aboard the Royal Hudson Steamtrain.

### Botanical Garden
**VanDusen Botanical Garden** and oak garden contains a wide variety of ornamental plants skilfully arranged into sub-gardens, displayed among lakes and mountain vistas. It features a popular Elizabethan-style maze hedge. Website: http://www.hedgerows.com/vandusen

## MORE ATTRACTIONS IN VANCOUVER
**Vancouver Art Gallery**, 750 Hornby street, tel: 682-4668; website: http://www.vanartgallery.bc.ca, located in a splendid heritage building, has a permanent Emily Carr exhibition along with important visiting paintings, sculptures and masks.
**Vancouver Police Centennial Museum,** 240 E. Cordova Street, one block east of Main Street, tel: 665-3346, has its claim to fame as the place actor Errol Flynn lay after his untimely death, and a weapons display along with confiscated contraband.
**Hotel Vancouver, Cathedral Place,** Georgia and Hornby streets and the **Canadian Craft Museum,** 639 Hornby Street, tel: 687-8266, are showcase buildings. Start with the tourist sport of lobby-walking through the hotel, then cross the street and visit the showcases of crafty excellence. The **Museum Shop** is Vancouver's best outlet for one-of-a-kind Canadian crafts.
**Vancouver Port Public Viewing Centre,** 1300 Stewart, tel: 666-6129, arranges free narrated tours of the port loading and docking facilities.
**BC Place Stadium** and **BC Sports Hall of Fame & Museum** on Beatty Street at the foot of Robson Street, tel: 687-5520, tickets to events, 280-4444, or 299-9000 and extension 4255, both stand near a tribute to **Terry Fox**, a Canadian hero who raised money to fight cancer. The massive air-supported domed stadium hosts major sporting events, consumer shows and concerts. The athletes' museum is interactive and features a tribute to Roger Bannister and the Four-Minute Mile.
**Old Hastings Mill Store Museum,** located at Jericho Park, 1575 Alma Street, tel: 734-1212, 263-4097, houses a collection of artefacts and "junque" from early Vancouver. Admission: donation.
**Forest Alliance of British Columbia Information Centre,** 1055 Dunsmuir Street, tel: 685-7507, is a great place to learn about wood, how much of it people use, how the forest is harvested and what steps are in place to protect it. Website: http://www.forest,org.
**University of British Columbia**, Canada's third largest university, is on Point Grey Road, tel: 822-2211, and the **UBC Botanical Garden**, 6804 SW Marine Drive, tel: 822-4186, one of the oldest in Canada, pays tribute to Asian plants and has a native plant garden. Garden website: http:///www.hedgerows.com. The university hides a scientific surprise open to all adventurers. Home to a particle accelerator, a **cyclotron**, producing muons and pions, the TRIUMF **Meson Facility,** 4004 Westbrook Mall, tel: 222-1047, has free 90-minute tours twice daily in summer, twice weekly in winter.

## North Shore

### TOP TEN ATTRACTIONS
### Capilano Suspension Bridge
This bridge, at 3735 Capilano Road, North Vancouver, tel: 985-74747, is the oldest tourist attraction in Vancouver. A gently swaying pedestrian bridge straddles a deep canyon amongst giant evergreen. Its restaurant and giftshop are popular. Website: http://www.capbridge.com.

### Peak of Vancouver
**Grouse Mountain Skyride**, top of Capilano Road, North Vancouver, tel: 984-0661, takes visitors to a plethora of activities starting with a gondola ride up the mountain,

followed by an optional theatre presentation, a mountain-top stroll with spectacular views and an optional **helicopter ride**, and ending with an optional dinner at the First Nations **híwus Feast House** and traditional button blanket dancing.

### Fish, Park and Canyon
**Capilano Fish Hatchery**, off Capilano Road, North Vancouver, tel: 666-1790, features the marvels of a salmon's life for free, along with a walk in the rainforest at the adjoining **Capilano River Regional Park**. Up Capilano Road a bit is the **Cleveland Dam**, tel: 987-1411, and its views of the Capilano Canyon from the water-shed area.

### Train/Boat Day Trip
The **Royal Hudson Steamtrain** day excursion, BC Rail Station, North Vancouver, reservations tel: 261-5100 or 631-3500, features a whistle-blowing, steam-chugging, clickety-clacking, rollicking good time aboard a 1939 steam engine that once carried King George and Queen Elizabeth. The train steams up scenic Howe Sound to Squamish and back. Or you may take a boat back.

### Suspension Bridge 2
**Lynn Canyon Ecology Centre** and **Lynn Canyon Suspension Bridge**, 3663 Park Road, North Vancouver, tel: 981-3154, 432-6350, are an informal environmental information hand-out centre and a free swaying suspension bridge over a deep gorge leading to a pleasant walk in the rainforest.

### Walled Garden
**Park & Tilford Gardens**, #440-333 Brooksbank Avenue, North Vancouver, tel: 984-8200, comprise a free demonstration garden with an exceptional Rose Garden, herb garden and hanging basket garden, all near muffin shops and coffee houses.

### Rainforest Walk
**Seymour Demonstration Forest and Vancouver Watershed**, over the Second Narrows bridge to the third exit (Lillooet Road) and follow the gravel road to the forest, tel: 987-1273, offers free tours and educational programmes or just walks. A 5,200-hectare (13,000-acre) reserve, its trails combine a gentle stroll through mixed age conifer forests with stops of interest illustrating how a multiple-use forest is managed.

### Petting Zoo
**Maplewood Farm** for kids, 405 Seymour River Place, North Vancouver, tel: 929-5610, is a hands-on petting zoo with billy goats, rabbits and sheep for children to touch and learn. Website: http://www.maplwoodfarm.bc.ca.

### Public Market
**Lonsdale Quay**, 123 Carrie Cates Court, North Vancouver, tel: 986-6111, is a public market, all delicious and fresh, with restaurants including one serving bubble-and-squeak, and a friendly

## Organised Sightseeing Tours

### VANCOUVER
Several companies offer unique transportation and fun ways to take in several of Vancouver's local attractions in a short time.

#### Land Tours
**Early Motion Tours Ltd.**, #1, 1380 Thurlow Street, tel: 687.5188. Personalised city tours in classic cars.
**Olde Tyme Carriage Rides**, Gastown Steam Clock or Canada Place, tel: 329-8611.
**Gray Line of Vancouver**, tel: 879-1105. Narrated coach tours, one- and half-day.
**Landsea Tours**, tel: 254-8968. Narrated small coach tours.
**Vancouver Trolley Company**, tel: 451-5581; website: http://www.vancouvertrolley.com. Day pass on red-trolley bus.
**West Coast City and Nature Sightseeing**, tel: 451-1600. Narrated small coach tours.

**Town Tours**, tel: 278-5251. Narrated small coach tours of Victoria and Vancouver.
**Vance Tours**, tel: 941-5660. Three daily narrated small coach city tours of Vancouver.
**Black Top and Checker Cabs**, tel: 731-1111 or 681-2181. Checker Cabs or Limo Service.
**Star Limousine**, tel: 488-0900. Night club tours by Rolls Royce, Lincoln or Cadillac.

#### Water Tours
**Starline Tours**, tel: 522-3506. Departing daily from New Westminster and Bridgepoint, trips up and down the Fraser River.
**Champagne Cruises**, tel: 688-6625. Sunset dinner cruise. Fishing and diving trips aboard luxury yachts.
**Harbour Cruises Ltd**, #1, North foot of Denman, tel: 687-9558. Several departures daily; narrated tours of the Port of Vancouver, lunch cruises of Indian Arm. Boat/train day-trip combinations.

### VICTORIA
#### Land Tours
**Gray Line of Victoria**, tel: (250) 388-5248. Narrated coach tours.
**Royal Blue Line Motor Tours**, tel: (250) 360-2249. Narrated tours.
**Tally Ho Horse Drawn Tours**, tel: (250) 383-2207. Well appointed horses and drivers.
**Old Cemeteries Society**, tel: 598-8870. Regularly scheduled quality tours, interesting history tales.
**Victoria Heritage Walking Tours**, tel: (250) 388-0205. Informative, fascinating guide.

#### Water Tours
For boat tours and whale-watching day-tours, cross the street from the Empress Hotel and descend the stairs to the marina. All tour boat companies operate out of an office there.

floor of shopping outlets. The preferred method of arrival is via the public transit **Seabus**, tel 521-0400. It docks alongside the market.

### By the Sea
**Ambleside Beach**, foot of 15th Avenue in West Vancouver, tel: 987-4488, and the **West Vancouver Centennial Seawall Promenade**, 2400 block Marine Drive at Dundarave Pier, are both popular seaside walks. Ambleside "beach for people" features a skateboard bowl plus there's a special "dogs-only beach", probably the only one of its kind in the world (retrievers love it). The promenade meanders for 2 km (1¼ miles) along the seafront. Restaurants and coffee houses nearby.

## Vancouver Outskirts

### TOP EIGHT ATTRACTIONS
#### Heritage Village: Burnaby
**Burnaby Heritage Village & Carousel**, 6501 Deer Lake Avenue, Burnaby, off Highway 1, tel: 293-6500, features historically costumed animators actively working in a restored village circa 1890s through 1925, along with a 1912 musical carousel. Website: http://www.burnabyparksrec.org.

#### Forest Awareness: Maple Ridge
**UBC Research Forest**, travel 8 km (5 miles) north of Highway 7 (Lougheed Highway) on 232nd Street, and **Pelton Reforestation Ltd**, 12930–203 Street, tel: 465-5411, are both in Maple Ridge, a suburb 50-minutes east of Vancouver. Created to do research work in forest ecology, UBC runs an integrated resource and watershed management facility. There are a number of well maintained trails through the rainforest. To visit Pelton's reforestation centre, the largest in North America (perhaps in the world), growing hundreds of millions of trees for new forests, phone for a visitor appointment.

#### Day Adventure: New West
**Irving House Historic Centre**, 302

Royal Avenue, corner of Merrivale, tel: 521-7656 or 527-4640, and the nearby **New Westminster Museum** showcase respectively the 14-room home of riverboat pioneer Captain Irving and the fascinating history of BC's first capital city.

Visitors like to combine these museums with a stopover at **Westminster Quay Public Market**, 810 Quayside, New Westminster, tel: 520-3881, for a fresh lunch; a visit to an authentic **Russian submarine**; then step aboard the historic **Samson V**, tel:521-7656, a permanently moored sternwheeler that once picked up snags along the Fraser River. Its Also fun to go on a **Paddlewheeler River Adventure**, in front of the market, tel: 5525-4465. **Starline Tours**, tel: 522-3506, depart daily from New Westminster and Bridgepoint for trips up and down the Fraser River, and in March run sea-lion watching tours.

#### Fur Trader Days: Fort Langley
**Fort Langley National Historic Site** and the adjoining village, 47 km (29 miles) east on Highway 1, tel: 513-4777, is a log palisade, preserved 1858 home of the HBC fur trading post, and a buzzing hive of activity with historic animators to explain the site. History buffs will love the opportunity to welcome the fur brigade as it was done in the 1800s, only recreated on the first weekend in August.

#### Zoo: Aldergrove
**Greater Vancouver Zoological Centre**, 5048, 264th Street, Aldergrove, tel: 856-6825, with over 840 animals and 115 species is a popular spot with families who like elephants, rhinos, tigers and baby animals. Bring a picnic and enjoy the petting zoo too.

#### Fish From the Sea: Richmond
**Steveston Fishing Village**, tiny **Steveston Museum**, 3811 Moncton Road, tel: 271-06868, and the **Gulf of Georgia Cannery National Historic Site**, 12138, 4th Avenue, tel: 664-9009, are grouped together in Richmond, an active

village where today's commercial fishing boats come to dock. Its seaside restaurants are the place to eat the freshest fish 'n'chips, and view an historic salmon cannery and its turbulent history.

#### Historic Mining: Britannia Beach
The **BC Museum of Mining National Historic Site**, on Highway 99, 52 km (38 miles) north of Horsehoe Bay, Britannia Beach, tel: 688-8735, is an historic copper mine featuring a ride on an underground train and the accoutrements of a hard rock mine. Nearby **Porteau Cove** offers beachfront picnicing, camping and for scuba divers an underwater wreck.

#### Major Show Garden: Bridal Falls
**Minter Gardens**, Highway 1, 90 minutes east of Vancouver at Bridal Falls, exit 135, tel: 1-800-661-3919, is a beautiful, lush 11-hectare (27-acre) garden of dazzling designs, topiary, carpet bedding, a maze garden, restaurants and a plant shop, all set against the magnificence of Mount Cheam.

## Victoria

### What's Up
To access Victoria via BC Ferries see *Getting Around: BC Ferries*. Begin your trip to Victoria with a stop at the **Victoria InfoCentre**, 812 Wharf Street on the Inner Harbour, tel: (250) 953-2033, fax (250) 382-6539, reservations: (250) 953-2022, toll free: 1-800-663-3883.

### TOP TEN ATTRACTIONS
#### The RBCM
The **Royal British Columbia Museum**, 675 Belleville Street, next to the Legislative Buildings, across from the bus depot and Empress Hotel, tel: (250) 387-3014, and **Helmcken House** are side by side.

The RBCM is a highly regarded museum with life-sized vignettes of natural history, a large First Nations exhibit, totem poles and argillite sculptures, a material found only on the Queen Charlotte Islands. It's an outstanding museum with life-like

## Whistler Attractions

● **What's Up**
To discover all the activities in Whistler, drop in (or write to) **Whistler Travel InfoCentre**, 2097 Lake Placid Road (Box 181), Whistler, BC, V0N 1B0, tel: 932-5528, fax: 932-3755. Also for Whistler information, tel: 932-3434, 664-5614, toll free: 1-800-766-0449, website: www.whistler-blackcomb.com.

● **Village Walk**
The favourite attractions in Whistler besides the village itself are its shops and eateries; skiing and snowboarding facilities, and snowmobile areas in the winter; **Blackcomb and Whistler mountains**; and year-round sports activities including the famous bone-crushing bike ride down the mountain. There are numerous street festivals year round. In summer visitors can ride the gondolas up the mountains.

● **Squamish**
For **sawmill tours** and **woodfibre plant tours**, Weldwood of Canada Sustainable Forests, tel: 892-9766; or for free mill tours, tel: 892-6623.

displays of early life in BC. Travel to the bottom of the ocean, stroll through a coastal rainforest, or walk down a street of the 1920s. This museum collects, researches, preserves, stores and exhibits objects of human and natural history.
    Tour the adjoining **Thunderbird Park** and the first doctor's home.

*Legislative Tours*
**BC (Provincial) Legislative Buildings**, 501 Belleville, called "parliament," overlooking the Inner Harbour, tel: (250) 387-3046 or (250) 387-0952, were once called the Birdcages. Designed by Francis Rattenbury, free tours of the marbled and domed interior cover the Diamond Jubilee Window and the Legislative Chambers.

*Coal Baron's Castle*
**Craigdorroch Castle**, 1050 Joan Crescent, tel: (250) 592-5323, **Government House Gardens**, 1401 Rockland Avenue, tel: 387-2080, and the **Art Gallery of Greater Victoria**, 1040 Moss Street, tel: (250) 384-4104, are all within a few blocks. The castle, home of the Dunsmuir coal barons, has ongoing guided tours; the gardens are attached to the home of the lieutenant-governor, representative of the Britsh Crown, and open as a courtesy to the public; the Art Gallery features an authentic Shinto

Shrine among other works.
*Afternoon Tea*
**CP Empress Hotel**, 721 Government Street, Inner Harbour, tel: (250) 384-8111, is popular for the tourist sport of lobby-walking as well as its very expensive afternoon tea for which reservations are required.

*Inner Harbour Walk*
The Inner Harbour has a cluster of attractions including the **Pacific Undersea Gardens,** 490 Belleville Street, tel: (250) 382-5717, **Royal London Wax Museum**, 470 Belleville Street: tel, (250) 388-4461, **Miniature World**, 649 Humboldt Street inside the Empress Hotel, tel: (250) 385-9731, and **Crystal Garden**, behind the Empress Hotel, tel: (250) 381-1213. Street musicians perform along the waterside, octopi and salmon swim in an enclosed underwater world, life-sized wax figures of royalty, rulers and rogues smile perpetually; displays depicting historic scenes in miniature delight chidren, while butterflies and tiny monkeys roam in a tropical environment under glass.

*Butchart Gardens: Brentwood*
The Butchart Gardens, 20 km (13 miles) from downtown Victoria at 800 Buenvenuto Drive, tel: (250) 652-5256, is a world-famous garden, begun in 1904, and meticulously cared for by Mrs Butchart's successors. The 20-hectare (50-acre) estate is a must-see. Particularly recommended are **Night Illuminations**, fireworks in July and August. Nearby are the **Victoria Butterfly Gardens**, 1461 Buenvenuto Avenue, in Brentwood Bay, tel: (250) 652-3822, where the indoor weather is always perfect for the little creatures that flutter by.

*Hatley Castle Gardens: Sooke*
Hatley Castle and gardens at Royal Roads University, 2005 Sooke Road, Sooke, tel: (250) 391-2511, are a Dunsmuir creation and today a free attraction featuring a large Japanese garden, a formal Italian garden and a majestic view of the Olympic Mountains. Arguably the best value in Victoria.

*Jolly Olde England*
**Anne Hathaway's Cottage**, 429 Lampson Street of Esquimalt Road, tel: (250) 388-4353, is an exact replica of the original in Shottery, England, and features hilarious guided tours. It is part of a complex of Tudor-style buildings, including the **Olde England Inn** where afternoon tea is a ritual.

*Maritime History*
The **Maritime Museum of BC**, 28 Bastion Square, tel: (250) 385-4222, once the Provincial Courthouse, has a large gallery devoted to Victoria's naval presence and the story of the Hangin' Judge, Matthew Begbie.

*Maritime Setting*
**Fort Rodd Hill National Historic Park** and **Fisguard Lighthouse**, 604 Belmont Road, outskirts of Victoria, tel: (250) 363-4662, an 18-hectare (44-acre) waterfront park, was once a coastal artillery installation and is of interest to World War II history buffs. A self-guided tour or on-site interpreters explain the importance of the site to the security of the West Coast. Bring a picnic as there are no food outlets on site.

## MORE ATTRACTIONS IN VICTORIA

**Carr House**, 207 Government Street, tel: (250) 387-4697. Birthplace of Emily Carr.

**Craigflower Farmhouse and Schoolhouse**, Admirals and Craigflower roads, tel: (250) 387-4697. Heritage buildings, heritage gardens and the first farm in Victoria.

**Point Ellice House & Gardens**, 2616 Pleasant Street, tel: (250) 387-4697. An Italianate Victorian residence from 1861, saved from industrial development. One of the most complete collections of Victoriana in its original setting in Western Canada.

**Forest Products tours**, Western Forest Products, tel: (250) 685-6351. To attend free tours in Sooke, also Jordan River tours.

**Mount Newton Seed Orchard**, Timberwest, tel: (250) 652-4211. To attend free tours in Saanichton.

### What's Up

These folks will get you oriented: **Tourism Association of Vancouver Island**, #304, 45 Bastion Square, Victoria, tel: (250) 382-3551, fax : (250) 382-3523. Information about all places listed below as well as the Gulf Islands, Tofino/Ucluelet/Long Beach is available from this source.

## TOP ATTRACTIONS

### Chemainus

There's the **world's largest outdoor art gallery**, half way between Victoria and Nanaimo, tel: (250) 246-4701, famous murals, a permanent summer festival, live dinner theatre, restaurants, shopping and warm hospitality. Also a free **sawmill tour,** MacMillan Bloedel, tel: (250) 246-3221 for times.

### Duncan

The **City of Totems**, throughout the little city, tel: (250) 746-4421, contains more than 40 authentic native-made totems on display, self-guided tours or guided tours from the railroad station, and the world's thickest totem pole.

**British Columbia Forest Museum**, 2829 Drinkwater Road, RR#4, tel: (250) 746-1251, features trains, a logging museum, and a demonstration of conservation and logging.

**Cowichan Heritage Centre**, 200 Cowichan Way, tel: 746-8119, fax: 746-4143, hosts demonstrations of totem pole carving, native knitting and story telling; also eight bighouses, a restaurant, special feasts and dancing presentations.

**Whippletree Junction**, 5.5 km (3½ miles) south of Duncan on Highway 1, tel: (250) 748-1100, is old-fashioned boardwalk with a lovingly reconstructed turn-of-the-20th-century town with shops; no charge for admission.

### Ladysmith

Namely the **Black Nugget Museum**, 12 Gatacre Street, tel: (250) 245-4846, and **heritage buildings self-guided tour,** first stop 26 Gatacre Street then throughout town, tel: (250) 245-2112.

### Nanaimo

**Bungy Zone**, 35 River Road, Box 399 Station A, V9R 5L3, tel: (250) 755-1266, toll free: 1-800-668-7771, fax: 755-1196, is a fun jump off a bridge with an attached cord.

**Newcastle Island**, accessible by ferry from Nanaimo's Maffeo-Sutton Park, tel: (250) 391-2300, features 14 km (9 miles) of marked trails, native middens, pavilion and visitors centre.

**Nanaimo Heritage Walks** are self-guided walks, first stop Nanaimo Visitor InfoCentre, Beban House, 2290 Bowen Road, tel: 756-0106, toll free: 1-800-663-7337, fax: (250) 756-0075, then follow interpretive signs. Also some guided tours available. Includes Swy-a-lana Lagoon, Lions Great Bridge, Bastion, Coal Seam and Dallas Square.

**Mill tours, Harmac Pacific**, tel: (250) 722-4201, are free tours; learn about the forest industry from source; a fascinating experience; wear closed-toe shoes.

### Qualicum Beach

**The Old School House Gallery & Art Centre**, 122 Fern Road West, tel: 752-1723, fax: 752-2600, puts on displays by local artists and hosts various events.

### Port Alberni

The **Forest Information Centre**, Macmillan Bloedel, tel: (250) 724-7890, will arrange free tours of woods. Contact **Mill Tours**, Alberni Pacific Division, tel: (250) 724-7410, or **Alberni Specialties**, tel: (250) 724-7890, to attend free tours of the mills.

### Pacific Rim National Park

The park is divided into three units: **West Coast Trail**, **Broken Group Islands** and **Long Beach.** For information contact Pacific Rim National Park, BC, V0R 3A0, tel: (250) 726-4212.

### What's Up

For information about attractions, accomodation and BC ferry access to the entire Sunshine Coast, contact **Southwestern BC Tourism**, #204, 1755 West Broadway, Vancouver, V6J 4S5, tel: 739-9011, toll free: 1-800-667-3306, fax: 739-3306. Also contact **Sechelt Visitor Centre**, 45, 5788 Cowrie Street, Trail Bay Mall, tel: 885-0662, fax: 885-0691.

### Seed Orchard Tours

Canadian Forest Products., tel: 885-5905 to attend free tours.

# Culture

## Entertainment Services

Tickets for all entertainment events: **TicketMaster**, tel: 280-4444.

**Dance Centre**, 400–873 Beatty Street, Vancouver, tel: 606-6400, fax: 606-6401; website: http://www.vkool.com/dancecentr.

**Great Northern Ticket Service**, 1334 Seymour Street, Vancouver, tel: 683-3515, fax: 669-8422; email: gnts@intouch.bc.ca.

**Vancouver Cultural Alliance/Arts Hotline**, 100–938 Howe Street, Vancouver, tel: 681-3535, fax: 681-7848; website: http://www.culturenet.ca/vca/.

## Music

**Concert Line** for entertainment happenings in Vancouver, rock & pop, or country & folk, tel: 299-9000 and extension 3080.

**British Columbia Boys Choir**, 2062 Esquimalt Avenue, West Vancouver, tel: 322-5240, fax : (250) 753-8280; website: http://www.yes.netlBCBC/.

**Jazz Hotline** for latest news on current events, tel: 872-5200.

**Coastal Jazz & Blues Society**, 316 West 6th Avenue, Vancouver, tel: 872-5200, fax: 872-5250. Presents a year-round programme of concerts featuring the best of jazz and world music in a variety of concert halls, nightclubs and free stages; including the acclaimed du Maurier Ltd. International Jazz Festival Vancouver in June.

**Dal Richards Orchestra**, 72–550 Beatty Street, Vancouver, tel: 681-6060, fax: 681-1066. Old-fashioned swing band.

**Early Music Vancouver**, 1254 West 7th Avenue, Vancouver, tel: 732-1610, fax: 732-1602; website: http://home.istar.ca/~earlymus.

**Vancouver Cantata Singers**, 5115 Keith Road, West Vancouver, tel: 921-8588, fax: 921-7194.

**Vancouver Opera**, 5th Floor, 845 Cambie St, Vancouver, tel: 682-2871, fax: 682-3981; website: http://www.vanopera.bc.ca. Also tel: 299-9000 and 8058. Performances of 20th-century opera and timeless masterpieces from October to May at the Queen Elizabeth Theatre. Ticket information: TicketMaster, tel: 280-3311; Vancouver Opera Box Office, tel: 683-0222.

## Top Shows

Especially popular with visitors are:
● Theatre Under the Stars
● Kitsilano Showboat
● Bard on the Beach.

Community theatre also has some attractive offerings, tel: 299-9000 and 3085.

**Vancouver Recital Society**, 304–873 Beatty Street, Vancouver, tel: 602-0363, fax: 602-0364; website: http://www.interchg.ubc.ca/vrs.

**Vancouver Symphony Orchestra**, 601 Smithe Street, Vancouver, tel: 684-9100, fax: 684-9264; website: http://www.culturenet.ca/vso/. Also tel: 2990-9000 and extension 8056. This major symphony orchestra performs in Vancouver's Orpheum Theatre and other Lower Mainland venues, as well as outdoors during the summer. Reservations, tel: 280-3311, 280-4444.

## Performing Arts

**Arts Club Theatre**, 1585 Johnston, Vancouver, tel: 687-5315, fax: 687-3306. The best in live theatre is offered year-round at two Granville Island locations: main stage and the Revue. Reservations suggested, tel: 687-1644. Also tel: 299-9000 and extension 8060.

**Bard on the Beach Shakespeare Festival**, 1101 West Broadway, Vancouver. Summer presentations at Vanier Park, tel: 737-0625, fax 737-0425; website: http://www.faximum.com/bard.

**Famous People Players**, c/o Bank of Montreal, 2609 Granville Street, Vancouver, tel: 665-2564, fax: 665-7258. Have a famous look-alike (how about the Queen of England?) come to your next Vancouver or Victoria party.

**Firehall Arts Centre**, 280 East Cordova Street, Vancouver, tel: 689-0926, fax: 684-5841. Experimental productions and old theatre.

**Ford Centre for the Performing Arts**, 777 Homer St, Vancouver, tel: 844-2801, fax: 844-2818. Also tel: 299-9000 and extension 8049. Broadway productions and big crowd-pullers like Showboat.

**Hoarse Raven Theatre**, 1160 Rossland Street, Vancouver, tel: 258-4079, fax: 253-4690. Contemporary plays, lots of enthusiasm.

**Kitsilano Showboat Society**, 2300 Blk Cornwall, Vancouver, tel: 733-7297, fax: 733-7297. Entirely made up of enthusiastic amateurs, tap dancers, singers and more on a seaside outdoor stage. Inexpensive and a Vancouver institution; old-fashioned fun.

**Presentation House**, 333 Chesterfield Avenue, North Vancouver, tel: 986-1351. Various plays.

**Queen Elizabeth Theatre and Playhouse**, Georgia and Hamilton Street, tel: 665-3050. Ballets, visiting musicians.

**Theatre under the Stars**, Malkin Bowl, Stanley Park, tel: 687-0174. Popular Broadway musical type productions during July and August. Shows are nightly, weather permitting, except Sunday. Curtain time is 8.30pm. Dress warmly.

**Vancouver Civic Theatres**, 649 Cambie Street, tel: 665-3050, fax: 665-3001; website: http://www.city.vancouver.bc.ca/the.

**Vancouver East Cultural Centre**, 1895 Venables Street, tel: 254-9578. The full gamut of entertaining live theatre.

**Vancouver Playhouse Theatre**, 160 West 1st Avenue, Vancouver, tel: 872-6622, fax: 873-3714; website: http://www.winefest.bc.sympatico.ca.

Also tel: 299-9000 and extension 8052 or 873-3311. Celebrates dramas of whimsy, romance, sorrow and comedy.

### Cinemas (Movie Theatres)
To find out what movies are on and when, tel: 299-9000 and 3106. For discount cinema times, tel: 299-9000 and 3456. For film reviews, tel: 299-9000 and 3100. For top picks, tel: 299-9000 and 3101.

### Comedy
Who says Canadians have no sense of humour? Check it out.
**Vancouver TheatreSports League,** 104–1177 West Broadway, Vancouver, tel: 738-7013, fax: 738-8013; website: http://www.vtsl.com. Hilarious improvisation, talented players, various venues.
**Yuk Yuk's,** 750 Pacific Blvd. South, Vancouver, tel: 687-5233, 299-9000 and extension 5233. International stand-up comedy; the best in professional stand-up.

## Victoria

### Entertainment Services
**"Terrifvic" Jazz Party,** Box 1719, Station E, Victoria, tel: (250) 381-5277, fax: (250) 381-3010.
**Victoria Flower and Garden Festival,** 910 Falmouth Road,tel: (250) 382-3658, fax: (250) 386-3312.

### Music
**Victoria Jazz Society,** Box 8542, Victoria, tel: (250) 388-4423, fax: (250) 388-0447.
**Victoria Symphony,** 846 Broughton Street, tel: (250) 385-9771, fax: (250) 385-7767.
**Pacific Opera Victoria,** 1316/B Government Street, tel: (250) 385-0222, fax: (250) 382-4944. Producing quality opera since 1980.

### Performing Arts
**McPherson Playhouse,** 3 Centennial Square, Victoria, tel: (250) 386-6121, fax: (250) 386-0805.

**Kaleidoscope Playhouse,** 520 Herald Street, tel: (250) 383-8124, fax: (250) 383-8911.
**The Ridge Playhouse,** 4980 Wesley Road, tel: (250) 658-6311.
**Belfry Theatre,** 1291 Gladstone Avenue, tel: (250) 385-6815, fax: (250) 385-6336.

## Nightlife

Clubs and bars with a variety of entertainment from strip shows to dinner theatre are listed in local newspapers. Most night clubs have a cover charge and so do some pubs in the evening if there is special entertainment. Some dine and dance restaurants require a minimum charge per person. Some clubs have a dress code; pubs are usually casual dress. Pub hours may vary but are generally 11am–2am. Because of liquor laws, no drinks can be sold after 1am.

## VANCOUVER
### Pubs and Lounges
**Hollywood North Cabaret,** 856 Seymour Street, tel: 682-7722.
**Jake O'Grady's,** 3684 East Hastings Street, tel: 298-1434. Sunday night jam.
**Kits on Broadway,** 1424 West Broadway, Vancouver, tel: 736-5811. Friendly neighbourhood pub atmosphere in Vancouver's popular Kits area.
**The Raven Neighbourhood Pub,** 1052 Deep Cove Road, North Vancouver, tel: 929-3834, 299-9000 and extension 2111. Excellent pub grub, renovated.
**Tugs Pub – Lonsdale Quay Hotel,** 123 Carrie Cates Court, North Vancouver, tel: 986 6111. Big screen sports, Top 40 music, great food.
**Yale Pub,** Yale Hotel, 1300 Granville Street, tel: 299-9000. Cheap and atmospheric.

### After Hours
**Richard's on Richards,** 1036 Richards Street, Vancouver, tel: 687-6794, 299-9000 and extension 6794. "The club so famous, they named a street after it."

**Sonar,** 66 Water Street, Vancouver, 683 6695. Memorable West Coast cuisine, urban culture, casual atmosphere, plus some of the best live music acts anywhere.
**Big Bam Boo Club,** 1236 West Broadway, tel: 733-2220, 299-9000 and extension 2220. Live music, cover, dress code, ladies night, extreme dance parties.
**Roxy Nightclub,** 932 Granville Street, tel: 684-7699, 299-9000 and extension 7699. Combo pub and nightclub, rock and roll the specialty.

### Casinos
Casinos in the Greater Vancouver area are usually located in major hotels. Their proceeds are shared with local charities.
**Great Canadian Casino Company Ltd.,** Holiday Inn, 1133 West Hastings, tel: 682-8415. Excitement every night! Roulette, blackjack. Daily 6pm–2am.
**Royal Diamond Casino,** 106B–750 Pacific Boulevard South, Plaza of Nations, tel: 685-2340. Noon–2am.

## VICTORIA
### After Hours
**Hermann's Jazz Club,** 735 View Street, tel: (250) 388-9166.
**Merlin's,** 107, 1208 Wharf Street, tel: (250) 381-2331.
**Sweetwaters Niteclub,** 27, 560 Johnson Street, tel: (250) 383-7844.

### Casino
**Great Canadian Casino Company Ltd,** 3075 Douglas Street, tel: 389-1136.

# Festivals

## Vancouver & Whistler

### January
- January 1: Polar Bear Swim
- Chinese New Year Festival

### February/March
- Numerous trade fairs

### April
- International Wine Festival

### May
- Vancouver International Children's Festival
- Hyack Festival, New Westminster.

## Events Info

- ● Thurday's *Vancouver Sun* is the newpaper that covers all the week's entertainment and festival events.
- ● **Festivals and events hotline:** To find out what's happening have a pencil handy, tel: 299-9000 and extension 3232.
- ● **Activities for kids:** tel: 299-9000 and 3084.
- ● **Events for teens:** tel: 299-9000 and 4812.

### June
- Canadian International Dragon Boat Festival
- Aboriginal Cultural Festival
- DuMaurier International Jazz Festival
- VanDusen Outdoor Flower and Garden Show
- Bard on the Beach
- Kitsilano Showboat Amateurs

### July
- July 1: Canada Day Celebrations
- Dancing on the Edge Festival
- Vancouver Folk Music Festival
- Vancouver International Comedy Festival
- The Vancouver Chamber Music Festival
- Italian Days, Vancouver Italian Community Centre
- Annual International Pow-wow, Mission
- Country and Blues Festival, Whistler
- Benson and Hedges Symphony of Fire: fireworks competition

### August
- BC Day Celebrations
- Pacific National Exhibition: country fair
- Greater Vancouver Open (PGA golf tournament)
- Powell Street Festival (Japanese)
- Annual Festival of the Written Arts, Sechelt
- Squamish Open Annual Regatta
- Vancouver Wooden Boat Festival
- Classical Music Festival, Whistler.
- Abbotsford International Air Show (every second year)
- Vancouver International Comedy Festival
- Symphony of Fire: pyro-technicians
- Whistler Summer Theatre Festival

### September
- Molson Indy Vancouver
- The Fringe Theatre Festival
- Bluegrass Music Festival, Chilliwack.
- Sand Sculpture Exhibition, Harrison Hot Springs
- Jazz Festival, Whistler.
- International Street Performers Festival, Whistler
- Coho Festival, West Vancouver

### October
- Mid-Autumn Moon Festival
- BC Home Show
- Oktoberfest
- Vancouver International Writers Festival
- Vancouver Ski and Snowboard Show: Sale and Swap

### November
- Christmas at Hycroft
- Christmas Craft Fairs

### December
- Christmas at Canada Place
- Sinter Klaas, New Westminster
- Christmas Carol Ship Parade

## Victoria & Vancouver Island

### January
- Polar Bear Swim
- Chocolate Festival
- Pacific Cup Old-timers Hockey Tournament

### February
- Focus On Women Arts Festival
- Flower Count

### March
- Artists' Studio Tours
- Playmakers Seniors' Cup Hockey Tournament

### April
- TerrifVic Jazz Party
- Antiques and Collectables Fair, Vancouver Island

### May
- International Children's Festival
- Swiftsure Lightship Classic
- Victoria Day Parade
- Garden Tours
- Heritage on the Hoof, Victoria
- Horse Logging Demonstrations, Chemainus
- National Forestry Week, Duncan
- Flatwater Racing Regatta, Long Beach
- Victoria Music Festival
- Tea Cup Races, Inner Harbour
- Queen's Birthday Celebrations
- Decorated Boat Parade, Victoria
- Victoria Exhibition
- Artists in Action Festival
- Annual Gorge Regatta, Victoria

### June
- Oak Bay Tea Party
- Jazz Fest
- International Folkfest
- Victoria International Boat Race
- Bay Day Children's Festival
- Sidney Days

**July**
- Canada Day Celebrations
- Saanich Strawberry Festival
- Old Time Fiddle Contest and Jamboree
- Pacific Rim Summer Festival
- Victoria International Airshow

**August**
- Victoria International Festival
- First People's Festival
- Symphony Splash
- Fringe Theatre Festival

**September**
- Classic Boat Festival
- Kids' Fest
- Sannichton Fair

**October**
- Royal Victoria Marathon
- Salmon Run

**November**
- Christmas Craft Fairs

**December**
- Santa Claus Parade
- Lighted Boat Parade

# Shopping

## Vancouver & Area

### Historic Shopping Districts

**Robson Street**, stretching from Hornby Street to the West End, is an area of fashionable stores, boutiques and international eateries, coffee houses and restaurants with outside patios; good for a stroll both day and evening.

**Chinatown**, centred on Keefer and Pender streets, is a hive of bustling Asian shops and markets as well as an example of early Vancouver architecture. It is within easy walking distance from Gastown.

**Gastown**, on Water Street, is in the historic heart of the city once known as Granville. Close to Canada Place, it features an assortment of souvenir stores and First People's art stores set in refurbished warehouses. Look for the mini-sections: **Blood Alley** and **Gaoler's Mews**.

**Kitsilano district**, lining Fourth Avenue between Burrard and Alma, has a fashionable bohemian atmosphere; full of health food stores and ethnic restaurants.

**Yaletown**, in the 500 to 1200 blocks of Mainland Street, is an area of renovated warehouses and features an eclectic and somewhat artsy selection of funky pubs, chic boutiques and art galleries. It prides itself on being a young, trendy "happenin' place".

**Sinclair Centre**, 757 West Hastings Street near Canada Place and the Waterfront SeaBus terminal, is a heritage building transformed into a small mall with boutiques and a self-service restaurant. No attached parking.

### Shopping Malls

A number of excellent shopping malls, most anchored by the same cookie-cutter department stores, are convenient and offer free underground or adjacent parking. You can browse, stop for lunch or even stay for a movie in the evening. All are accessible by public transit.

**Pacific Centre**, Georgia and Howe streets, downtown, almost 200 stores set underground with a three-storey waterfall and glass skylights. This popular mall is anchored by Eatons and The Bay. Open seven days a week, tel: 299-9000 and extension 7467.

**Metrotown**, BC's largest shopping complex is in Burnaby, on Kingsway between Willingdon and Nelson streets, and is accessible by SkyTrain, Metrotown Station. Over 380 shops include anchors Eaton's, Sears and The Bay department stores. Several adjoining shopping centres: Metrotown Centre, Eaton Centre, and Station Square. At Station Square there are 12 Cineplex Odeon and Famous Players movie theatres, a games arcade, recording studio and many restaurants. Tel: 299-9000 and extension 4700.

### Public Markets

**Granville Island Market**, at the south end of the Granville Island Bridge, is an urban success story, a visitor-friendly oasis of public market and eateries in a trendy neighbourhood with theatres, charter boats, breweries, bookstores and art studios – a thriving mix. For information, tel: 299-9000 and extension 5784.

**Lonsdale Quay Market**, 123 Carr Cates Court, North Vancouver, accessible by SeaBus, offers fresh fruits, fish and vegetables to fashion, gifts and restaurant adventures. For information, tel: 299-9000 and extension 6261.

**Westminster Quay Public Market**, at the foot of 8th in New Westminster, overlooks the Fraser River and stands near the Russian submarine, boardwalk, floating paddleboat museum. Fresh food, fish and vegetables; restaurants. For information, tel: 299-9000 and extension 5085.

## Victoria

### Historic Shopping Districts

**Government Street** shopping district, starting at the Empress Hotel, extends for several blocks and features china stores, tartan shops, Rogers' Chocolates, gift shops, First People's arts and souvenir stores.

**The Bay Downtown**, 1701 Douglas Street, is an historic building housing all the modern goods the former royal-chartered fur trading company, established 1604, is presently famous for.

**Bastion Square**, north on Government Street near the Maritime Museum, is an area of historic buildings and artists' shops.

**Victoria Eaton Centre**, corner of Government and Fort, a single complex of several refurbished historic buildings, features places to buy Canadiana along with a shiny shopping mall.

**Market Square**, between Yates, Wharf and Johnston streets, includes some 40 shops, gift stores and restaurants as well as the Centennial Fountain and an Elizabethan Knot Garden.

**Antique Row**, on Fort Street from Blanchard to Cook, is roughly equivalent to Kensington Church Street in London, and is the place where the best antiques and collectables are found.

**Chinatown** and **Fantan Alley**, Fisguard at Government Street through the Gate of Harmonious Interest, has *dim sum* restaurants and Asian goods shops. Fantan Alley, the narrowest street in Canada, features artists' studios and little boutiques.

## Whistler

A series of enclosed pedestrian-only outdoor civic squares, designed with alpine-style detailing, includes stores selling ski apparel and accessories, West Coast native art, fashion, Canadian gift items, sportswear, jewellery and fashions.

# Sport & Leisure

## Vancouver on the Move

Sometimes its seems as if the whole city of Vancouver is skating, walking, biking, running or on the move. Here's your guide to joining in.

### Birding

**Reifel Bird Sanctuary**, 5191 Robertson Rd., Delta, tel: 946-6980. Over 3 km (2 miles) of trails lead to marshland habitats supporting more than 240 species of birds. Nominal fee to support sanctuary.

### Charterboats

Charterboats are available for sports fishing, power or sail, marine cruising, day tours or dinner cruises. The best place to find a charter is on the water side of the yellow building called Bridges on Johnson Street, Granville Island. Vancouver's charterboat trade is highly competitive and services are not as expensive as elsewhere. **Boat Charter Tips**, tel: 299-9000 and extension 9778.

**One Stop Charter Centre**, 310, 990 Beach Avenue, tel: 681-2915, fax: 682-3802; website: http://-www.intergate.bc.ca/business/boat.
**Carousel II Charters**, 1601 West Georgia, tel: 687-4377.
**Silver Blue Charters**, tel: 689-1524. Forty-one-foot luxury yacht located at Granville Island. Fishing and cruising.
**Pride of Vancouver Charters Ltd.**, north foot of Burrard Street, next to Pan Pacific, tel: 687-5533.

### Cycling

Vancouver has few designated bike right-of-ways, but there are interesting routes to cycle around

False Creek, in certain beach areas and along the Stanley Park SeaWall in the designated lanes. It is illegal to cycle on sidewalks and police do ticket cyclists for traffic violations. Helmets are mandatory. Bicycles are permitted on the SeaBus on Saturdays, Sundays and holidays. They are not allowed on the buses or SkyTrain.

You may join a tour, **Velo-City Cycle Tours**, tel: 924-0288, fax: 929-8822. Their website is at: http://www.velocity.com.

## Action Stations

Here are a few places to catch the best Vancouver action:
● **Jericho Sailing Centre**, 1300 Discovery, tel: 224-0615. Quick lessons and rental equipment for windsurfing.
● **Adventure Fitness**, 1510 Duranleau, Granville Island, tel: 687-1528. Quick lessons, kayaks, canoes and tours.
● **Sewell's Marina**, Horseshoe Bay, West Vancouver, tel: 921-3474. Small self-piloted boats for ocean-going fun.
● **Ecomarine Ocean Kayak Centre**, 1668 Duranleau Street, Granville Island, tel: 689-7575. Kayak and canoe rentals.

The main cycling event of the year is the **Gastown Grand Prix** held in July. The race starts in the morning with all categories and makes a 900-metre (1,000-yard) circuit around the city streets for a total of 60 km (37 miles), equalling 65 laps.

Rent a bike for a spin around Stanley Park at one of these shops:
**Bayshore Bicycles Ltd – Denman**, 745 Denman Street, tel: 2664-9820.
**Bayshore Bicycles Ltd – Westin**, 1601 West Georgia Street, tel: 264-9820.
**Sports Bicycle Rental and Espresso Bar Inc.**, 1798 West Georgia Street, tel: 688-5141.

### Golf

A popular year-round sport in Vancouver. Every year the **BC Open** is held in June.

**The West Coast Golf Shuttle** will pick you up at your hotel and shuttle you to a course, tel: 730-1032, fax: 730-1072. Their website is at: http://www.golf-shuttle.com.

There are several private golf courses close to the city centre and about 20 public courses in the metropolitan area; a few public courses are listed here. In general, Vancouver courses tend to be a bit steep and somewhat challenging. For general information, tel: 299-9000 and extension 9761.

**Fraserview Golf Course**, 7800 Vivian Drive, tel: 327-5616. Par 71, 6,165 yards.

**University Golf Club**, 5185 University Boulevard, tel: 224-1818. Par 72, 6,147 yards.

**McCleery Golf Course**, 7170 MacDonald Street, tel: 257-8191. Par 72, 6,168 yards.

**Langara Golf Course**, 290 West 49th Avenue, tel: 257-8355. Par 71, 6,103 yards.

### Horseracing

**BC Jockey Club**, Exhibition Park, Vancouver, tel: 254-1631. Enjoy thoroughbred racing action from April to October, starting at 6.30pm Monday, Wednesday and Friday; 1.15pm Saturday, Sunday and holidays. Full facilities including clubhouse on site.

### Horse Riding

Vancouver has several riding stables and horses for hire. The serious equestrian set gravitate to the suburb of Maple Ridge.
**Southlands Riding Club**, 7025 Macdonald, tel: 263-4817. Indoor and outdoor riding areas. They don't rent horses but you can call them about equestrian events.
**Maple Ridge Equ-Sport Centre**, 21973, 132nd Avenue, Maple Ridge, tel: 463-1331. Centre for the horsey set.
**Alpine Riding Academy**, near Buntzen Lake, tel: 469-1111. Trail rides. Reservations required.
**Cheekeye Stables**, Box 312, Brackendale, BC, V0N 1H0, tel: 898-3432. Less than one hour from Vancouver, enjoy guided adventure trail rides through coastal

## Spectator Sports

The National Hockey League (NHL) team, the **Vancouver Canucks**, iinvite you to join them and their enthusiastic supporters at GM Place from September through May, tel: 299-9000, extension 3055, or 254-5141.

Vancouver's National Basketball Association (NBA) team is the **Vancouver Grizzlies**, and they go through the hoops at GM Place from October to May, tel: 299-9000 and extension 3072.

The Canadian Football League (CFL) presents Grey Cup champions, **BC Lions Football Team** at the BC Place Stadium.

rainforests to private glacier-shrouded beach houses.

### Indoor Rock Climbing

**Cliffhanger Indoor Rock Climbing Centre**, 106 West Ist Avenue, Vancouver, tel: 874-2400, fax: 874-5620; website: cliffhanger.bc.ca.
**Inside Edge Climbing Gym Inc.**, #2, 1485 Welch Street, North Vancouver, tel: 984-9080, fax: 980-3270.

### Running/Fitness

For information on sports and fitness activites and what's happening in Vancouver, tel: 462-7133, 299-9000 and 3040; website: www.runningroom.co.
**Vancouver International Marathon Society**, Box 3213, Vancouver, V6B 3X8, tel: 8872-2928, fax: 872-2903; website: http://www.wi.bc.ca

### Scuba Diving

Divers know the area's water as the Emerald Sea. The most popular city-ocean areas for scuba and snorkelling are: Whytecliff Park, Lighthouse Park, Porteau Cove, Tuwanek Point and Cates Park. Most diving near Vancouver takes place in Howe Sound and Indian Arm. Surf diving is the usual type of diving and and a long shore current or rip current is present. Consult a dive shop before diving. To dive in the outer harbour, permission is

The season is from June to late October, tel: 299-9000 and extension 3355 or 930-5466.

If you enjoy baseball, the Pacific Coast League's **Vancouver Canadians** play at the Nat Bailey Stadium from April to September on Sunday afternoons and weekday evenings, tel: 299-9000 and extension 2255 or 872-5232.

Professional soccer (European football) is handled by the **Vancouver Eighty-Sixers** between July and October at Burnaby's Swanguard Stadium in Central Park, Kingsway and Boundary, tel: 299-9000 and extension 8666.

necessary. Contact the **Vancouver Port Corporation**, tel: 666-2405. Wet suits are needed in BC waters, especially off the west coast of Vancouver Island.

For information on diver's equipment and supplies, tel: 299-9000 and 9756. Scuba diving rental stores are:
**Diver's World**, 1523 West Third Avenue, tel: 732-1344.
**Diving Locker**, 2745 West Fourth Avenue, tel: 736-2681.
**Adrenalin Sports**, 1512 Duranleau, Granville Island, tel: 682-2881.

### Sea Kayaking

Sea kayaking has become a popular way to explore coastal areas.
**Ecomarine Ocean Kayak Centre**, Granville Island, tel: 689-7575. Rents kayaks and provides instruction.
**Sage Wilderness Experiences**, 1370 Main Street, North Vancouver, tel: 983-3108; Website: http://www.refer-all.com/sage/. Sea-kayaking.

### Ski Hills

BC's Coastal Range provides year-round skiing including summer skiing on the high-altitude The 7th Heaven Horstman Glacier on Blackcomb Mountain in Whistler. There is snow at higher elevations on Vancouver's North Shore mountains from roughly November through March. The nearest skiing and snowboarding areas to Vancouver are visible from the downtown area: **Grouse**, **Seymour** and **Cypress mountains**. Intermediate to top skiers go to the **Whistler-Blackcomb** area, about a 2-hour drive. **Mount Baker**, in the US state of Washington, is 120 km (75 miles) south of Vancouver.

## Snow and Ski Reports
Ski Hotline, tel: 280-1234 or tel: 299-9000 and 3070.
Whistler Conditions, tel: 687-6761, 932-4211, 664-707.

## Downhill Skiing & Snowboarding
**Cypress Bowl Recreations ski hill**, Cypress Mountain, West Vancouver, tel: 922-0825, fax: 926-9441.
**Grouse Mountain ski hill, the Peak of Vancouver**, 6400 Nancy Green Way, North Vancouver, tel: 984-0661, 984-7234.

## Cross-Country Skiing
There is cross-country skiing from December through March at **Cypress bowl**. Its Hollyburn Lodge has food service; busy on weekends. There are cross-country ski trails at Whistler in the Lost Lake and Cheakamus Lake areas. The best cross-country skiing is at **Manning Park**, a 3-hour drive from Vancouver.

## Sport Fishing
All sports fishing activities require a licence, either a salt-water licence or a fresh-water licence. In addition to the numerous lakes and streams in the Greater Vancouver area, where you can simply spend the day or go on an overnight camping trip, you can rent a small power boat, hire a charter, or fish from one of the wharves, piers or sea-wall areas. Rock cod, ling cod, sole, flounder, red snapper, halibut and perch are common catches. In some areas you can catch crab.
**Sport fishing information:** Sports Fishing Institute of British Columbia, tel: 663-600, toll free: 1-800-663-6000; website: www.sportfishing.bc.ca.
**Fish and Wildlife Service,** government office: tel: 582-5200.

**Fish Hotline:** tel: 1-900-451-6611.
**Sewell's Marina**, Horseshoe Bay, tel: 921-3474. Tackle, licences and where the fish are biting.
**M&M Charters**, 1500 Charland Avenue, Coquitlam, tel: 937-3962, fax: 937-7650; website: http://www.vaninfo.com/m&m.html.
**Coho Sports**, 4152 Fentinon Street, Vancouver, tel: 435.7333, fax: 431-8566.
**Vancouver Sportfish Centre Dock**, 566 Cardero Street, tel: 689-7108.
**Next Step for BC Fisherman's Unique Tours**, 200–1001 Columbia Street, New Westminster, tel: 522-4331, fax: 517-6169; website: www.onestart.net/bcfish.
**Granville Island Sport Fishing Museum**, 1502 Duranleau Steet, tel: 683-1939; website: http://www.netminder.com/gisfm.

## Tennis
The tennis season is from March through October but sometimes you can play during the winter. There are 180 public courts, some of them outdoors and free. You'll find courts at: Stanley Park, Queen Elizabeth Park, Kitsilano Beach Park, Jericho Beach Park and at most community centres around the city. Night-lit public courts are on the Langara College campus, on 49th Avenue, between Cambie and Maia. Vancouver Parks & Recreation will route you to whoever is currently in charge of booking courts, tel: 257-8400. For Stanley Park, tel: 605-8224.

## Windsurfing
Windsurfing schools supply boards, wet suits and life jackets as well as instructions. The rental-instruction packages are from one to six hours.
**Windsure Windsurfing School**, 1300 Discovery, Jericho Beach, tel: 224-0615.

## Victoria on the Move

### Charterboats
**Island Breeze Sailing Ltd.**, Box 1233, Victoria, V8W 2T6, tel: (250) 361-3773, fax: (250) 361-3778. Two and a half-hour sailing trips from Victoria's Inner Harbour.

**Newport Yacht Charters**, 1327 Beach Drive, Victoria, tel: (250) 595-2628.
**Springtide Charters Ltd**, 4336 Crownwood Lane, Victoria, tel: (250) 658-6061, toll free: 1-800-470-3474, fax: (250) 651-0779. Two zodiacs for whale watching or diving, 23-foot for fishing, 36-foot for harbour tours.

### Cycling/Rollerblading
**Sports Rent**, 611 Discovery Street, tel: (250) 385-7368. Equipment for hiking, camping, surfing; bikes rollerblades, canoes, kayaks.
**Island Outback Expeditions**, 960 Tulip Avenue, tel: (250) 389-2975. Bicycle tours.

### Diving
**Ocean Centre**, 800 Cloverdale Avenue, tel: (250) 475-2202.

### Sea Kayaking
**Intertidal Explorations Kayak and Sailing Co.**, 2010 Stanley Avenue, tel: (250) 595-4774.
**Ocean River Sports**, 1437 Store Avenue, tel: (250) 381-4233.

### Water Fun
**Crystal Pool**, 2275 Quadra Street, tel: (250) 380-7946.
**Recreation Oak Bay**, 1975 Bee Street, tel: (250) 5995-7946. Pool, 150-foot water slide, sauna, whirlpool.
**Sannich Commonwealth Place**, 4636 Elk Lake Drive, tel: (250) 727-7108. Family fun, wavepool, diving boards, waterslides.

## Whistler on the Move

Ask for information at the **Whistler Travel InfoCentre**, 2097 Lake Placid Road, tel:932-5528, fax: 932-3755, about heli-skiing, golf, snowboard school, hiking, mountain biking, horseback riding or climbing.

### Ski Mountains
Rated by top ski magazines, consumers guides, skiiers and snowboarders as the best in North America (yes, Colorado was in the running) the number one rated ski resort in North America, triple

## Victoria: Parks, Birding, Beaches & Whales

● **Beacon Hill Park**, Douglas and Dallas roads. Permit park, kids' petting zoo, three little lakes, duck ponds, picnic areas, pitch and putt, flowers.
● **Swan Lake Nature Sanctuary**, 3873 Swan Lake Road, tel: 479-0211. Bird sanctuary, floating boardwalk, nature in the raw, marshes.

● **Beaver and Elk Lake Parks**, Halburton and Sayward roads. Lakeside beaches.

**Out to Sea:**
● **Seaker Adventure Tours**, departing from Victoria's Inner Harbour, tel: (250) 480-0244. Whale watching adventures, five departures daily.

are food concessions, picnic sites and a shore-side trail. Be warned that on hot days parking may be difficult.

## Outdoor Adventures

### VANCOUVER

**Eco-Tours**

The great attraction is the outdoors and these folks will help you get the most out of your West Coast experience.
**ATS Adventure Tourism Services**, 50 East 48th Avenue, Vancouver, tel: 803-8448, fax: 324-1123; website: http://www.ultranet.ca/ats.
**Vancouver All Terrain Adventures Ltd.**, 4191 Dominion Street, Burnaby, BC, V5G ICS, tel:.434-2278, fax: 434-9155; website: http://www.all-terrain.com.
**Vancouver Eco-Adventures**, 5646 Westport Road, West Vancouver, BC V7W 1V1, tel: 921-8739, fax: 921-8730; website: http://ww.vancouver-bc.com\vancouvereco-adven.
**Wild Spirit Adventures Ltd.**, PO Box 2825, Vancouver, BC, V6B 4A6, tel: 874-3782.
**Jeep Safaris By Outer Limits Expeditions Ltd**, 2044 West 44th Avenue, Vancouver, BC, V6W 2E9, tel: 803.8448, fax: 324.1123; website: http://www.members.-aol.com/edwardsson.

**River Rafting**
**Canadian Outback Adventure Company Ltd**, 100, 657 Marine Drive, West Vancouver, tel: 921-7250, fax: 921-7860; website: http://www.canadianoutback.com
**Hyak Wilderness Adventures**, 1975 Maple Street, Vancouver, tel: 734-8622, fax: 734-5718; website: http://www.hyak.com/hyak.
**REO Rafting Adventure**, Suite 355, 535 Thurlow, Vancouver, tel: 684-4438, fax: 684-9536; website: http://www.reorafting.com.
**Great Expeditions**, 5915 West Blvd, Vancouver, BC V6M 3X1, tel: 257-2040, fax: 257-2037; website: http://www.greatexpeditions.com
**Vancouver Jet Ventures Ltd**, 6882 Gilley Street, Burnaby, BC, VSJ 4W7, tel: 313-6088.

crown winner. Whistler and Blackcomb mountains have over 100 trails for novices through to experts and the longest downhill drop in North America. Summer and winter, fully enclosed gondolas whisk skiiers or summer visitors to the top of the twin mountains for spectacular views. Website: http://www.whistler.net.

    **Guest Relations – Whistler Mountain**, Box 67, 2320 London Lane, Whistler, BC, V0N 1B0, tel: 932-5616, 299-9000 and extension 5700. Soar skyward on the Whistler Express highspeed gondola for all-season enjoyment, from skiing to magnificent alpine scenery and mountain-top dining.

    **Guest Relations – Blackcomb Mountain**, 4545 Blackcomb Way, Whistler, BC, V0N 1B4, tel: 932-3141, 873-4131, 687-1032, 299-9000 and extension 7547. The "mile-high mountain" (5,280 vertical feet) offering both winter and summer skiing plus other activities. State-of-the-art lift technology, great service and endless variety.

## Vancouver Beach Blanket Guide

Which Vancouver beach? Here's a quick overview so you know what to bring along with your beach blanket.
**Ambleside Beach**, foot of 15th Street, West Vancouver, tel: 922-1211. A great beach for swimming, windsurfing, sunning, walking and sunsets. Nearby shopping and restaurants.
**Wreck Beach**, located in an out-of-the-way area below the cliffs of Point Grey on the western tip of

UBC grounds, is basically for nudists.
**Second Beach**, Stanley Park, tel: 257-8400, A popular family beach with a (pay) pool. Offers supervised and secured ocean-side swimming in chlorinated water. Food and drink concession, close to Ceperly Park picnic facilities, playground, pitch n'putt and pay-tennis.
**Third Beach**, Stanley Park, tel: 257-8400. A large stretch of sand with an ocean view, great for sunsets. it's a quiet beach, no music allowed, close to picnic tables, food concessions and the well-equipped and monitored **Variety Kids Waterpark**, a professional paddler's paradise. Also close to the Vancouver Aquarium.
**English Bay**, West End. One of the oldest and most popular West End beaches and site of the well-known New Year's Day Polar Bear Swim, and the July Sea Festival and annual fireworks displays.
**Sunset Beach**, West End, close to False Creek and the Aquatic Centre. This isn't a suitable beach for swimming but it's popular for viewing sunsets or watching boats sail by.
**Kitsilano Beach Park & Pool**, north foot of Arbutus Street, tel: 257-8400. A grassy-sloped mecca for hedonistic sun-worshippers with enclosed pool, children's playground and a large beach volleyball area. A popular young adult beach with bars and restaurants across the street.
**Jericho, Locarno and Spanish Banks**, north foot of Discovery Street, tel: 257-8400. This chain of beaches is over 3 km (2 miles) long. Besides being ideal for swimming and wind-surfing, there

## Rainforest Walks

● **Pacific Spirit Park**, 33rd and Camousen. Endowment lands near UBC, Vancouver.
● **Beaver Lake**, Pipeline Road in Stanley Park, Vancouver.
● **Seymour Demonstration Forest**, Second Narrows bridge to Lilooet Road, exit to gravel road and follow signs, North Vancouver.
● **Lighthouse Park**, NW Marine Drive to Beacon Lane, West Vancouver.
● **Capilano Canyon**, Capilano Road, left at Regional Park sign, North Vancouver.

### VICTORIA

**Freedom Adventure Tours**, Box 8606, Victoria, V8W 3S2, tel: (250) 480-9409.
**Coastal Connections**, Box 8360, Victoria, V8W 3R9, tel: (250) 480-9560, toll free: 1-800-840-4453. Interpretive nature hikes throughout Victoria and Vancouver Island.
**Trek Canada Tours Ltd.**, Box 267, Cobble Hill, V0R 1L0, tel: 743-7759.

### WHISTLER

**Whistler Snowmobile Guided Tours**, P.O. Box 463, Whistler, BC, V0N 1B0, tel: 932-4086. Experience the Whistler others don't see with a scenic snowmobile tour to view cedar groves that are over 1,200 years old. Reservations suggested.

# Further Reading

## General

*Banners and Bands: A Guide to the Festivals of the Pacific Northwest*, by Eileen Marrett. Upper Case Publishing, 1991.
*British Columbia: Visions of the Promised Land*, by Brand Lee White. Flight Press, 1986.
*Guide to Western Canada*, by Frederick Pratson. Globe Pequot Press, 1987.
*Guidebook to Ethnic Vancouver*, by Ann Petrie. Hancock House, 1982.
*Raincoast Chronicles*, by Edward Howard White. Harbour Publications, 1983.
*Sunshine and Salt Air*. Harbour Publications, 1987.
*The National Dream*, by Pierre Berton. McClelland Stewart.
*The Vancouver Trivia Book*, by Craig O. Henderson. Polestar Press, 1985.
*Vancouver*, ed. by Chuck Davis & Shirley Mooney. Vancouver Board of Trade, 1986.
*Vancouver*, by Eric Nicol. Doubleday, 1978.
*Vancouver: Sights & Insights*, by Donald Stainsby, drawings by George Kuthan. Macmillan of Canada, 1962.

## History

*Barkerville Days*, by Fred W. Luddith. Mitchell Press, 1969.
*Beyond the Island: An Illustrated History of Victoria*, by Peter A. Baskerville. Windsor Publications, 1986.
*British Columbia: A Centennial Anthology*, ed. by Reginald Eyre Watts. McClelland & Stewart, 1958.
*British Columbia, a History*, by Margaret Ormsby. Macmillan, 1958.
*British Columbia's Logging History*, by Ed Gould. Hancock House Publishers, 1975.

*Canada, the Story of British Columbia*, by the Rev. F. A. Peake. McGraw Hill Co. of Canada, 1966.
*Distant Neighbors: A Comparative History of Seattle and Vancouver*, by Norbert MacDonald. University of Nebraska Press, 1987.
*Early Vancouver*, seven vols. self-published by Major J. S. Matthews, 1933–59.
*Heritage Vancouver*, by Richard Edward Allen. Josten's Publications, Winnipeg, 1983.
*Island in the Creek: The Granville Island Story*. Harbour Publications, 1988.
*The Journals of George M. Dawson: British Columbia, 1875–78*, ed. by Douglas Cole & Bradley Lockner. University of BC Press, 1989.
*Malaspina and Galiano, Spanish Voyages on the Northwest Coast*, by Donald C. Cutter. Douglas & McIntyre, 1991.
*The New El Dorado or British Columbia*, by Kinahan Cornwallis. Thomas Cautley, London, 1858.
*The Pacific Coast Scenic Tour*, by Henry T. Finck. Charles Scribners & Sons, 1907.
*The Pacific Northwest: Its discovery and early exploration by sea, land and river*, by Edward W. Neiffield. Hancock House Publishing, 1990.
*Understanding Vancouver*. City Planning Dept, 1970.

## People

*The Canadians*, by Andrew H. Malcolm. Times Books, 1985.
*Hundreds and Thousands: The Journals of Emily Carr*. Clarke, Irvin & Co., 1966.
*Saltwater City, An Illustrated History of the Chinese in Vancouver*, by Paul Yee. Douglas & McIntyre, 1988.

## The Outdoor Life

*Bicycling Greater Vancouver and the Gulf Islands*, by Maggie Burtinshaw and Mary Ellen Bradshaw. Gordon Soules Publishing, 1990.
*Easy Hiking Around Vancouver*, by Jean Cousins and Heather Robinson. Douglas & McIntyre, 1990.

*Horse Trail Guide, Southwest BC.* H. T. Publications, Cloverdale, 1990.
*109 Walks in British Columbia's Lower Mainland,* by Mary and David Macaree. Douglas & McIntyre, 1990.
*Salmon Fishing British Columbia,* by Mike Cramond. Heritage House, 1990.
*West Coast River Angling,* by Eric Carlisle. Hancock House, 1990.

## Other Insight Guides

The 190 books in the *Insight Guides* series cover every continent and include 40 titles devoted to the United States and Canada, from Alaska to Florida, from Seattle to New Orleans. Destinations in this particular region include:

*Insight Guide: Canada.* A companion volume to this book. Stunning photojournalism seeks out Canada's most exciting information and details, from its extensive US border to its Arctic wastes.

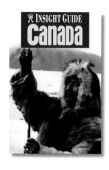

*Insight Guide: Montreal.* A behind-the-scenes look at this beautiful, prosperous city with a French accent.

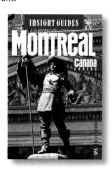

*Insight Pocket Guide: Toronto* Perfect for people in a hurry, this small book comes with insider's information and labour-saving hints from Insight's Toronto-based correspondent.

*Insight Pocket Guide: British Columbia.* Carefully selected itineraries and personal recommendations for independent travellers compiled by Insight's local expert.. Complete with a pull-out map.

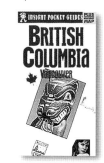

# ART & PHOTO CREDITS

*All photography by STUART DEE except for:*

**Archives, Canada/C.W. Jeffreys** 40
**Bodo Bondzio** 185, 196, 197, 200, 201, 210, 211, 214
**Canadian Pacific Ltd** 31, 36
**Ronald Grant Archives** 91
**Greenpeace/Keziere** 43
**Pat Kramer** 20, 23, 49, 50, 55, 68, 100, 102/103, 162, 166, 180, 194
**The Ladd Company** 89
**Paramount/Charles Bush** 90
**Province of British Columbia** 168/169
**Tourism Association of Vancouver Island** 186, 188
**Universal Pictures** 88
**Harry M. Walker** 2
**Western Canada Wilderness Committee** 109
**Vancouver Public Library/Stanley Young** *24/25*, 29, 30, 32, 33, 34/35, 40, 41, 106, 107
**Stanley Young** 38, 39, 42

*Maps* **Berndtson & Berndtson Publications**
*Cartographic Editor* **Zoë Goodwin**
*Production* **Mohammed Dar**
*Design Consultants* **Carlotta Junger, Graham Mitchener**
*Picture Research* **Hilary Genin**

# Index

*Numbers in italics refer to
photographs*

66 I was first drawn to the Insight Guides by the excellent "Nepal" volume. I can think of no book which so effectively captures the essence of a country. Out of these pages leaped the Nepal I know – the captivating charm of a people and their culture. I've since discovered and enjoyed the entire Insight Guide series. Each volume deals with a country in the same sensitive depth, which is nowhere more evident than in the superb photography. 99

*Sir Edmund Hillary*

# The World of Insight Guides

**400 books in three complementary series cover every major destination in every continent.**

## Insight Guides

Alaska
Alsace
Amazon Wildlife
American Southwest
Amsterdam
Argentina
Atlanta
Athens
Australia
Austria
Bahamas
Bali
Baltic States
Bangkok
Barbados
Barcelona
Bay of Naples
Beijing
Belgium
Belize
Berlin
Bermuda
Boston
Brazil
Brittany
Brussels
Budapest
Buenos Aires
Burgundy
Burma (Myanmar)
Cairo
Calcutta
California
Canada
Caribbean
Catalonia
Channel Islands
Chicago
Chile
China
Cologne
Continental Europe
Corsica
Costa Rica
Crete
Crossing America
Cuba
Cyprus
Czech & Slovak Republics
Delhi, Jaipur, Agra
Denmark
Dresden
Dublin
Düsseldorf
East African Wildlife
East Asia
Eastern Europe
Ecuador
Edinburgh
Egypt
Finland
Florence
Florida
France
Frankfurt
French Riviera
Gambia & Senegal
Germany
Glasgow

Gran Canaria
Great Barrier Reef
Great Britain
Greece
Greek Islands
Hamburg
Hawaii
Hong Kong
Hungary
Iceland
India
India's Western Himalaya
Indian Wildlife
Indonesia
Ireland
Israel
Istanbul
Italy
Jamaica
Japan
Java
Jerusalem
Jordan
Kathmandu
Kenya
Korea
Lisbon
Loire Valley
London
Los Angeles
Madeira
Madrid
Malaysia
Mallorca & Ibiza
Malta
Marine Life in the South
    China Sea
Melbourne
Mexico
Mexico City
Miami
Montreal
Morocco
Moscow
Munich
Namibia
Native America
Nepal
Netherlands
New England
New Orleans
New York City
New York State
New Zealand
Nile
Normandy
Northern California
Northern Spain
Norway
Oman & the UAE
Oxford
Old South
Pacific Northwest
Pakistan
Paris
Peru
Philadelphia
Philippines
Poland
Portugal
Prague

Provence
Puerto Rico
Rajasthan
Rhine
Rio de Janeiro
Rockies
Rome
Russia
St Petersburg
San Francisco
Sardinia
Scotland
Seattle
Sicily
Singapore
South Africa
South America
South Asia
South India
South Tyrol
Southeast Asia
Southeast Asia Wildlife
Southern California
Southern Spain
Spain
Sri Lanka
Sweden
Switzerland
Sydney
Taiwan
Tenerife
Texas
Thailand
Tokyo
Trinidad & Tobago
Tunisia
Turkey
Turkish Coast
Tuscany
Umbria
US National Parks East
US National Parks West
Vancouver
Venezuela
Venice
Vienna
Vietnam
Wales
Washington DC
Waterways of Europe
Wild West
Yemen

## Insight Pocket Guides

Aegean Islands★
Algarve★
Alsace
Amsterdam★
Athens★
Atlanta★
Bahamas★
Baja Peninsula★
Bali★
Bali Bird Walks
Bangkok★
Barbados★
Barcelona★
Bavaria★
Beijing★
Berlin★

Bermuda★
Bhutan★
Boston★
British Columbia★
Brittany★
Brussels★
Budapest &
    Surroundings★
Canton★
Chiang Mai★
Chicago★
Corsica★
Costa Blanca★
Costa Brava★
Costa del Sol/Marbella★
Costa Rica★
Crete★
Denmark★
Fiji★
Florence★
Florida★
Florida Keys★
French Riviera★
Gran Canaria★
Hawaii★
Hong Kong★
Hungary
Ibiza★
Ireland★
Ireland's Southwest★
Israel★
Istanbul★
Jakarta★
Jamaica★
Kathmandu Bikes &
    Hikes★
Kenya★
Kuala Lumpur★
Lisbon★
Loire Valley★
London★
Macau★
Madrid★
Malacca
Maldives
Mallorca★
Malta★
Mexico City★
Miami★
Milan★
Montreal★
Morocco★
Moscow
Munich★
Nepal★
New Delhi
New Orleans★
New York City★
New Zealand★
Northern California★
Oslo/Bergen★
Paris★
Penang★
Phuket★
Prague★
Provence★
Puerto Rico★
Quebec★
Rhodes★
Rome★
Sabah★

St Petersburg★
San Francisco★
Sardinia
Scotland★
Seville★
Seychelles★
Sicily★
Sikkim
Singapore★
Southeast England
Southern California★
Southern Spain★
Sri Lanka★
Sydney★
Tenerife★
Thailand★
Tibet★
Toronto★
Tunisia★
Turkish Coast★
Tuscany★
Venice★
Vienna★
Vietnam★
Yogyakarta
Yucatan Peninsula★

**★ = Insight Pocket Guides**
**with Pull out Maps**

## Insight Compact Guides

Algarve
Amsterdam
Bahamas
Bali
Bangkok
Barbados
Barcelona
Beijing
Belgium
Berlin
Brittany
Brussels
Budapest
Burgundy
Copenhagen
Costa Brava
Costa Rica
Crete
Cyprus
Czech Republic
Denmark
Dominican Republic
Dublin
Egypt
Finland
Florence
Gran Canaria
Greece
Holland
Hong Kong
Ireland
Israel
Italian Lakes
Italian Riviera
Jamaica
Jerusalem
Lisbon
Madeira
Mallorca
Malta

Milan
Moscow
Munich
Normandy
Norway
Paris
Poland
Portugal
Prague
Provence
Rhodes
Rome
St Petersburg
Salzburg
Singapore
Switzerland
Sydney
Tenerife
Thailand
Turkey
Turkish Coast
Tuscany

UK regional titles:
Bath & Surroundings
Cambridge & East
    Anglia
Cornwall
Cotswolds
Devon & Exmoor
Edinburgh
Lake District
London
New Forest
North York Moors
Northumbria
Oxford
Peak District
Scotland
Scottish Highlands
Shakespeare Country
Snowdonia
South Downs
York
Yorkshire Dales

USA regional titles:
Boston
Cape Cod
Chicago
Florida
Florida Keys
Hawaii: Maui
Hawaii: Oahu
Las Vegas
Los Angeles
Martha's Vineyard &
    Nantucket
New York
San Francisco
Washington D.C.
Venice
Vienna
West of Ireland